TROPHIES
OF
GRACE

By DEAN HULCE

Copyright © 2016 by Dean Hulce

Trophies of Grace
by Dean Hulce

Printed in the United States of America.

ISBN 9781498470032

All rights reserved solely by the author. The author guarantees all contents are original and do not infringe upon the legal rights of any other person or work. No part of this book may be reproduced in any form without the permission of the author. The views expressed in this book are not necessarily those of the publisher.

Unless otherwise indicated, Scripture quotations taken from the
King James Version (KJV)–*public domain*.

Scripture quotations taken from the New King James Version (NKJV).
Copyright © 1982 by Thomas Nelson, Inc. Used by permission. All rights reserved.

Scripture quotations taken from the New American Standard Bible (NASB).
Copyright © 1960, 1962, 1963, 1968, 1971, 1972, 1973, 1975, 1977, 1995
by The Lockman Foundation. Used by permission. All rights reserved.

Scripture quotations taken from the English Standard Version (ESV).
Copyright © 2001 by Crossway, a publishing ministry of Good News Publishers. Used by permission. All rights reserved.

Scripture quotations taken from the Holy Bible, New Living Translation (NLT). Copyright ©1996, 2004, 2007 by Tyndale House Foundation.
Used by permission of Tyndale House Publishers, Inc.

Scripture quotations taken from New Life Version (NLV).
Copyright © 1969 by Christian Literature International.

Scripture quotations taken from the Living Bible (TLB). Copyright © 1971
by Tyndale House Foundation. Used by permission of
Tyndale House Publishers Inc., Carol Stream, Illinois 60188. All rights reserved.

Art provided by Dallen Lambson

Dallen's work can be seen and ordered at:
www.lambsonart.com
Lambson's Wildlife Art
1242 E. Alameda Rd.
Pocatello, ID 83201
1-800-756-4275

www.xulonpress.com

This Devotional Belongs to

Sammry Norman Jr

Love mom and dad
Christmas 2023

Study to show thyself approved unto God, a workman that needeth not to be ashamed, rightly dividing the word of truth.

2 Timothy 2:15

DEDICATION PAGE

If I could go back and do It all over again, I would do it better and allow God to work through me starting at a younger age. This work is dedicated to Him first and foremost. He alone has allowed me to become who I am and He directs my hands as I type, to His glory. It is because of His grace that I know that I will spend eternity with Him. Thank you my Heavenly Father.

To my wife, Linda, I don't deserve you or your love. Thank you for staying with me and loving me through the years. I couldn't have done this without your support.

To Ryan, Nick, Cory Ann and Micah, you guys inspire me. Chloe, Hunter and Harli, may you come to know Jesus at a young age and may He direct your paths through life.

Mom and Dad, thank you for all that you raised me to believe, in what God did in sending His son Jesus, in Jesus who came to live, die and be raised again for the redemption of my soul and the Holy Spirit who is here to guide me day in and day out. I wish that Dad could be here today to see what his children have become in God's service.

To all those friends and family that have believed in me and my abilities, your encouragement made it work. Dan, Doug, Shorty, Rick, Dave, Steve, Tim, Brandt, Mike and many others are not only friends but brothers.

FORWARD

I first met Dean during an extended prayer and visioning retreat at The Cielo Vista Ranch, a gathering like none other. Six men with year-round access to an 80,000+ acre Ranch would typically write their narratives for what they will do and accomplish. But not for this crew. For four extended days these men humbly sought the heart of God in prayer, Scripture, discerning conversations, and more prayer. After intense wrestling for what the LORD would have done a Theological Mandate was declared, "This Sanctuary is to reveal My power and My divine nature so be still and know that I am God."

This Ranch is truly a Sanctuary. God's creative order is just as the Psalmist references. The sun, the moon, the stars, the animals, the very foundation of the Earth all have a creative rhythm declaring His glory. Yet we mortal humans are distinct. We stand in this Sanctuary, awkward. We are the only element in all of Creation which does not naturally bring Him glory. Our sin sets us apart in desperate need of His grace and redemptive plan (II Corinthians 5:13-21).

We need these daily moments. Each carefully crafted in prayer, these devotions will inspire because they are so very practical.

As a hunting guide, Dean patiently positions hunters for access to a trophy. What happens next depends upon how the hunter receives his instruction. But one thing is for certain. When you are with Dean, you are family (Ephesians 1:3-11).

May these devotionals bless you as much as they have blessed me

Rick Kindschi

January

Jeremiah 29:11

For I know the plans I have for you, declares the Lord, plans for welfare and not for evil, to give you a future and a hope.

JAN 1

TROPHIES OF GRACE

2 Corinthians 2:14
"But thanks be to God! For through what Christ has done, He has triumphed over us so that now wherever we go He uses us to tell others about the Lord and to spread the Gospel like a sweet perfume."

Linda and I along with our sons (mostly Linda) have put together a fairly good number of trophy mounts in our home and camp. These are similar to a football, tennis or basketball player's showcase where he or she would display their awards. Each of the "trophies" on display carries a special memory or triumph in life.

If today you know Christ as your personal Savior, you are a trophy of His grace.

One definition of God's grace is this, "the free and unmerited favor of God, as manifested in the salvation of sinners and the bestowal of blessings."

So as Christians we can think of ourselves as God's trophies on display in heaven for eternity. Because of His grace we are justified, purified and His forever more. We were purchased with the very blood of God's only Son (John 3:16).

Joseph Price said, "if it is God who justifies you, who can bring a charge against you?"

So if we are TROPHIES OF GOD'S GRACE, who can stand against the power of an almighty God. Stand firm.

JOURNAL ENTRY

JAN 2

DAMAGED ARMOR

Ephesians 6:11
"Put on the whole armor of God that ye may be able to stand against the wiles of the devil."

This verse and the few that come after it talk about the armor that God gives us to combat Satan. We sometimes picture this as new, smooth and shiny. But this armor has been into battle. It is going to be dented, beaten on, scratched and scared. God tells us that trials and attacks will come and we need to be prepared. If we are not facing these attacks, our armor won't look like we've been to battle. If this is the case, then we need to consider if we are on God's battlefield or not.

Recently I read this little saying. It makes a lot of sense when we talk of the spiritual battlefield.

"Show me a Knight in shining armor, and I will show you a man that has not yet had his metal truly tested."

How's your armor? Is it in need of some polishing, some dent removal and some reinforcement? Ephesians 6 is all about the need for armor, the armor is only needed if we are in Gods army. If there are no dents or other damage, then consider where your allegiance is. Does it need repair? Good it shows that you've been at war. If it is still shiny, get in the battle.

JOURNAL ENTRY

_____

_____

_____

_____

_____

_____

_____

JAN 3

LIVING SACRIFICES

Romans 12:1
"Therefore, I urge you, brothers and sisters, in view of God's mercy, to offer your bodies as a living sacrifice, holy and pleasing to God —this is your true and proper worship."

I read this verse this morning and wondered, what really is a "living sacrifice"? Am I a good example of a "living sacrifice"? Am I sold out for my God?

Until Christ came and was sacrificed, animals had to be killed for sacrifice. They had to give their "all", they were, in today's terms, "all in". We are called to "die to our own desires". In Galatians 5:24, Paul wrote,

"Those who belong to Christ Jesus have crucified the flesh with its passions and desires."

I wish that I lived this every day, all day, but I don't. However, this is what we are called to... To "offer yourselves as a living sacrifice" this is "true worship"... That's what I want. How about you?

Go "all in"!

JOURNAL ENTRY

___

___

___

___

___

___

___

___

___

JAN 4

LIKE A ROARING LION

1 Peter 5:8-9
"Be alert and of sober mind. Your enemy the devil prowls around like a roaring lion looking for someone to devour. Resist him, standing firm in the faith, because you know that the family of believers throughout the world is undergoing the same kind of sufferings."

One of my favorite, all-time movies is, "Ghosts In The Darkness". I'm not sure why, because I am not usually one for blood and gore. The two stars of that movie are two huge male lions that I associate with these verses. These two lions roam at night, in the darkness, searching for some to devour.

These verses describe this very thing. But we are called to be sober. Not just sober physically, but spiritually... prepared to resist Satan at every turn. If we "sleep", or doze off in our spiritual life, Satan is waiting right there to overtake us.

So prepare yourself, stay spiritually awake, and don't convince yourself that you can't stray off of God's path just a little ways. Off His path is darkness and this darkness is where Satan lurks to take us down.

Instead, "Submit yourselves therefore to God, resist the devil, and he will flee from you", James 4:7

And finally there is a reward for remaining sober and resisting.

James 1:12 – "Blessed is the man that endureth temptation: for when he is tried, he shall receive the crown of life, which the Lord hath promised to them that love him."

JOURNAL ENTRY

JAN 5

JOY DOESN'T MEAN

Romans 15:13
"May the God of hope fill you with all joy and peace as you trust in him, so than you may overflow with hope by the power of the Holy Spirit."

A Christian is supposed to be joyful... There are many verses that talk about this. Sometimes this doesn't feel possible. But we forget that joy doesn't mean always walking around with a big smile. It does mean being fulfilled in what God provides. More in spiritual fulfillment than belongings, but God provides all our needs if we trust Him to do it.

Being joyful in good times is easy. We can carry a smile when things are going our way and we can be joyful even when some of the things are falling into place for us. But how about when most things are coming down on top of us, when it feels like our world is crumbling around us? Then how do we do? It is when we shouldn't have joy and we still have it that we are living as we are called to Romans 15:13.

I read a little piece on Facebook the other day that said, "The smile on my face doesn't mean my life is perfect, it means I appreciate what I have and what God has blessed me with."

That's what joy is.

JOURNAL ENTRY

_____
_____
_____
_____
_____
_____
_____
_____
_____
_____

JAN 6

PRAYERS FOR AUTHORITIES

1st Timothy 2:1-2
"I urge, then, first of all, that petitions, prayers, intercession and thanksgiving be made for all people; For kings and all those in authority, that we may live peaceful and quiet lives in all godliness and holiness."

Wow this is tough... When we agree with someone's viewpoint or their platform it is easy to do. But in today's world of totally partisan politics, the thought of praying for those in authority is a "hard pill to swallow". The verse doesn't say, "if you agree with their views" or "if you like them"... It says, "all those in authority". It's easier when your "guy" or "girl" is in office... But no matter whom it is we are called to pray.

Can you imagine how things could be different if we all sincerely did this? We could change our world. The promise that goes with this would make it worthwhile, "that we may live peaceful and quiet lives in all godliness and holiness."

Let's give this a try, make it a point daily.

JOURNAL ENTRY

JAN 7

Romans 13:9
The commandments, "You shall not commit adultery," "You shall not murder," "You shall not steal," "You shall not covet," and whatever other command there may be, are summed up in this one command: "Love your neighbor as yourself"

When we look within ourselves or outward at others and see sinful hearts or behaviors we can see selfishness at the core. When we move away from God it is always because we want what we want, not what God wants for us. Each step away from where we should be makes it harder to come back.

So if we truly love our neighbors as ourselves we break the selfish cycle. The next time we are tempted to make a sinful choice, remember we can't follow God when we are looking out for ourselves first.

Philippians 2:3-4 "Do nothing from selfish ambition or conceit, but in humility count others more significant than yourselves. Let each of you look not only to his own interests, but also to the interests of others."

JOURNAL ENTRY

_____

_____

_____

_____

_____

_____

_____

_____

_____

_____

_____

JAN 8

BE ENCOURAGED

Zephaniah 3:17
"The LORD your God in your midst, the Mighty One, will save; He will rejoice over you with gladness, He will quiet you with His love, He will rejoice over you with singing."

I saw these four comments (below) and with the verses that accompany each, I wanted to bring encouragement to others this morning.

1. Remember that your Character should always be stronger than your Circumstances.
    "Rejoice always, pray continually, give thanks in all circumstances;
    for this is God's will for you in Christ Jesus." 1 Thessalonians 5:16-18

2. Remember that your Struggles always lead to Strength.
    "And we know that in all things God works for the good of those
    who love Him, who have been called according to His purpose."
    Romans 8:28

3. Remember that God's timing is always perfect.
    "For I know the plans I have for you declares the Lord; plans to
    prosper you and not to harm you, plans to give you hope and a
    future." Jeremiah 29:11

4. Remember that God will never leave your side.
    "Be strong and courageous. Do not be afraid or terrified because
    of them, for the Lord your God goes with you; He will never leave
    you nor forsake you." Deuteronomy 31:6

SO BE ENCOURAGED AND WHEN YOU GET THE CHANCE, ENCOURAGE SOMEONE ELSE.

JOURNAL ENTRY

_____

_____

_____

_____

_____

_____

JAN 9

Romans 8:28
"And we know that God causes all things to work together for good to those who love God, to those who are called according to His purpose."

This verse doesn't promise that all things will be easy for those who love God. However, they promise that they will "work together for good".

There is a line in the movie **_LINCOLN_** where Abraham Lincoln says,

"A compass, I learnt when I was surveying, it'll... it'll point you True North from where you're standing, but it's got no advice about the swamps and dessert and chasm that you'll encounter along the way. If in pursuit of your destination, you plunge ahead, heedless of obstacles, and achieve nothing more than to sink in a swamp... What's the use of knowing True North?"

This is a great line that is true in human thinking. However, in a life where God is allowed to fill us and we are loving and trusting Him, we need not worry about the swamps, desserts and chasms of life. This is true in the outdoors as well. We can see the big dipper and the North Star, we can have a compass in our hand... we can follow them day and night ... but we will still come up against obstacles.

God will get us through them. And, if we trust Him to do so, we will be blessed each time we come out of one of them and HE will be glorified. This is only true if we are filled with a love for God and that we have that personal relationship with Him.

Allow God to direct your *compass" in life and His "true north" will always be reachable, with Him as our guide.

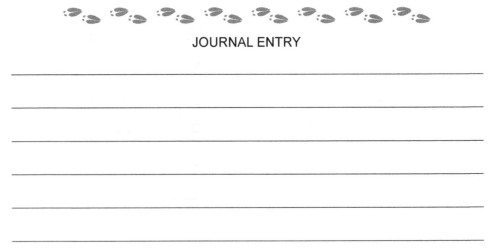

JOURNAL ENTRY

January

JAN 10

TIME IN THE WORD

Joshua 1:8
"This Book of the Law shall not depart from your mouth, but you shall meditate on it day and night, so that you may be careful to do according to all that is written in it. For then you will make your way prosperous, and then you will have good success."

Dr David Jeremiah once said, "The Bible that is falling apart usually belongs to someone who isn't."

I have my dad's original bible and I have to be careful even turning a page as I fear it falling apart. There are markings all over the pages. It was obviously very used.

We can't expect God to talk to us, if we are not willing to listen. God can talk to us in many ways but when we read the bible we are hearing God's Words written for us, to hear Him.

We can't keep any relationship going without listening and conversing with a person. The same is true of a relationship with God. Open your bible, wear it out.

Psalm 119:18 "Open my eyes that I may see wonderful things in your law."

JOURNAL ENTRY

_____
_____
_____
_____
_____
_____
_____
_____

JAN 11

PLANTING SEEDS

Matthew 25:35-40
"For I was hungry and you gave me food, I was thirsty and you gave me drink, I was a stranger and you welcomed me, I was naked and you clothed me, I was sick and you visited me, I was in prison and you came to me. Then the righteous will answer him, saying, Lord, when did we see you hungry and feed you, or thirsty and give you drink? And when did we see you a stranger and welcome you, or naked and clothe you? And when did we see you sick or in prison and visit you? And the King will answer them, Truly, I say to you, as you did it to one of the least of these my brothers, you did it to me."

Throughout our lives when, we serve others, we have no way of knowing how it effects their lives. As the verse above states, "Lord when did we see you hungry and feed you..."

This weekend I was told a story about a disabled veteran who was served by some others. He was treated to a very special hunt and at the end of the weekend he spoke from his wheelchair... "A short time back I loaded a pistol and held it to my head, when I pulled the trigger the round didn't fire." He pulled out a loaded round of ammo, held it up and continued. "Because of this hunt, I will ever need this again."

We are called to serve each other, to love each other and to look out for each other... We have no idea the eternal impact we have by our actions.

Our job is to "plant seeds" and "water" them... God does the rest. Like putting in a food plot for a fall hunt, if we don't first put the seeds in the ground there isn't much chance that it will produce a harvest come season.

1 Corinthians 3:7 "It's not important who does the planting, or who does the watering. What's important is that God makes the seed grow."

JOURNAL ENTRY

_____

_____

_____

_____

_____

_____

JAN 12

1 Corinthians 15:58
"Therefore, my dear brothers and sisters, stand firm. Let nothing move you. Always give yourselves fully to the work of the Lord, because you know that your labor in the Lord is not in vain."

In this chapter the apostle Paul has written about Christ's resurrection and then the future resurrection of those that have a trust in Christ.... At the very end of the chapter come these two verses.

Here we are told to "stand firm" and to "give ourselves full to the work of God"

Standing firm isn't easy. Satan is always trying to move us away from God's work and we are easily moved. Our lives here on earth are so short. What is more important than what we do for God? Don't be discouraged or pushed off course. Paul's directives to us here come with a promise, "because you know that your labor in the Lord is not in vain."

Charles Stanley said this: "Disappointment is inevitable. But to become discouraged, there's a choice I make. God would never discourage me. He would always point me to himself to trust him. Therefore, my discouragement is from Satan. As you go through the emotions that we have, hostility is not from God, bitterness, unforgiveness, all of these are attacks from Satan."

Stand firm and give yourselves fully.

JOURNAL ENTRY

JAN 13

JUST ASK, HE WILL ANSWER

Matt 7:7
"Ask and it will be given to you, seek and you will find, knock and the door will be opened to you."

It had been a long morning. Jim and I had hunted up a big ridge above Uyak Bay on Kodiak Island since daylight, and now it was approaching noon. We had fought brush all the way. We were looking for a place to glass for blacktail deer. Finding no openings in the brush big enough, we finally decided to walk back down through a mile of narrow creek bottom.

Walking in this type of confined area, in the middle of brown bear haunts, was not the best idea, but it was easier than where we had been walking.

A few minutes into our descent, we jumped a deer and the thick brush soon swallowed it up. Instinctively, I let out a call like a distressed fawn, in an attempt to call it back. Instead of a deer coming to the call, a huge, half-ton, charging bear came crashing in looking for an easy meal. Luckily for me, Jim panicked and pulled the trigger on his rifle, stopping the bear at about twenty feet.

As the bear turned to leave, I started praying for God's protection for Jim and myself. We escaped out of the creek bottom to the ridge above. We were in a bad spot and needed to get out quickly; God provided the way and saved our lives that day.

Too many people are not persistent in their asking, seeking, and knocking, so they are unable to find the way out of their problems. God promises to provide a way out of our problems. It is sure, but it is conditioned upon our determination to ask, seek, and knock until He opens the best door.

Remember that the way that we think is the best isn't always so. Sometimes we think the valley is the place to get out, when it was really the ridge top. To find the way, we have to ask.

Isa. 55:8-9 "For my thoughts are not your thoughts, neither are your ways my ways, declares the Lord. As the heavens are higher than the earth, so are my ways higher your ways and my thoughts than your thoughts."

JOURNAL ENTRY

_____

_____

_____

January

JAN 14

NO WEAPON FORMED UP AGAINST US

Isaiah 54:17
"No weapon formed against you shall prosper, and every tongue which rises against you in judgment You shall condemn. This is the heritage of the servants of the Lord, and their righteousness is from Me, Says the Lord."

I'm not sure about everyone else, but I know there are days when I certainly feel like there are weapons coming against me that intend to destroy me. Yet at the end of the day, I still stand, and the Lord stands alongside of me.

I read a short note yesterday that said, "God never said that the weapons wouldn't form, He just promised that they wouldn't prosper." If we have a personal relationship with God, and weapons come against us in life, we have the promise that they will not prosper. Our God still sits on His throne in heaven, and He is still in control.

Most of us would prefer to think of a godly or sacred place as some bright dwelling, filled with good, positive feelings. We don't want to think that something as ugly and brutal as combat could be involved in any way with God's spiritual realm. However, would any true Christian say that Calvary Hill was not a sacred space?

The weapons of man—a sword, a hammer and spikes, a crown of thorns, a whip and even a brutal cross—were all brought against Christ, but in the end not one of these weapons won. Three days after Christ died, He rose again. Even the weapon of death didn't stand up against God's power.

So take on God's armor and trust that, while they might be built to hurt us, no weapon formed against us shall prosper.

JOURNAL ENTRY

_____

_____

_____

_____

_____

_____

_____

JAN 15

APPLE SEEDS

John 4:35-38
"Do you not say, 'There are yet four months, and then comes the harvest'? Behold, I say to you, lift up your eyes and look on the fields, that they are white for harvest. "Already he who reaps is receiving wages and is gathering fruit for life eternal; so that he who sows and he who reaps may rejoice together "For in this case the saying is true, 'One sows and another reaps.' read more.
"I sent you to reap that for which you have not labored; others have labored and you have entered into their labor."

We are called to sow seeds concerning Christ and what He did for us, His love and the hope we have through Him. We are called to sow in faith, faith that there will be a harvest and it might not be us involved in the harvest... But we do our part.

There are four principals of sowing and reaping:

- You reap what you sow. If you sow apple seeds, you get apples, not sugar cane.
- You can only reap if you sow. If you don't sow the seeds, how will it grow?
- The harvest takes time. Wait on the harvest. Tend to the crop. In due season we shall reap (if we faint not).
- You will reap more than what you sow.

A friend recently told me, his uncle planted an Oak tree in his yard about 20 years ago with an acorn he picked up at a local park. Every year that tree yields thousands of acorns. Consider the apple tree; planted with one seed. Think of how many apples that tree produces just in one season. Then think how many seeds are in those apples. Now think of this; any man can count the number of seeds in an apple, but only God can count the number of apples in a seed! Praise the Lord for His magnificence!"

What a great thought... We can plant one seed about Christ. That one seed can multiply into millions in heaven. Our job is just to sow seeds.

Remember the APPLE SEEDS.

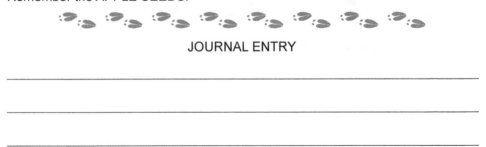

JOURNAL ENTRY

_____

_____

_____

January

JAN 16

TRUE FRIENDSHIP

Ecclesiastes 4:9-10
Two are better than one; because they have a good reward for their labor.
10 For if they fall, the one will lift up his fellow: but woe to him that is
alone when he falls; for he hath not another to help him up.

There aren't too many times you will find me quoting a yogi, guru from India. However, Paramahansa Yogananda, the one believed to have brought yoga to our country, once said, "There is a magnet in your heart that will attract true friends. That magnet is unselfishness, thinking of others first; when you learn to live for others, they will live for you."

I agree that to build true friendship there has to be a condition of unselfishness in our lives. When we are willing to give of our time, our life, our efforts and even sometimes our money? When the other person's needs become more important than our own... This is how true friendship begins and lasts.

Linda and I have struggled since January to prepare our house for sale... This past weekend two friends came and stayed with us and worked selfishly all weekend to help us. We were burned out and because of the love of friends it pushed us forward again. Giving up of one of the few beautiful summer weekends would only be done by true friends.

To have true friends, be a true friend. Give of yourself to others... Friends will appear in your life.

Proverbs 18:24 A man who has friends must himself be friendly, but there is a friend who sticks closer than a brother.

JOURNAL ENTRY

_____

_____

_____

_____

_____

_____

JAN 17

REJOICE WITH GLADNESS

Philippians 4:4
"Rejoice in the Lord always: and again I say, Rejoice."

It's easy to rejoice in the Lord when things are good; we can do that easy enough. But when things get tough and we don't see our way out of a situation or when we plan for one thing and a disaster hits... Then, can we truly rejoice?

Yesterday was one of those days for me. It started out good enough with some great meetings etc... Then during lunch, the bottom fell out. After reading an email, I had to tell my wife that what we had planned for was not going to happen... A mistake was made and things weren't going to go as planned. Disappointed, she said little. But soon her countenance changed from quite discouragement to Cheery, uplifting and positive, it was amazing...... She was joyful in the midst of what seemed like disaster to me. Then it hit me, God knows what is happening right now, He has all of this in His control. Why should I be discouraged?

Then tonight on Facebook I came across a post that read,

"Don't wait for things to get better. Life will always be complicated. Learn to be happy right now, otherwise you will run out of time."

While this quote didn't mention God having control, it still played right into my life. What good did it do to get discouraged? Why stay down? Just before I got the "bad news" at lunch, I had a meeting with a customer that just a year or so ago had lost everything in a fire... Whenever I saw him through that time I was astounded by his cheerfulness. He didn't allow a circumstance in his life keep him down.

Philippines 4:4, doesn't say, "Rejoice in the Lord" sometimes or when we feel like it or when things are going our way... It says "ALWAYS"! No matter what you are facing today, God knows and cares more than we can imagine. Rejoice, because the option is to allow one of the few short days we have on this earth to get past us while we are miserable... What a waste!

Psalm 68:3 "But let the righteous be glad; let them exult before God; Yes, let them rejoice with gladness."

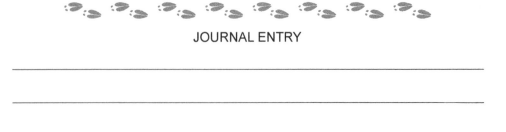

JOURNAL ENTRY

_____

_____

_____

January

JAN 18

Matthew 4:18-20
"As Jesus was walking beside the Sea of Galilee, he saw two brothers; Simon called Peter and his brother Andrew. They were casting a net into the lake, for they were fishermen. Come, follow me, Jesus said, and I will send you out to fish for people. At once they left their nets and followed him."

I love to fish... It is very relaxing for me. I'm not sure of many things more relaxing than sitting on a bank or in a boat wetting a line. The only thing better might be a meal of fresh fish. We can sit in the living room or on the deck and talk fishing for months on end, we can dream of fishing at night. But if we don't get onto the water we will be eating franks and beans instead of perch fillets.

When Jesus called to Peter and Andrew He didn't say come catch some fish... No, He said "I will send you out to fish for people." He didn't promise them a harvest, just a calling.

We get so caught up in the fear of fishing that we forget that God is in the boat with us. The ultimate Guide is directing us and has our back. Or we are so concerned about making sure that everything is perfect, that the house or the church is pretty or the "fish" won't bite. We are so tied up that we don't do the fishing at all.

Paul Harvey said, "Too many Christians are no longer fishers of men but keepers of the aquarium."

Don't worry about the aquarium or if you have the right equipment. Just remember, you have the right guide and He just wants us to fish.

Galatians 6:9 "Let us not lose heart in doing good, for in due time we will reap if we do not grow weary."

Don't grow weary, keep fishing

JOURNAL ENTRY

_____

_____

_____

_____

JAN 19

BE STILL AND KNOW

Numbers 20:8
"Take the staff, and assemble the congregation, you and Aaron your brother, and tell the rock before their eyes to yield its water. So you shall bring water out of the rock for them and give drink to the congregation and their cattle."

Moses had been traveling in the wilderness for quite some time. He was waiting to get into the land that the Lord had promised. His whole life was set on that mission and yet because he didn't trust God to do something on His own, that land was never seen by Moses.

Moses was tired of Gods people grumbling. Instead of trusting what God had said, "tell the rock before their eyes to yield its water"... Moses got angry and used his anger instead by striking the rock. This isn't what God had commanded.

How many times in life do we go ahead of God by trying to do things ourselves when we really should be waiting on the Lord? When God says, do it this way and we think we know better? Instead of resting on what the Lord has promised, we move ahead and push, because we have to provide the answer in our timing not His. It could be one little thing, but it will become a pattern of impatience and self reliance. While we don't even know it we've set God's plan aside for our own. Not that they are all bad plans, but they are not Gods plans.

I may have used the example before of my Jr High Sunday school music leader. It seemed as though every week we sang the same song. At the time we would snicker amongst ourselves... But the meaning and the words stuck

HE OWNS THE CATTLE ON A 1000 HILLS

He owns the cattle on a thousand hills,
The wealth in every mine;
He owns the rivers and the rocks and rills,
The sun and stars that shine.
Wonderful riches, more than tongue can tell
He is my Father so they're mine as well;
He owns the cattle on a thousand hills -
I know that He will care for me.

Think about it... How many times do we jump ahead of God? He says, "Trust Me", "Wait for Me" and it seems right for little while... But then we grow tired of waiting and take matters into our own hands. Maybe the waiting was our lesson. Maybe God needed for us to see that He could provide for us without our back breaking exhausting effort.

And maybe we needed to listen to the Psalmist when he wrote down God's word...

Psalm 46:10 He says, "Be still, and know that I am God..."

January

JAN 20

TRIALS WILL COME, "CONSIDER IT ALL JOY"

James 1:2-4
"Consider it all joy, my brethren, when you encounter various trials, knowing that the testing of your faith produces endurance. And let endurance have its perfect result, so that you may be perfect and complete, lacking in nothing."

Training for a sporting event, a long race or a mountain climb can be very strenuous; it can be painful and tedious. I'm not one that enjoys exercise for the sake of exercise... But putting a goal at the end, a carrot hung in front of me, as it were, and I can put up with the discomfort... I can usually "endure".

God allows our faith to be tested, He allows us to face trials of many kinds. In the Old Testament, He allowed Job to lose everything he had except for his wife and a few friends, which weren't much help anyhow. God allows these things to come upon us for the strengthening of our faith and the building of our character.

Walt Disney said it like this...

"All the adversity I've had in my life, all my troubles and obstacles has strengthened me... You may not realize it when it happens, but a kick in the teeth may be the best thing in the world for you."

God doesn't allow these things for a hardening of our hearts but to allow us to grow into a closer relationship with Him.

I read a small saying the other day and it struck me as not only being true but had a great lesson in it. "The same boiling water that softens potatoes hardens eggs. It's all about what you're made of, not your circumstances."

It's how we go into a trial or testing that determines how we come out. If we go in with our hearts set on God and in joy we will come out stronger and closer to the Lord... If we go in already negative, we will only dig the hole deeper.

The trials will come, "consider it all joy"

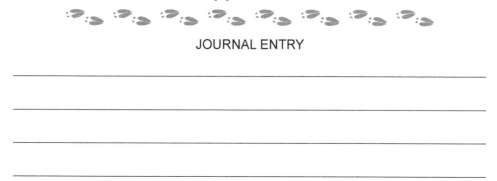

JOURNAL ENTRY

_____

_____

_____

_____

JAN 21

THE BATTLE BELONGS TO THE LORD

Ephesians 6:12
"For our struggle is not against flesh and blood, but against the rulers, against the authorities, against the powers of this dark world and against the spiritual forces of evil in the heavenly realms."

I've never been much of a fighter. Coming from a family with 5 boys you would think that I would have had a lot of fights... But all my brothers were half my size and I always felt like I couldn't go all out. My wife cries when she sees fights, she's not much of a fighter either.

That being said, we are involved in a fight every day of our life. It is more of an ongoing battle than a short fight. If you are standing for God you will be in a continual battle with demonic powers. These powers will do all that they can to bring us down. There are many times in life that we feel under attack by people when in fact it is evil powers.

In Numbers chapter 13 we read about 12 men that Moses sent to spy on Canaan. After 40 days they returned. 10 of them were fearful. There were giants in the land. The city was fortified. They couldn't see past the impossible situation before them.

But Caleb had hope. He was ready and willing to fight for the land that God had promised him.. Caleb knew that with God all things are possible. He knew that God is bigger than anything that stood before him. He knew that the battle was not his but the Lord's. The Israelites were fearful. They grumbled, and they mourned for those days back in Egypt. But Caleb and Joshua followed God wholeheartedly regardless of those things they had seen.

Lord forgive us for the times we grumble and complain. Forgive us for not facing our giants with hope. Forgive us for giving up and giving in to despair. Grant us a heart like Caleb, ready and willing to fight. Give us the hope and the strength to stand up against whatever may come. The battle is Yours Lord.

Numbers 14:6-9 "Joshua son of Nun and Caleb son of Jephunneh, who were among those who had explored the land, tore their clothes and said to the entire Israelite assembly, The land we passed through and explored is exceedingly good. If the Lord is pleased with us, he will lead us into that land, a land flowing with milk and honey, and will give it to us. Only do not rebel against the Lord. And do not be afraid of the people of the land, because we will devour them. Their protection is gone, but the Lord is with us. Do not be afraid of them."

THE BATTLE BELONGS TO THE LORD!

JOURNAL ENTRY

JAN 22

"AIM SMALL, MISS SMALL"

Philippians 3:12-14

"Not that I have already obtained all this, or have already arrived at my goal, but I press on to take hold of that for which Christ Jesus took hold of me. Brothers and sisters, I do not consider myself yet to have taken hold of it. But one thing I do: Forgetting what is behind and straining toward what is ahead, I press on toward the goal to win the prize for which God has called me heavenward in Christ Jesus."

I love to shoot traditional archery gear. It is truly an art form. I can walk through the woods and pick out a leaf or a twig on the ground at 30 yards and hit it most every time. Now put a full grown deer at that same distance and I will miss it most of the time... Why, because I'm shooting at the entire deer, not at some as small as a twig.

I have a good friend that is a very good shot with his archery equipment. He can set up a target anywhere from 15 to 75 yards and keep his arrows in the center. He is always using the phrase, "aim small, miss small" and it works for him. This saying means that if we don't focus on the small important target we will miss our mark. This same concept is true in life, if we don't concentrate on what is important we will go off in every direction, not doing what we should be doing.

Deuteronomy 7:6 says that we are a holy people. No one can be holy on their own, but if we "aim small" and strive towards holiness, we become better and better all the time. Verse 6... "For you are a holy people to the LORD your God; the LORD your God has chosen you to be a people for His own possession out of all the peoples who are on the face of the earth."

Again, we can never attain holiness without a trust in Christ as our Savior. But once we have that relationship, we are then holy in God's eyes... But we will still struggle in our own hearts and lives.

So strive to be holy... Like in archery, the more you practice the better you will be. "AIM SMALL, MISS SMALL"

JOURNAL ENTRY

___

___

___

___

JAN 23

CHILD OF THE KING!

Hosea 4:6
"My people are destroyed for lack of knowledge."

Do you know that with a life connected to Christ we are free? Do we know what that truly means? Freedom from so much and freedom for so much, true freedom.

In the Bible God is called the King of kings and Lord of Lords. And in Romans 8:17 it tells us, "and if children, then heirs—heirs of God and joint heirs with Christ, if indeed we suffer with Him, that we may also be glorified together." So we are children of the king... And not just any king but truly the King of kings!

So why do we act like something less than God's children? Why are we less than we should be?

I think that Abraham Lincoln was one of my favorite Presidents... He stood for what he believed, even to the point of death. During Lincoln's presidency, he signed the Emancipation Proclamation, which freed all American slaves. But there are documented cases where slave owners hid the Proclamation, and slaves continued serving in bondage because they were ignorant of the change that had taken place. This has been exactly Satan's strategy against the church. If Satan can keep a Christian ignorant or in unbelief about who they have become and their rights as a child of the King, he can keep them in bondage even though the law of liberty in Christ Jesus has been put into effect!

Don't let Satan tell you that you are weak, worthless or that your life has no meaning. If you know Christ, allow God to use you in a mighty way... Remember, you are a CHILD OF THE KING!

JOURNAL ENTRY

_____

_____

_____

_____

_____

January

JAN 24

Psalm 27:1
"The Lord is my light and my salvation, whom shall I fear?
The Lord is the stronghold of my life, of whom shall I be afraid?"

When you've guided hunters for a few slow days of hunting you get to know a lot about them. You're always looking for something to break up the monotony of the long days. This was the case with Bill... Bill was a hunter from northern Illinois who walked with a pronounced limp. After a couple days of slow elk hunting somehow conversation turned to his limp.

Bill told me a horrific story of falling from a tree stand on to a metal fence post. He explained in depth the terrible details of being impaled, the surgeries and then the long years of recovery... All because he didn't wear a safety harness. A very simple insurance against pain or death.

It made me realize that Christ can be a safety harness of sorts. He insures us a life without ultimate death (eternal life). But in this life Christ also, like a tree stand harness, allows us a freedom to move about without fear.

While a harness attaches us to the tree and would seem to limit us, it actually is giving us freedom without fear. We know that if we make a misstep we are not in danger of disaster. Yes, we may feel a little pain if we fall, but our safety harness will hold us and allows us an assurance that we are safe.

Going through life without a relationship with Christ is like leaning out over the edge of a tree stand. You might be OK for today, but eventually you will pay the ultimate consequence.

Be safe and strap into the eternal safety harness. If you don't have this safety harness in your life, please feel free to contact me with any questions. If you already have the connection with Christ, share it with those around you. You wouldn't watch your friends lean out of a tree stand with mentioning a safety harness... Don't let them live without knowing Christ, the ultimate "Safety Harness".

Strap in.

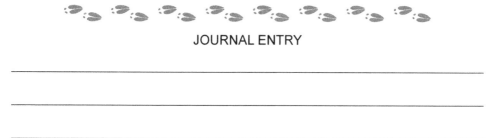

JOURNAL ENTRY

JAN 25

Mark 6:31
"Then, because so many people were coming and going that they did not even have a chance to eat, he said to them, "Come with me by yourselves to a quiet place and get some rest."

For many people there is nothing better than a quick nap in the afternoon. Some like a 5 minute quick snooze while other people have to sleep for an hour to get rested. Most of my life neither kind of naps were possible. Except for when I have been sick I can count on both hands the times I've napped in the last 20 years. Until this year I've finally learned the joy of napping and sweet rest.

God gives us rest if we seek Him out and find our rest in Him. He allows our spirit to find rest and comfort.

Tomorrow I will head out for a couple days of rest thanks to a few good friends. They saw the need and blessed me with the opportunity. I don't have to feel as though I'm missing out on anything... I can close my eyes and regain some strength.

The great hockey player of the 1900's, Gordie Howe, gave his all on the ice. He explains effort and restful reward like this. "You find that you have peace of mind and can enjoy yourself, get more sleep, and rest when you know that it was a one hundred percent effort that you gave–win or lose."

So it is with the life of a Christian. When we give our all for God, we know that we will be rewarded with the rest we deserve... But like salvation, we need to just accept that gift and allow rest to come over us.

All of us need a rest; there is no shame in it. Allow yourself the pleasure of a renewing of your body and mind. Work hard in what God has called you to, but then take the time to refresh so you can again move forward with strength.

Hebrews 4:11 "Let us, therefore, make every effort to enter that rest, so that no one will perish by following their example of disobedience."

Sweet Rest

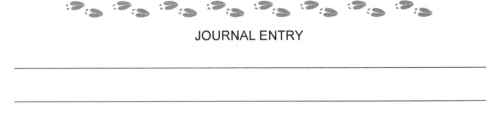

JAN 26

Titus 2:14
"Who gave Himself for us to redeem us from every lawless deed, and to purify for Himself a people for His own possession, zealous for good deeds."

A few years ago while on a deer hunt, I spent a morning with a good friend, Brandt. That morning will live on in our memories forever, funny to mine, sad to Brandt's.

That morning a huge 150" 9 point buck chased a doe right out in front of us. Brandt proceeded to fire several (5-6) shots at the buck, but each and every shot missed its mark (quite funny now, looking back). Brandt's head just hung at his chest... The best I could do was to tell him, "This won't make any difference in your life come tomorrow morning". After a couple hours at the rifle range, Linda took Brandt out for the afternoon hunt. About sunset I got a call asking me to come pick the two of them up as they had shot at a buck. When I arrived Brandt was standing over a great 13 point buck... Bigger than the morning's buck. Brandt had redeemed himself. But we still laugh at the morning's fiasco.

I can't speak for anyone else but I know that like Brandt did with the deer, I miss the mark in life on a daily basis. Romans 3:23 tells us that, "All have sinned and fallen short of the glory of God"... We all need to be redeemed. The important thing is to know that my redemption has been taken care of once and for all by what Christ did for me 2,000 years ago (John 3:16). I don't have to go back and redeem myself.

So next time you miss the mark in life, know that Christ paid the price for that. If you've accepted His gift to you then you are already redeemed... If you haven't accepted that gift, know that your redemption has already been paid... You just have to accept it.

Big Daddy Weave recorded a song called "Redeemed"... The first verse says it well...

"Seems like all I could see was the struggle
Haunted by ghosts that lived in my past
Bound up in shackles of all my failures
Wondering how long is this gonna last
Then You look at this prisoner and say to me "son
Stop fighting a fight it's already been won"

I am redeemed, You set me free
So I'll shake off these heavy chains
Wipe away every stain, now I'm not who I used to be
I am redeemed, I'm redeemed"... REDEEMED

JAN 27

NOTHING TO FEAR

2 Timothy 3:1-9

"But know this, that in the last days perilous times will come: For men will be lovers of themselves, lovers of money, boasters, proud, blasphemers, disobedient to parents, unthankful, unholy, unloving, unforgiving, slanderers, without self-control, brutal, despisers of good, traitors, headstrong, haughty, lovers of pleasure rather than lovers of God, having a form of godliness but denying its power. And from such people turn away! For of this sort are those who creep into households and make captives of gullible women loaded down with sins, led away by various lusts, always learning and never able to come to the knowledge of the truth. Now as Jannes and Jambres resisted Moses, so do these also resist the truth: men of corrupt minds, disapproved concerning the faith; but they will progress no further, for their folly will be manifest to all, as theirs also was."

For those that have watched biblical prophecy take place, we have been amazed at the speed in which we've been hurled forward towards "end times". I don't know if we are 1 day, 1 year or 100 years from Christ calling His children home... But this I know, today we are closer than yesterday.

Looking into Bible prophecy for yourself can be scary business. Not even a Hollywood disaster movie does justice to what Revelation predicts we must go through before Jesus comes. Understandably, even true believers get frightened by what they read in their Bibles, despite that verse that says "perfect love casts out all fear." If you haven't yet acquired "perfect love" then you may want to learn to face and conquer your fears concerning what we may face soon.

I must admit that there have been times when I have feared for what we may face as those that are willing to stand for Christ... But lately I've come to an excitement instead of fear. As Paul wrote in Philippians 1:21, "For to me, to live is Christ and to die is gain." What do I have to lose? Nothing... Just to gain.

God is calling His children together and we will need to become a true family in Him, If we know Him... We truly have "nothing to fear".

JOURNAL ENTRY

_____

_____

_____

_____

January

JAN 28

1 Peter 3:15
"But in your hearts revere Christ as Lord. Always be prepared to give an answer to everyone who asks you to give the reason for the hope that you have. But do this with gentleness and respect,"

I've read that NFL players train and prepare for appropriately 2000 hours a year. However, the average starting player actually has 4 minutes of playing time (actual action) per game, times 16 games equals, 60 minutes of action per year. Think about it, training 2000 hours for one hour of action.

Peter tells us to "be prepared (or trained) to give an answer". How long have you prepared this week, this month, this year to speak to others about a God that even gave His only Son (John 3:16)? It's embarrassing to think that grown men playing a game prepare hundreds of times more than we do, to play a game.

Abraham Lincoln once said, "Give me six hours to chop down a tree and I will spend the first four sharpening the axe".

Lincoln knew the meaning of being prepared to get the job done.

Many of you read this short lesson each morning, which is great. Keep it up... But I hope that it inspires you to dig deeper, to spend more time looking into God's Word yourself. I challenge you to prepare to give an answer for why you follow God...

I challenge you... be prepared!

JOURNAL ENTRY

___

___

___

___

___

___

___

JAN 29

STAND THE TEST

James 1:12
"Blessed is the one who perseveres under trial because, having stood the test, that person will receive the crown of life that the Lord has promised to those who love him."

Our lives are filled with trials... Today mine was filled with high winds and driving rain... Along with very unseasonably warm temperatures. When guiding for deer this can be (and this week is) and recipe for disaster. But I keep telling myself that I can't do much of anything about nature... It's taken me years to realize I can only control the things that God has put under my control. Once we realize that God has control of everything and allows only certain things to fall within our realm of influence only then do we allow ourselves to totally trust Him. We will have pain and trials. We will go through bad times... But we can trust Him 110%

Vince Lombardi once said... "Once you agree upon the price you must pay for success, it enables you to ignore the minor hurts, the opponent's pressure, and the temporary failures."

Satan will attack God's people. We will face temporary pain and suffering. But we know, without a shadow of a doubt that God will carry us through.

Stand the test!

JOURNAL ENTRY

JAN 30

FAITH DON'T COME IN A BUSHEL BASKET,

Galatians 3:6
"Just as Abraham believed God, and it was counted to him as righteousness"?

With these words, "Abraham believed God," Paul shows us that faith in God is the highest worship, the greatest allegiance, the ultimate obedience, and the most pleasing sacrifice. If you have faith to truly believe God has your best in mind, you will discover that faith is all-powerful. Its power is immeasurable and infinite. Faith gives God the greatest honor anyone can give Him. Giving God honor is believing Him, considering Him truthful, wise, righteous, merciful, and all-powerful. In short, it's recognizing that He is the Creator and Giver of every good thing. Reason doesn't do this; only faith does.

In the Lynn Austin novel, "Candle in the Darkness" Lynn writes, "Faith don't come in a bushel basket, Missy. It come one step at a time." Decide to trust Him for one little thing today, and before you know it, you find out He's so trustworthy you be putting your whole life in His hands.

Faith makes God real to us. Where there is no faith, God has no majesty or divine power. The life without faith (trusting that God is who He says He is and will do what He says He will do) cannot draw on the power of God. True faith in God, is giving up of our personal desires... and knowing that His ways are best. When we have that kind of faith we are showing the greatest wisdom, the highest justice, and the best worship, while offering the most pleasing sacrifice.

"Faith don't come in a bushel basket"... But it can...

JOURNAL ENTRY

_____

_____

_____

_____

_____

_____

JAN 31

QUALITY CROP

2 Corinthians 8:9
"For you know the grace of our Lord Jesus Christ, that though he was rich, yet for your sake he became poor, so that you by his poverty might become rich."

I've found that I'm happiest when I can make others happy... I'm most fulfilled when I can see others getting not only their needs but some of their desires met as well. This is true in marriage, friendships and often while serving strangers.

I recently heard a story that showed the benefit of helping others...

There was a farmer who grew excellent quality corn. Every year he won the award for the best grown corn. One year a newspaper reporter interviewed him and learned something interesting about how he grew it. The reporter discovered that the farmer shared his seed corn with his neighbors. "How can you afford to share your best seed corn with your neighbors when they are entering corn in competition with yours each year?" the reporter asked.

"Why sir," said the farmer, "Didn't you know? The wind picks up pollen from the ripening corn and swirls it from field to field. If my neighbors grow inferior corn, cross-pollination will steadily degrade the quality of my corn. If I am to grow good corn, I must help my neighbors grow good corn."

So it is with our lives... Those who want to live happy and fulfilled lives are those that help enrich the lives of others. If Christ had remained in heaven instead of coming and giving (even to the point of His life on the cross) where would we be today?

You can choose to be happy today and invest in the happiness of others.

Grow a quality crop of happiness!

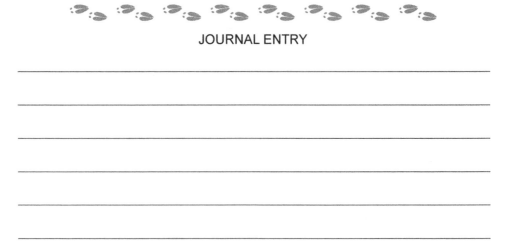

JOURNAL ENTRY

_____

_____

_____

_____

_____

_____

February

John 3:16

For God so loved the world that he gave his one and only Son, that whoever believes in him shall not perish but have eternal life.

FEB 1

Psalm 23:1-4
1 The Lord is my shepherd, I lack nothing. 2 He makes me lie down in green pastures, He leads me beside quiet waters, 3 He refreshes my soul. He guides me along the right paths for his name's sake. 4 Even though I walk through the darkest valley, I will fear no evil, for you are with me; your rod and your staff, they comfort me.

I'm starting my 30th year of guiding this year. It doesn't seem possible until I look back on all of the great friends that I've made over that time. I do have some friends that always tell me they wouldn't go on a guided hunt as they would always prefer to do it all themselves.

There are some places hunting on your own is not legal and if you want to hunt there you are required to have a licensed guide with you. Why? To protect you from the dangers. For instance a non-resident hunter in Alaska is required by law to have a guide for grizzly bears, sheep etc... Without a guide your life is in danger in many situations on these trips.

This is the case with life in general. We have a need for a guide in our lives. Most everyone has heard and/or memorized the 23rd Psalm. These verses speak of a shepherd that is caring for His sheep.

Life is dangerous and we could also use a guide. He is always there and all too often we ignore His advise and guiding. When we do this we end up in terrible trouble. Stick close to your Guide in life.

When times are dark your Guide will light your way for you. He holds the light that illuminates our way in life.

Psalms 119:105 Thy word is a lamp unto my feet, and a light unto my path.

Use your guide regularly.

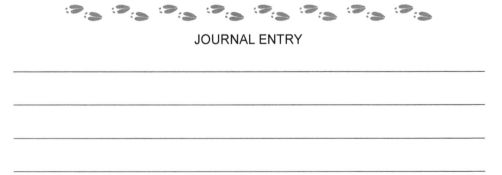

FEB 2

HAVE THE OLD THINGS PASSED AWAY?

2 Corinthians 5:17
Therefore if any man be in Christ, he is a new creature: old things are passed away; behold, all things have become new.

A caterpillar is an interesting insect in many ways. However, it would rarely be called beautiful. At some point in its life it creates this shell called a cocoon around itself. This cocoon isn't very pretty either. Sometime later it emerges from this shell a totally new and different creation. Now it is amazingly beautiful... AND IT FLIES!!

This a great symbol of lives that come to trust in Christ, "old things are passed away, all things are new". We no longer have to crawl through life struggling to get over obstacles on our own efforts, we are released to fly.

If the new creation, the beautiful butterfly, tried to carry the shell of the caterpillar around so it could live in its old life... It will never be able to fly. Once one comes to Christ, we are free from carrying the burdens of our past. Like the caterpillar turned butterfly we have lift under our wings in life. Christ is what lifts us.

Let go of your past... Learn to fly... You are a new creation.

JOURNAL ENTRY

FEB 3

COUNT IT ALL JOY

James 1:2-8

2 Consider it pure joy, my brothers, whenever you face trials of many kinds, 3 because you know that the testing of your faith develops perseverance. 4 Perseverance must finish its work so that you may be mature and complete, not lacking anything. 5 If any of you lacks wisdom, he should ask God, who gives generously to all without finding fault, and it will be given to him. 6 But when he asks, he must believe and not doubt, because he who doubts is like a wave of the sea, blown and tossed by the wind. 7 That man should not think he will receive anything from the Lord; 8 he is a double-minded man, unstable in all he does.

It's interesting that James had no doubt that we would face trials... It is inevitable. He said "when" not "if". We will face trials and many WILL be unjust. But God doesn't give us these trials to break down our faith, but to build it up.

Trials in themselves don't produce faith, but when trials are received with faith, it produces perseverance or patience. Yet patience is not automatically produced in times of trial. If difficulties are received without unbelief or with grumbling, trials can produce bitterness and discouragement. This is why James directs us to "count it all joy". Counting it all joy is faith's response to our trials.

Later in verses 6 & 7 James tells us to ask without doubting. God wants us to build our faith and patience and then to come to Him and ask; believing that our heavenly father truly wants His children to be happy.

This week as you face trials, and you will, first count it as joy because you can rest assured that if you do... You will be blessed. When someone else takes the recognition that you deserve, count it as joy. When the rug has been pulled out from under you... Again, count it all as joy. Even if your home has been taken from you... Count it all as joy!

Trust that God is working in you and HE will bless you if your heart is right and you come and ask Him for His will.

JOURNAL ENTRY

_____

_____

_____

_____

FEB 4

YOU ARE IMPORTANT

Psalm 8:3-4
When I consider your heavens, the work of your fingers, the moon and the stars, which you have set in place, 4 what is mankind that you are mindful of them, human beings that you care for them?

When you consider what a small piece of the overall universe we are a part of, it truly is amazing that God even cares a little about our "insignificant" lives.

The comedian, Steve Martin said this, "If you've got a dollar and you spend 29 cents on a loaf of bread, you've got 71 cents left; but if you've got seventeen grand and you spend 29 cents on a loaf of bread, you've still got seventeen grand. There's a math lesson for you."

To God, we are always worth the seventeen grand to Him, plus much more. The payment for each of us was the death of His son. Yet, as an indescribably small part of an indescribably huge universe, God still cares about each and every one of his children.

What do we have to be concerned about in life, really?

Matthew 6:26 says, Look at the birds of the air; they do not sow or reap or store away in barns, and yet your heavenly Father feeds them. Are you not much more valuable than they?

JOURNAL ENTRY

___

___

___

___

___

___

___

___

FEB 5

MAKE A DIFFERENCE IN SOMEONE'S LIFE

John 13:35
By this all people will know that you are my disciples,
if you have love for one another

Jesus said these words just after "lowering" Himself to wash his disciple's feet. At the time they didn't know what He was doing and argued that He shouldn't be doing it. But Christ was the perfect example of what we should be...

Christ gave 100% of himself, to the point of death. If we use His example we will give up our "lives" daily. If we do this, by putting others needs above our own, many people will see that we are different from the world.

I've been so blessed to be able to serve some special needs families over the last 20 years. Getting to sit side by side with a child and their parent when someone's first deer was taken is an amazing experience. The families of these young people have always gone out of their way to thank me for what I've done. But the truth is that I am that one that was blessed. What I was given from these experiences far outweighed what I gave.

Practice giving of yourself daily. Start with small steps and you will get addicted to the joy that it brings. Life is short, make a difference!

JOURNAL ENTRY

FEB 6

YOUR OBITUARY

Galatians 5:24
Those who are Christ's have crucified the flesh with its passions and desires.
Four years ago I sat with my brothers and wrote my dad's obituary. It was a tough thing to do, but was also a way to honor a good man. If someone were to write your obituary today, what would stand out? Would the things of this world be first and boldest in the words? Or would it be what you did for Christ that would shine brightest?

Paul wrote to the Galatian people to crucify the flesh with its passions and desires. Not only put it to death, but kill it where it's obvious to you and others that it is dead. By killing the worldly things, it only leaves Godly things.

When my obituary is written, I hope that it won't be written of the things I have accomplished for men, not about my hunting, not even about my family... but instead, for what I did to serve God. This is what's important in life.

You can strive to become wealthy, but if you don't honor God through it, what will it get you? You can build a powerful organization, but if you aren't building better God loving people what good have you done?

Matthew 16:24 says, "... If anyone wants to be my disciple he must first deny himself..."

Think for a minute about what your obituary would say... And start rewriting it today.

Don't settle in life for the bad, don't even settle for the good. But instead, search out the best.

JOURNAL ENTRY

FEB 7

DO WHAT YOU'RE CALLED TO DO

2 Timothy 4:2-5
Preach the word; be prepared in season and out of season; correct, rebuke and encourage—with great patience and careful instruction. 3 For the time will come when people will not put up with sound doctrine. Instead, to suit their own desires, they will gather around them a great number of teachers to say what their itching ears want to hear. 4 They will turn their ears away from the truth and turn aside to myths. 5 But you, keep your head in all situations, endure hardship, do the work of an evangelist and discharge all the duties of your ministry.

When I first read these verses I thought that it was stressing the others in our world that are giving out false information. They preach what people want to hear, not the truth.

But this passage starts and ends with a verse of instruction and challenge. The more false teaching there is, the more I/we are responsible to speak the truth.

Not that it doesn't matter to God what others are doing but God has called each of us for a purpose and we are to do the work He has set for us.

A great read is Philippines 3. In verse 14 it says, "I press on toward the goal to win the prize for which God has called me heavenward in Christ Jesus."

Move forward, in whatever God has called you to do. There will be those around that will teach falsely, but keep speaking the truth. Fulfill your calling. Serve God by serving others.

JOURNAL ENTRY

FEB 8

STAND FIRM TO THE END

John 15:18-25

18 "If the world hates you, keep in mind that it hated me first. 19 If you belonged to the world, it would love you as its own. As it is, you do not belong to the world, but I have chosen you out of the world. That is why the world hates you. 20 Remember what I told you: 'A servant is not greater than his master'. If they persecuted me, they will persecute you also. If they obeyed my teaching, they will obey yours also. 21 They will treat you this way because of my name, for they do not know the one who sent me.

I remember hearing these verses as a child. We were warned that if we stood for Christ we would be hated. Well I stood for Christ in school and I got laughed at but not hated. It was like a badge of courage to me.

Our world has changed... Yesterday morning I saw a post on FaceBook by a news agency about Josh Dugger and the sexual sin he admitted to, from 15 years ago, when he was a boy. I read the comments and it was clear that 99% of those that were commenting had not heard the whole story that they were commenting on. They just hated what the family stood for.

I wrote my opinion on sin and forgiveness. WOW!! Within minutes I was totally bombarded by 36 people that hated this young man and the entire Duggar family. They hated the Duggers and me at that point because we spoke of God. I tried to respond in a loving, biblical way, but to no avail.

We must realize now that we now live in a world where if we stand for the one true God we will be hated. But there is hope and a great promise...

Matthew 10:22 assures us; "You will be hated by everyone because of me, but the one who stands firm to the end will be saved.".

Stand firm.

JOURNAL ENTRY

_____

_____

_____

_____

_____

FEB 9

Romans 12:4-5
4 For just as each of us has one body with many members, and these members do not all have the same function, 5 so in Christ we, though many, form one body, and each member belongs to all the others.

We deal with such pain in our physical bodies. As we grow older the injuries we had at a younger age come back to give us discomfort. And as we feel pain we deal with it... We don't ignore it hoping that it will go away. We don't throw a body part away because it is hurting.

The same needs to be true with the Christian family, we are a body. The hand cannot work without the arm, the shoulder, the neck etc... We need each other to survive and thrive. When you see a part of the body/family hurting, rush to it and love it back to health. You wouldn't look down at your leg, seeing blood gushing out and think, "someone else will take care of that"... You would care for it. The same should be true with the body of Christ.

Desmond Tutu once wrote, "You don't choose your family, they are God's gift to you, as you are to them."

Treat each part of your Christian family as a precious gift from God. Care for it, love it and keep it healthy.

JOURNAL ENTRY

___
___
___
___
___
___
___

FEB 10

FIND YOUR MOUNTAIN

Matthew 14:22-23

22 Immediately Jesus made the disciples get into the boat and go on ahead of him to the other side, while he dismissed the crowd. 23 After he had dismissed them, he went up on a mountainside by himself to pray. Later that night, he was there alone...

Is there any place more special than a mountain? When a person needs to just get away to think and pray there is no better place. When I am in the mountains I can't wait for morning to come, to see the sunrise as it illuminates God's amazing creation. It is a special time.

In these two verses, Jesus had just come off of a hard day of speaking and feeding the 5,000 and was mourning the death of John the Baptist. He was no doubt physically worn down and feeling for John's family. Jesus sent everyone away and went to the mountain.

Do you have a "mountain" to get away to? A place where you can be alone in prayer, a place where there are no distractions?

There is nothing wrong with needing time to refresh in life. We all try to act strong for the appearance to those around us. But take the time to refresh physically, emotionally and spiritually... Even the son of God did.

Find your mountain.

JOURNAL ENTRY

_____

_____

_____

_____

_____

_____

_____

_____

FEB 11

Colossians 3:13
Bear with each other and forgive one another if any of you has a grievance against someone. Forgive as the Lord forgave you.

We've all been hurt so badly by someone that it is extremely difficult to even think about forgiving them, let alone actually forgiving them. I believe that it is impossible to truly forgive someone an offense without the help of God... Why? Because, since the original sin from Adam and Eve, humans have all carried a sin nature.

C.S. Lewis once said, "To be a Christian means to forgive the inexcusable because God has forgiven the inexcusable in you."

Life is too short, to spend any time holding a grudge against someone. The person that you can't forgive is not the one being brought down... It's the one that can't forgive.

Let it go, forgive as God forgave you. The freedom and rest you will receive will be well worth it.

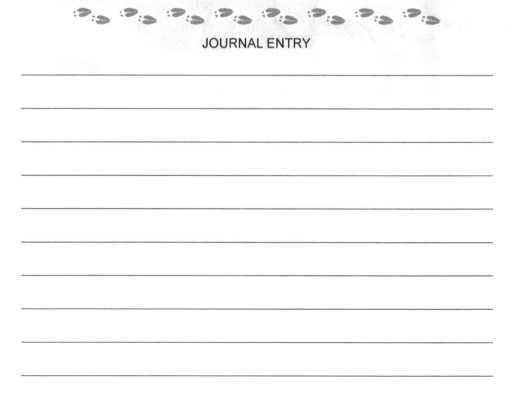

JOURNAL ENTRY

FEB 12

SLOW DOWN... SEE BEYOND

Luke 12:27
"Consider how the wild flowers grow. They do not labor or spin. Yet I tell you, not even Solomon in all his splendor was dressed like one of these."

God's creation is an amazing thing. When we look around at the beauty of nature in its entire splendor, a small wildflower, a crystal stream, a floating eagle on the afternoon thermals, a deer browsing on summer growth, how can someone look around and say, there is no Creator?

Yet, so many of us see this all with our eyes daily and it rarely gets to our hearts. Being an avid outdoorsman, I love to see game animals and have probably been guilty of looking past the beauty of the big picture to see something else. To see a bull elk is a fantastic sight, but if we miss the golden aspens, the seeping springs, the magpie or the mountain... We may have missed the best parts of creation.

Slow down, release the "pinpoint focuses" of life and learn to appreciate the whole picture. Slow down, breath in deep and appreciate the breath. Slow down, and learn to see all that God has blessed you with.

Lao Tzu gave good advice with one small quote. "Nature does not hurry, yet everything is accomplished."

Learn to see beyond your focus of this moment. God has so much for us to see and appreciate

JOURNAL ENTRY

_____

_____

_____

_____

_____

_____

_____

FEB 13

A TIME TO LAUGH

2 Samuel 6:14
And David danced before the Lord with all his might;
and David was girded with a linen ephod.

Our world has a misconception about Christians and fun. Billy Joel sang the song, "Only the Good Die Young". In that song he sang, "I'd rather laugh with the sinners than cry with the saints Sinners are much more fun..."

So untrue, God wants His children to have all the fun possible. He wants us to be filled with Joy, to dance, to celebrate... And then He wants us to wake up the next morning with a clear conscience.

Don't let the world see you looking like you are in mourning all the time. What kind of testimony is that?

Ecclesiastes 3:1 & 4 There is a time for everything, and a season for every activity under the heavens: 4 a time to weep and a time to laugh, a time to mourn and a time to dance,

Don't let the world believe that "the sinners are much more fun"... We've got the market cornered on Joy. Let it show!

JOURNAL ENTRY

FEB 14

Proverbs 4:23
Above all else, guard your heart,
for everything you do flows from it.

In the last 50 years we have seen a total twisting of what Love is. Love has become a physical thing and certainly not a spiritual thing. When people talk about emotional love their thoughts quite often go to Valentine's Day. But when it comes to today's real feeling towards someone else of the opposite sex the old Tina Turner song comes to mind, "What's Love Got To Do With It".

If we want to get to what love is supposed to be we need to go back to God's word. There is no place else to go, because without God's word there is no basis for love in this world. If God isn't real then there is not right and wrong and no love. God set the standard. And while we cannot truly attain the perfect Agape love that God shows us, we can learn to love by His example.

God's love was manifest in the fact that Christ gave up His life for His children, you and I. That alone is enough of a basis to know what love should be. Giving totally of yourself for the well being of someone else. When you put someone else's thoughts, wishes and desires, needs and dreams above your own.

Proverbs 4:23 tells us to guard our heart, why, because EVERYTHING else flows from it. That just shows you how important our heart is to our well being. So today as you exchange valentines and eat a heart shaped cookie, remember, God's love is the standard. Love as He loved us.

Happy Valentine's Day

JOURNAL ENTRY

___
___
___
___
___
___

FEB 15

COMFORT ZONE

Joshua 1:9
Have I not commanded you? Be strong and courageous. Do not be frightened, and do not be dismayed, for the Lord your God is with you wherever you go.

We've read of heroes in the Bible, men and women that did great things. Men and women who seemed to be fearless but they were all people like you and me. Most of them questioned if they were capable of doing what they were called to do.

Take Moses for instance... God told him to get God's people free from the Egyptians and over and over again Moses argued that he couldn't do it. After other excuses he said that he had a slow tongue. In Exodus 4:11-12 God told Moses this,

"Who gives man his mouth? Who makes him deaf or dumb? Who gives him sight or makes him blind? It is I, the Lord. 12 Now, go! I will help you to speak, and I will tell you what to say."

When God calls you and me, He doesn't ask us to do anything He hasn't prepared us for, anything He hasn't already given us the tools to get the job done. We can ALWAYS count on the old saying, "if God calls you to it, He will see you through it".

2 Timothy 1:7 gives us great confidence in knowing these things...

"For God gave us a spirit not of fear but of power and love and self-control."

Life begins at the end of your comfort zone... Live it!

JOURNAL ENTRY

FEB 16

REVIVE, REFRESH AND BE RENEWED

Isaiah 40:31
31 but those who hope in the Lord will renew their strength. They will soar on wings like eagles; they will run and not grow weary, they will walk and not be faint.

Finally, I believe winter is over. Even spring felt somewhat like winter this year. Just last week, we had heavy frost three mornings in a row. Early this morning it is 56 glorious degrees and the sun is just starting to come up. It gives new hope, new life and it renews my strength.

The Bible tells us in many places that God will renew us, revive us and He will restore us.

Psalms 51: 10 Create in me a clean heart, O God and renew a steadfast sprit within me.

Psalms 85:6 Will you not revive us again. That Your People may rejoice in you again.

God uses many things to renew, revive and restore us. He often uses His people to do this for others. Are you available? Are you looking for opportunities to refresh others? Are you asking God to use you?

It makes my day when someone responds to a morning devotional saying, "I really needed this today to get me through" or "somehow you knew what I needed to restore me today". I take pride, not in myself, but in the fact that God has allowed me to do that for some of you. He directs my thoughts and my typing, He alone gets the credit.

Proverbs 11:25 A generous man will prosper; he who refreshes others will be refreshed. Make it a point to refresh someone today. Pray for that opportunity, by doing so you too will be refreshed.

JOURNAL ENTRY

___

___

___

___

___

FEB 17

SLIP SLIDING AWAY

John 16:33
33 "I have told you these things, so that in me you may have peace. In this world you will have trouble. But take heart! I have overcome the world."

A few days ago I was turkey hunting with one of my oldest and dearest friends. Late in the afternoon he got a message that his wife's brother had just been diagnosed with a brain tumor. The doctors said that they would be doing surgery within a day or two. In the morning Steve packed and headed home to be with his wife and her family. He wanted to be with them to comfort them in this time of hardship. One of the greatest challenges we have is to somehow continue to believe God and to trust Him in the midst of horrendous devastation. When you see children being separated from their fathers and mothers by death., when you see families brought to their knees by sickness we start to wonder, "Where is God?"

What we need to realize is that God can be trusted, even when it seems as if He is not on our side. We have to point people to the fact that God has intervened in our planet by sending Jesus Christ. There we see the love of God most clearly. He gave His own son (John 3:16) to die a horrible, painful death, on a cross, for each one of us.

SIMON & GARFUNKEL'S song "Slip Sliding Away" has it somewhat right and somewhat wrong... "God only knows, God makes his plan. The information's unavailable to the mortal man"

We don't know all of God's plans, but we do know much of it as it is laid out in His word. The rest, we need to believe that even in the worst of times, He still loves us and cares. I think this is the best illustration. All of Job's 10 children died in a disaster that was totally out of his control. There was a wind storm that blew down the house. Job was confronted with the fact that because of something completely unexplainable, there are 10 fresh graves on the hill. So now what is he going to do?

His "loving" wife says to curse God and die. But Job said, "The Lord gave and the Lord has taken away. Blessed be the name of the Lord." Job shows us that even in the midst of losing his family, it is still possible to worship God even without explanations, even when we don't know all the reasons. Those who worship God under those conditions are especially blessed.

As we deal today with heartache and pain, with disaster and uncertainty, we can know that through it all, God is there for each of us. These things are easier with God in our life.

Lastly, remember that God created a perfect world that was brought down to this level by man's choice for sin. There will be a perfect place for us again, if we trust in Him.

FEB 18

PUTTING OFF THE OLD

Ephesians 4:22-24
22 You were taught, with regard to your former way of life, to put off your old self, which is being corrupted by its deceitful desires; 23 to be made new in the attitude of your minds; 24 and to put on the new self, created to be like God in true righteousness and holiness.

We just got back from a trip across the southern states. In Texas, while we were turkey hunting, we saw whitetail bucks without antlers and some still carrying their racks. Most bucks and bull elk across the country have dropped their antlers by this time of the year or are in the process right now.

Shedding antlers is very similar to what should happen to the children of God. When antlers shed it is removing old dead weight and replacing it with new living tissue. If the old antlers didn't fall off there would be no possibility of the new healthy, quite often bigger and stronger, antlers to grow.

If a Christian doesn't get rid of the old things of their life the sinful past there is no room for the new way of life. No matter how much we try to change and grow it just can't happen. Until the old is gone, the growth of the new is impossible.

In 2nd Corinthians, Paul writes that Christians are a new creation... Not just changed, but new.

2 Corinthians 5:17
17 Therefore, if anyone is in Christ, he is a new creation; old things have passed away; behold, all things have become new.

So if you haven't gotten rid of the old, do that or new growth can't happen. You are a new creation.

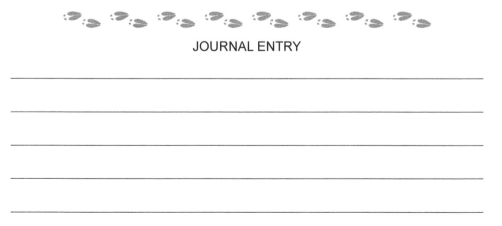

JOURNAL ENTRY

_____

_____

_____

_____

_____

FEB 19

PRAISE GOD FOR HIS PLAN.

1 Corinthians 9:19-23

For though I am free from all men, I have made myself a servant to all, that I might win the more; 20 and to the Jews I became as a Jew, that I might win Jews; to those who are under the law, as under the law, that I might win those who are under the law; 21 to those who are without law, as without law (not being without law toward God, but under law toward Christ), that I might win those who are without law; 22 to the weak I became as weak, that I might win the weak. I have become all things to all men, so that I might by all means save some. 23 Now this I do for the gospel's sake, that I may be partaker of it with you.

Most of us were taught at a young age to not care about what others thought of us. We were told it doesn't matter what anybody else thinks and we shouldn't change to meet what someone else wants us to be. Yet here the apostle Paul writes, "I have become all things to all men".

I've learned that God puts us in places so that we can relate to others in that same place. It might be a lifestyle, vocation, hobbies, pain, sickness or even tragedy. God will move us to a place where we can be used by Him to reach and serve others. Just today I was able to counsel someone because of what God brought me through.

If you are going through a bad time right now, just think, God could be preparing you help someone else get through something similar or worse. Look at your circumstance today, is God preparing you to be His tool to care for someone else. Imagine, God chose you for a very special purpose.

Or perhaps you've felt like you have drifted from place to place in life not knowing what is next... Take a moment to look back and see how God has connected the dots of your life to build you into what He needs you to be. Don't waste the lesson.

Remember as you struggle with pain or discouragement today or confusion of not knowing what tomorrow will bring the words of Isaiah, in chapter 55, verses 8-9;

8 My thoughts are not your thoughts, neither are your ways my ways, declares the Lord. 9 as the heavens are higher than the earth, so are my ways higher than yours and my thoughts your thoughts.

JOURNAL ENTRY

___

___

___

FEB 20

FULFILL THE GREAT COMMISSION.

Matthew 28:16-20

16 But the eleven disciples proceeded to Galilee, to the mountain which Jesus had designated. 17 When they saw Him, they worshiped Him; but some were doubtful. 18 And Jesus came up and spoke to them, saying, "All authority has been given to Me in heaven and on earth. 19 Go therefore and make disciples of all the nations, baptizing them in the name of the Father and the Son and the Holy Spirit, 20 teaching them to observe all that I commanded you; and lo, I am with you always, even to the end of the age."

Someone yesterday shared a story with me after reading the mornings devotional. It struck me and I would like to share it. This person shared with me how they heard God calling them to do something, and they responded. She wrote, "I was moved to witness to my atheist father-in-law. Almost didn't make the call. Never heard any affirmation from him, but the next day he had massive heart failure and died. Glad I obeyed. Hope he heard."

She "hoped he heard". I do too, but that part is between the person and God himself... We're just called to listen and obey.

The verses above are called "The Great Commission". Throughout Christ's ministry He had shared with His disciples tasks to do, feed the hungry, care for the widows and orphans etc. But His last words to them were found in these verses.

Life is short, for some of us it could be very short, we don't know. God has left those here on earth, that know Him, for one purpose, to "Go therefore and make disciples of all the nations". When we hear that small quiet whisper what is our response? What do we have to lose? What does the other person have to gain?

Several years ago I came back to my desk after lunch. I shared a common area with several people, all of whom didn't have a relationship with Christ. I hit the button on my phone to listen to my messages. This is what came over the speaker, loud enough for all to hear; "Good afternoon Dean. Hey if you had a cure for cancer, would you be telling everyone about it? You know something much better, tell everyone.". No one in that office had to wonder what I believed after that.

Do you think God would ask us each to share about His Son, Christ if He didn't believe we could do it? We have nothing to lose and those around us have everything to gain!

Fulfill the Great Commission.

JOURNAL ENTRY

FEB 21

HEAR THE HORN BLOW

Hebrews 4:7
7 God again set a certain day, calling it "Today." This he did when a long time later he spoke through David, as in the passage already quoted: "Today, if you hear his voice, do not harden your hearts."

Robert Ruark was a journalist from New York City who traveled Africa with his wife on Safari. Ruark wrote of his adventures and his works have been read by millions... you either love his work or hate it. This morning I read several reviews on his book, "Horn of the Hunter". It is interesting how all but one of the reviews talked about the hunt, the adventure, the writing style etc. One review stood out to me, this review spoke of the "horn" itself that a person with a hunter's heart hears in life. If you are not a serious, buffalo plaid, camouflage clad hunter that eats, drinks and sleeps hunting you might not understand (unless you are married to one). This review spoke of hearing the "horn" and being drawn to it... a person sold out to the hunting lifestyle.

So it is with (or should be) with the Christian life, when we hear the voice of the Lord calling us to Him. Many will feel that they know God, some will even do things for God's service... but if you truly hear the "horn" calling to you, then you should be sold out to His calling and His service.

In 1st Kings 19:11-13 God spoke to Elijah... and Elijah heard. Why, because he was listening for the call, the "horn" blowing. 11 The Lord said, "Go out and stand on the mountain in the presence of the LORD, for the LORD is about to pass by." Then a great and powerful wind tore the mountains apart and shattered the rocks before the LORD, but the LORD was not in the wind. After the wind there was an earthquake, but the LORD was not in the earthquake. 12 After the earthquake came a fire, but the LORD was not in the fire. And after the fire came a gentle whisper. 13 When Elijah heard it, he pulled his cloak over his face and went out and stood at the mouth of the cave. Then a voice said to him, "What are you doing here, Elijah?"

Like Ruark's book, "Horn of the Hunter" we need to be truly in tune with what we hear. We can hear God's calling and not know what we heard, or we can hear and be sold out to a life of His calling. Quite often when God speaks it is in its still soft whisper and in order to hear it we must be close to Him. To hear the "horn" blowing we must be listening for His call, in tune to Him and close. Then we must respond.

HEAR THE HORN BLOW.

JOURNAL ENTRY

February

FEB 22

Acts 27:18-20

We took such a violent battering from the storm that the next day they began to throw the cargo overboard. 19 On the third day, they threw the ship's tackle overboard with their own hands. 20 When neither sun nor stars appeared for many days and the storm continued raging, we finally gave up all hope of being saved.

H ave you ever been in a storm so bad that it seemed like you might not survive? It is a terrible feeling.

Quite a few years ago I was with a group on Lake Superior when a storm blew up. We were a two hour boat ride out from shore fishing, when all of a sudden the captain said, "pull up the lines, we have to head in NOW". You could tell by the tone of his voice that there was a problem. Within minutes we felt the problem when strong offshore winds hit us. The morning trip out that had taken 2 hours was now going to be a 4 1/2 hour trip back to the dock. We were tossed back and forth from one wave to the next the whole time the Gordon Lightfoot song, "The Wreck Of The Edmund Fitzgerald" kept playing through my head. Lots of prayers were prayed as waves rained down on top of the boat.

God brought us safely through the storm that day, as He eventually brought the Apostle Paul through the storm in the scripture from Acts above. But not without first testing our faith in Him. There are many storms in life that we face on a yearly, monthly or even weekly basis... We wonder how we can possibly get through them without perishing in the process. But God sees our peril and knows what we are going through. We are never alone. He has control of the storms of our life.

In the book of Mark chapter 4 verse 39 we can read of another storm that was completely under Christ's control. He had been sleeping in the boat when the others woke Him to show Him the danger that they were all in... "He got up, rebuked the wind and said to the waves, "Quiet! Be still!" Then the wind died down and it was completely calm."

We need to realize that no matter what storms we face, if we give God control over it, He can calm it.

JOURNAL ENTRY

___

___

___

FEB 23

1 Peter 5:8(NIV)
"Your adversary the devil walks about like a roaring lion, seeking whom he may devour."

The late Keith Green sang a song that grows more and more relevant each day. "No One Believes In Me Anymore" is a song about satan and his power. Here's a small part of the song.

"Oh, my job keeps getting easier as time keeps slipping away
I can imitate the brightest light and make your night look just like day
I put some truth in every lie to tickle itching ears
You know I'm drawing people just like flies
'Cause they like what they hear
I'm gaining power by the hour they're falling by the score
You know, it's getting very simple now
Since no one believes in me anymore"

Satan is real. He's not a little red cartoon character with pointed ears, a pointed tale, and a pitchfork. He is far more cunning and diabolical than that. Satan is alive and well, and he seeks to destroy you. His scheme is to destroy anything and everything as well as anyone that has anything to do with God.

Satan seeks to destroy God's world and all that are in it. How else could we possibly explain all of the pain today. How could we explain child abuse, the Holocaust, suicide bombings etc? Satan is alive and "walking about like a roaring lion, seeking whom he may devour." satan is pure evil. He exists and he is totally devoted to his unholy cause.

Satan is your personal enemy, and you will never have a greater foe than the devil.

The good news is this... With Christ in your life satan has no power over you, unless you give it to him. Don't give him power over your life.

Luke 10:19 (NIV) 19 I have given you authority to trample on snakes and scorpions and to overcome all the power of the enemy; nothing will harm you.

JOURNAL ENTRY

___
___
___
___

February

FEB 24

SEPARATE YOURSELF

Psalm 15:1-2
O LORD, who may abide in Your tent? Who may dwell on Your holy hill? He who walks with integrity, and works righteousness, And speaks truth in his heart

This past week I saw someone selling moose antlers on the internet. He didn't have a price listed and when I inquired the price was considerably higher than I could afford. The seller then responded with a much lower, much more attractive price. And... When the seller told me the story of his desperate need for money to keep his family going, I agreed to his offer. After several attempts we were able to transfer money to him... And that was the last I heard from him. I think I was scammed.

This past week I saw someone selling moose antlers on the internet. He didn't have a price listed and when I inquired the price was considerably higher than I could afford. The seller then responded with a much lower, much more attractive price. And... When the seller told me the story of his desperate need for money to keep his family going, I agreed to his offer. After several attempts we were able to transfer money to him... And that was the last I heard from him. I think I was scammed.

I'm hurt, I'm angry, I'm a little embarrassed and I'm becoming aware of how our world is being turned over to satan.

The last few days have made it perfectly clear (much more beyond this antler incident) that we are living in a time where there is no longer a line between right and wrong for the majority of people, but just a wide gray band. Satan has blurred the difference between dark and light for the worldly... They don't really care about others, just their wants and desires.

2 Timothy 3:1-5 warns of what will become of those that don't belong to Christ's family in the last days...

1 But know this, that in the last days perilous times will come: 2 For men will be lovers of themselves, lovers of money, boasters, proud, blasphemers, disobedient to parents, unthankful, unholy, 3 unloving, unforgiving, slanderers, without self-control, brutal, despisers of good, 4 traitors, headstrong, haughty, lovers of pleasure rather than lovers of God, 5 having a form of godliness but denying its power. And from such people turn away!

As the children of God we need to be ever mindful that the world is watching. Don't allow anyone to think of us as those that live like the people described in 2 Timothy 3... Be honest and trustworthy, looking out for others.

SEPARATE YOURSELF

FEB 25

Psalm 5:1-3
1 Listen to my words, Lord, consider my lament. 2 Hear my cry for help my King and my God, for to you I pray. 3 In the morning, Lord, you hear my voice in the morning I lay my requests before you and wait expectantly.

Every one of us has things we carry that are painful, some of these things we've carried for many years. None of us are immune to this. But, we need to remember that God has given us a place to bring our pain and our need for God's help.

Go daily before the Lord to release that pain and to plead for God's help. King David went before the Lord every morning... then he waited. He was dealing with things that were far weightier than what most of us carry on a daily basis. Yet David totally expected God to answer him... and he waited

Psalm 18:3. Says, I will call upon the LORD, who is worthy to be praised: so shall I be saved from mine enemies."

Your answer to your pain might not come today... but continue to go before Him, and in His timing, HE will take care of it. Just wait on Him. "Wait expectantly" as David did.

JOURNAL ENTRY

FEB 26

TAKE A STAND

1 Peter 2:9
But you are a chosen race, a royal priesthood, a holy nation, a people for his own possession, that you may proclaim the excellencies of him who called you out of darkness into his marvelous light.

Wow! If you have a personal relationship with Christ you have been called out... A "royal priesthood". Do you act like that? Can others see that in you? Do you show off your love for God through your life? Or is it hidden so well that there is no way to tell us from the rest of the world?

We have no idea what impact we can have on others by one small action. Consider Tim Tebow... During the 2009 College Championship game, he wore his "eye black" inscribed with John 3:16. During that game 92 million people used Google to look that verse up. That's 92 million people!!!!! They all read a gospel message because one young man was bold enough to take a stand.

Israelmore Ayivor made a secular statement but it is true in the spiritual world as well... "Take a chance to standout. You can only have your head above water if you stick your neck out a bit. It's time to take off... Dare to rise!"

God is calling His people out. We are to be seen, to be heard, to stick your neck out, to stand up and stand out. Maybe you won't affect 92 million people... But if you affect just one that is all you are called to do today... And one tomorrow and then the next day etc... Take a stand!

JOURNAL ENTRY

FEB 27

THE COST OF SIN

Hebrews 12:15
15 See to it that no one falls short of the grace of God and that no bitter root grows up to cause trouble and defile many.

The headlines read, "VIDEO PUBLISHED ON NFL PROSPECT'S TWITTER ACCOUNT MAY HAVE COST HIM MILLIONS"

Not many of us had ever heard of Laremy Tunsil until a week or so ago. He was a college football player that was expected to be drafted in the first few picks last week. However, just before the draft someone posted a video of him doing drugs. Eventually the Dolphins selected him with their # 13 pick. But that drop may have cost Mr. Tunsil millions of dollars. Laremy admitted that it was him in the clip and that it was years earlier. And he said that it was a mistake that he regretted. This is an large example of how something that seemed harmless and small can have tremendous consequences later on... It the price of sin.

That's the way it is with sin too. It has a high cost, even though at the time it may seem so small. Seemingly harmless transgressions can end up doing great damage. The "root of bitterness"(from the verse above) or hatred in our lives can produce enormous spiritual harm to ourselves, others, and to our relationship with God.

If we have a relationship with Christ seemingly small sins can effect us and others in a big way, but we are forgiven. This doesn't mean there won't be consequences for our sin while still here in this life.

If you don't know Christ as your Savior, the cost of sin is much higher... That cost is death.

Romans 6:23 tells us that, "The wages of sin is death, but the gift of God is eternal life, through Jesus Christ our Lord."

We all deserve an eternal death, but God sent His Son to take the penalty for us, to provide an escape.

JOURNAL ENTRY

_____

_____

_____

_____

FEB 28

> **PREPARE TO GET THROUGH...**

Psalm 42:1-2
As the deer pants for streams of water, so my soul pants for you, my God.
2 My soul thirsts for God, for the living God. When can I go and meet with God?

I write daily words that go out to thousands, yet there are times I feel so very dry–so far away from the presence of God. In these moments of dryness, I have no great yearning to read the Word. My reading of the Bible is done mostly through a sense of obligation, a need to follow God's lead in my writing. When I'm dry and empty, I feel little "push" to pray. I know my faith is intact, and my love for Jesus is still strong. There is no desire in me to go after the sinful things of this world. It's just that I can't seem to touch God in those days and weeks of spiritual dryness.

Spiritual dryness can be a time of preparation for us. Most every well known godly person in the Bible that was used in a mighty way of God had to go through a dry/desert time. This includes Moses, Job, David, Elijah, Jesus, and Paul. Being in a place where we are dry, waiting, wanting, praying, examining, etc., is often a time of preparation for strength and refinement. Then, after this time is completed, the thing that we have been prepared for comes upon us. Sometimes this preparation is for hardship, sorrow, and pain. Other times it is for blessing, reward, and ministry. Remember, the Lord has not saved us to be trophies on His wall or shelf. We are His instruments to be used in the world. This usage requires that we be able to be used, able to be sent, able to trust the Lord in spite of what we see and feel. So, the time of spiritual dryness is a time of preparation.

We need to prepare our hearts to get through those deserts.

JOURNAL ENTRY

MARCH

Philippians 4:6

Do not be anxious about anything, but in every situation, by prayer and petition, with thanksgiving, present your requests to God.

MARCH 1

PRACTICE, PRACTICE, PRACTICE!

1 Samuel 16:7
But the Lord said to Samuel, "Do not consider his appearance or his height, for I have rejected him. The Lord does not look at the things people look at. People look at the outward appearance, but the Lord looks at the heart."

God has given me an eye for things in nature... I've been very blessed with the ability to see things that are out of place, things that just don't belong. One time I was driving down a gravel road on Kodiak Island and something caught my eye way off in the woods. I backed up (no traffic on the roads there) and walked back into the woods. Way back in there was a world class antler from a blacktail deer.

I can't take any credit for that ability, God blessed me with it. But the more we use the gifts that we are blessed with the keener they become. Discernment is a gift that God gives all His children, but if we don't use it and practice it regularly it doesn't become sharp.

There are so many false teachings and teachers in our world today...Things that are so close to the truth, yet fall short. We have to measure everything against the word of God... If it seems, "not quite right" study it further.

In Romans 12:2 Paul explained to the Romans... "And do not be conformed to this world, but be transformed by the renewing of your mind, so that you may prove what the will of God is, that which is good and acceptable and perfect."

Our hearts become renewed when we put our trust in Christ. Our minds are continually being renewed by Godly living, actions and thoughts.

Practice, practice, practice!

JOURNAL ENTRY

_____

_____

_____

_____

_____

MARCH 2

Ephesians 4:1-3&30
Therefore I, the prisoner of the Lord, implore you to walk in a manner worthy of the calling with which you have been called, 2 with all humility and gentleness, with patience, showing tolerance for one another in love, 3 being diligent to preserve the unity of the Spirit in the bond of peace... 30 Do not grieve the Holy Spirit of God, by whom you were sealed for the day of redemption.

Yesterday Linda told me about a young family that lost a 3 month old baby very unexpectedly. Recently we spent time with great friends whose 18 year old child had moved out under very bad conditions. I've known families who have been through battles of illness with their children, some to the point of death.

These parents grieve beyond my imagination The pain in their heart is something that is hard for anyone to bear. In the same way, I personally and all of us that would call ourselves "Christians", bring grief to our God. Our Lord is called ABBA in the scripture. This word means far more than "father"... It is a term that has no true translation in the English. It is an affectionate word that might come close to "Daddy" when used in the deepest loving sense.

So verse 30 said to "not grieve the Holy Spirit of God". This shows that our God, or ABBA is so much more than an unfeeling "dictator in the sky". He is hurt when we run away, when we make bad choices, when we turn our back to have our own way... And we all do.

I challenge you today to read Ephesians 4. Read it occasionally and do it with no distractions. Paul offers so much in this one short chapter.

As I think about "grieving the Lord" I'm reminded of an old Sunday school song, "Oh Be Careful". There are several verses but each one has the theme. At one time I thought the meaning of the song was that we had to be careful because God was watching and we might be in trouble... But is says " the father up above is looking down with love"... Don't grieve our ABBA.

JOURNAL ENTRY

_____

_____

_____

_____

MARCH 3

LISTEN CAREFULLY

1 Samuel 13:13-14

Samuel said to Saul, "You have acted foolishly; you have not kept the commandment of the Lord your God, which He commanded you, for now the Lord would have established your kingdom over Israel forever. 14 But now your kingdom shall not endure...

I've guided hunters and some fisherman for going on 30 years, I've often been amazed at the people that will pay for my services and yet, pay no attention to my direction. I once asked a hunter (right after he moved from the place I had placed him while I was calling turkeys), why do you pay me? His answer, "because I want your expertise." My response was, "save yourself some money because you are not listening anyhow".

How often we get good godly advice in our lives and just ignore it, thinking we know better than the one giving the advice. We often know right from wrong and we do the wrong out of impatience and selfish ambition. Thus was the case with King Saul... Samuel had given him a directive, yet Saul went ahead and did it this own way... For this one seemingly small infraction God pulled Saul's lineage from the leadership of Israel. If he had only listened!

We need to carefully listen to God's directives and then patiently wait for Him to move us. It's when we follow our own heart and our own desires that we will fail.

JOURNAL ENTRY

_____

_____

_____

_____

_____

_____

_____

MARCH 4

USE THE POWER

2 Timothy 2:21
Therefore, if anyone cleanses himself from these things, he will be a vessel for honor, sanctified, useful to the Master, prepared for every good work.

Driving across Southern Minnesota today we passed by 100's, if not 1000's, of giant wind turbines. Seeing it was a windy day, most of them were spinning feverishly harvesting the power of the wind and converting it to electric power. It is an amazing thing to see.

This reminded me of the power that we have available to us and responsibility we have to allow that power to work through us.

We each have a mission to accomplish, given by Jesus himself. Only by the outpouring of the Holy Spirit's Power can we expect to make a difference in this world. The promise of this divine ability recorded in Acts 1:8 was in fact the last thing Jesus said before his ascending return to heaven. "...you will receive power when the Holy Spirit has come upon you; and you shall be my witnesses both in Jerusalem, and in all Judea and Samaria, and even to the remotest part of the earth."

Jesus promised this over 2000 years ago and that promise has not changed–we are supernaturally equipped to preach the gospel to the ends of the earth. How are we using that power in our lives?

We cannot harvest anything from God like we harvest the wind power.... It's actually much easier than that. All we have to do is allow God to work in and through our lives.

Use the power!

JOURNAL ENTRY

MARCH 5

WHERE IS YOUR HOPE?

Romans 8:24-25
For in this hope we were saved. Now hope that is seen is not hope.
For who hopes for what he sees?
25 But if we hope for what we do not see, we wait for it with patience.

Where is our hope as we wait on the Lord to accomplish His work? What is our hope? Our biblical hope is different from human hope. What Hope Isn't

Hope is not "I hope my team wins the Super Bowl" or "I hope I get a raise." Biblical hope is not a "hope-so" but it is a "know-so". It isn't wishing for the best. It isn't waiting to see what happens and hope that it turns out well. Hope is not a feeling or an emotion. Biblical Hope is the knowledge of facts. If someone says to you that "I hope you have a good day," there is no guarantee that the day will go well. To have a biblical hope is to have a sure anchor of the soul, not hoping for rain because the forecast says that there is a 60% chance of rain and you hope that you get your garden watered. That is not hope... that is wishful thinking and it is totally undependable and has no power to make anything happen... It's just a wish. Human hope pales in comparison to biblical hope, as we shall read.

Paul gives us a great example of hope in Romans chapter 8. Whenever we encounter hopelessness in new believers and even among experienced Christians and there is doubt about their salvation, we can direct them back to Romans 8:24-25

A Christian's definition of hope is far superior to that of the world. Instead of wishing or hoping for something to happen, a believer knows that their hope is solid, concrete evidence because it is grounded in the Word of God and we know that God cannot lie (Heb 6:18; Num 23:19). The Christian has a hope that is "the assurance of things hoped for, the conviction of things not seen" (Heb 11:1). It is a hope that is like faith...a faith that cannot be moved by circumstances or what the eyes see because an unseen God is seen because He is faithful to us, His children.

Where is your hope?

JOURNAL ENTRY

___

___

___

___

MARCH 6

QUICK TO LISTEN, SLOW TO SPEAK

James 1:19-21

My dear brothers and sisters, take note of this: Everyone should be quick to listen, slow to speak and slow to become angry 20 because human anger does not produce the righteousness that God desires. 21 Therefore, get rid of all moral filth and the evil that is so prevalent and humbly accept the word planted in you, which can save you.

Though the Christian community places high regard on the talent of "pretty" speech, here James places the accent on listening. It is the person who listens intently to the Word of truth who moves forward in godliness.

As a boy and as a young man I can confess that I was quick to speak. Often I spoke without thinking too much first. Or I might have talked over others in a conversation. Even now, later in life, I have to tell myself to "stop and listen" and I've found that I learn a lot about others; their needs and passions. It doesn't really matter what they know about me... As long as they know that I care about them.

We will also find the more we intently listen, the slower we are to become quickly angered. We can discern an answer before we would if we were quick to speak. I've heard the statement many times, "there's a reason God gave us two ears and only one mouth". Good point.

In John 13:35 we are told "By this everyone will know that you are my disciples, if you love one another."

The world will also know that we love them if we are, "quick to listen, slow to speak and slow to become angry". This is different than the world's way... People will notice.

QUICK TO LISTEN, SLOW TO SPEAK

JOURNAL ENTRY

___

___

___

___

___

___

MARCH 7

WHAT IS YOUR FOUNDATION

Luke 6:47-48
Everyone who comes to me and hears my words and does them, I will show you what he is like: he is like a man building a house, who dug deep and laid the foundation on the rock. And when a flood arose, the stream broke against that house and could not shake it, because it had been well built.

This morning I can hear it pouring rain outside... I know that tomorrow I will be repairing some stuff that will be washed away around some of my roads and trails. I prepared yesterday for the upcoming storm and it won't be as bad as it could have been. I've also prepared for the storms that hit us in life...

If you grew up in the church, you probably heard the parable of the man building his house on the rock and the man who built his house on the sand when you were in Sunday school. Or you heard the song about the wise man and foolish man building their houses.

We can often focus on the foundation of the man whose house was built on the rock. He obeys the words of Jesus and his house stays up. We often tend to ignore that this man also goes through the storm. Both of these men go through the same storm, but there is a different outcome for each man. The only difference is their foundation.

We can learn a little bit of truth from this story. We learn that the Christian life isn't about escaping the storms that come our way. The Christian life is about weathering the storms with Jesus as our foundation. Jesus never said that the man who lives his words won't have any problems in life. He says that the man who does what he's said will be able to make it through these problems because he has Jesus as his foundation.

What is your foundation during the storms of life?

JOURNAL ENTRY

_____

_____

_____

_____

_____

_____

MARCH 8

A GOOD TURKEY HUNTER

James 1:14-15
... but each person is tempted when they are dragged away by their own evil desire and enticed. 15 Then, after desire has conceived, it gives birth to sin; and sin, when it is full-grown, gives birth to death.

I've been a turkey hunter for over 30 years and I hope that over that time I've gotten better at the fundamentals and art of turkey hunting. Anyone, if they sit long enough in the turkey woods can eventually kill a turkey. But a good turkey hunter perfects the talents that it takes to be consistently successful.

Satan would make a good turkey hunter... Really. To be a good turkey hunter you have to be somewhat cunning, thinking like a turkey and planning your next move. You have to be deceptive with the use of calls and decoys at times. Lastly to harvest a turkey you have to be willing to pull the trigger and kill it.

Consider Genesis 3:1-7 we can read the story of how man fell into sin. We can see how Satan offered a lie (the call), how Eve looked at the fruit (the decoy) and how they fell and lost everything (death). It sounds like a turkey hunt, doesn't it?

The difference between a good turkey hunter and satan is this, a good turkey hunter doesn't kill all of the turkeys he comes in contact with, he is selective and he has a respect for his quarry... Satan has no respect for any life and he strives to kill every person he can.

1 Peter 5:8 "Be alert and of sober mind. Your enemy, the devil, prowls around like a roaring lion looking for someone to devour."

There is no better killer than a cat and the king of the cats is the lion. Satan is like a cunning cat seeking to kill and devour you. Don't fall for his calls or decoys, stay out of range and protect yourself by surrounding yourself with Godly people and things.

JOURNAL ENTRY

___

___

___

___

___

MARCH 9

"IT'S A LOVE WITHOUT END, AMEN"

Luke 15:20
So he got up and went to his father. "But while he was still a long way off, his father saw him and was filled with compassion for him; he ran to his son, threw his arms around him and kissed him.

There is old George Strait song called, "It's a Love Without End, Amen"... It speaks of both the love of a parent and the love of our heavenly Father. The chorus is this...

"Let me tell you a secret about a father's love,
A secret that my daddy said was just between us."
He said, "Daddies don't just love their children every now and then.
It's a love without end, amen"

This is definitely true of our Heavenly Father and it should be true of earthly parents as well.

Luke 16 is written about a father that thought he had lost a son; he had taken his inheritance and ran off for the "good life"... No phone calls, letters, texts, or smoke signals... For all the father knew his son was dead. The son had hurt his father deeply but the father continues to look towards the horizon, hoping his son would return. When the son returned, the father not only welcomed him back, he ran to him and hugged him. Then he did more, he celebrated that son's return with a party.

How many of us have a child that chose a different path that we want for them, a child that has decided not to live a life that is our choice? We can't give up... We should be in continual prayer for them. Look to the horizon, never stop loving.

Our heavenly Father is the example of this... He waits patiently for His children. His heart has been broken by His children yet He waits for us to turn to Him and even after we've turned to Him and then turn away... He waits to hold us again in a close embrace.

Never give up, pray and trust God. Look to His example.

"IT'S A LOVE WITHOUT END, AMEN"

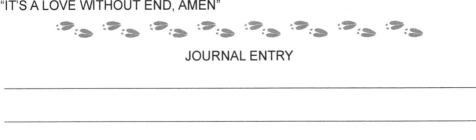

JOURNAL ENTRY

___

___

___

MARCH 10

DON'T ENVY THE GODLESS

Proverbs 28:13
People who conceal their sins will not prosper, but if they
confess and turn from them, they will receive mercy.

In the movie, "God's not dead", Mina's mother said, "Sometimes the devil allows people to live a life free of trouble because he doesn't want people turning to God. Their sin is like a jail cell, except it is all nice and comfy and there doesn't seem to be any reason to leave. The door's wide open. Till one day time runs out and the door slams shut and suddenly it's too late to get out."

As we go through life we see people that seem to be extremely comfortable in life. Some are comfortable financially, some emotionally and some just cruising with no apparent cares. Many of these folks are living lives less than what we would call "moral" or godly. If we are not careful we find ourselves envying these people for what we assume is an "easy life".

The above quote from "God's Not Dead" explains how and why this happens at times... Satan allows many to be very comfortable in this now to keep them happy in this world. They don't need a god that will "complicate" their seemingly "easy life".

Those that we assume to prosper in this life will pay for it for eternity.

Don't envy that life style. The rewards for it are not worth the fleeting pleasure.

JOURNAL ENTRY

MARCH 11

QUIT LIVING MEMORIES

Philippians 3:13-14
Brothers and sisters, I do not consider myself yet to have taken hold of it. But one thing I do: Forgetting what is behind and straining toward what is ahead, 14 I press on toward the goal to win the prize for which God has called me heavenward in Christ Jesus.

There is a saying in hunting that goes, "you are hunting memories". This means that you are spending your time hunting places that produced years ago, but things have changed and the animals just aren't there anymore. A hunter doing this usually gets discouraged and it is very unproductive.

The same can be true of our lives, aside from hunting. So many of us allow our past to drag us down and to have us waste so much of life. This is a trap of satan, don't fall into it. Satan wants us to dwell on the sin and shame of our past and that will continue to makes us unproductive in what God has called us to do. But just like "hunting memories" it will discourage us and make our walk unproductive.

When the apostle Paul wrote this he knew that if he "lived in his past", he could not be productive because the guilt would bring him down. Paul hunted down and killed Christians... How bad is your past? I bet it isn't that bad.

Psalm 103:12 As far as the east is from the west, so far hath he removed our transgressions/sins from us.

If God has removed your sins, let them go, quit living memories.

JOURNAL ENTRY

_____

_____

_____

_____

_____

_____

MARCH 12

NOTHING TO FEAR

Psalm 89:23
I will crush his foes before him and strike down his adversaries

Max Lucado once said, "One of the greatest gifts we can give people is the hope that their death is nothing to fear–you know, not that it has no fear in it, but the promise of scripture is that God will lead us through the valley of the shadow of death."

There is only one way to escape a fear in death and that is to know Jesus personally and have a relationship with Him. With a confidence in what comes after this earthly life, we can be totally without fear of death.

I saw in my dad an excitement for what came after this life here on earth... There was no fear, just an anticipation to get to heaven and see his Savior. As he neared death the anticipation, not the fear continued to build. I have the same hope and excitement. I know without a doubt that I will see my dad, my sister and grandmothers again. I also know that I will someday, when they pass, see so many friends and family again.

This hope isn't just a maybe kind of hope but an assurance kind of hope.

I pray that all of my friends and family will have that excitement and assurance.

NOTHING TO FEAR?

JOURNAL ENTRY

MARCH 13

LET YOUR LIGHT SHINE

2 Samuel 22:29
You are my lamp, O LORD; the LORD turns my darkness into light.

As the sun rose this morning I thought about how God illuminated the darkness in the world. I have pretty good navigational skills and see pretty well in the darkness... But things become much clearer and easier in the light of day than they do in the dark.

Why do we choose to live in the darkness when we can see clearly in the light? God has given us His Son that became the light of the world. Our job is first to except that Light, next to quit living in the darkness and then to share that light to those that are still living in the darkness of this world.

With our travels around North America, Linda and I (along with our kids) have visited, guided and operated lodges in some places that are extremely "dark". They are shaded by the cloak of satan... It doesn't take much to illuminate a place like that... Showing the love that Christ gives is a great start and the shadows recede like the darkness before a bright sunrise.

Matthew 5:14-16 "You are the light of the world. A town built on a hill cannot be hidden. 15 Neither do people light a lamp and put it under a bowl. Instead they put it on its stand, and it gives light to everyone in the house. 16 In the same way, let your light shine before others, that they may see your good deeds and glorify your Father in heaven.

LET YOUR LIGHT SHINE

JOURNAL ENTRY

MARCH 14

2 Peter 3:9
The Lord is not slow about His promise, as some count slowness, but is patient toward you, not wishing for any to perish but for all to come to repentance

I have to admit, I'm a little excited... I'm a Chicago cubs fan and have been for nearly 50 years. This year they have one post season victory under their belt... That's huge. They have struggled for years as a team (their last championship was 1908). You know you are in trouble as a team when you've been known for a few generations as the "Lovable Losers". But I have hung on as a fan and I always will... We Cubbies fans are very long suffering.

Our Lord could be a Cubs fan if He chooses to do so. He has a long suffering heart. As Peter wrote He is not slow as we would consider slowness... But (and I am so thankful for this) He is patient so that everyone will have a chance to come to Him.

How many people have you told about Christ recently? All of God's children look around and see what is happening and say, "Lord come quickly"... But He's waiting until everyone has a chance.

So do you want Christ to return and take us out of this mess? Then get busy sharing the Good News that Jesus is the Lord God and came to save. This is on all of us now... We have one job to do... Win souls for Christ. Eternity is a long time to live in anything less than heaven.

Share the Good News

Get busy!

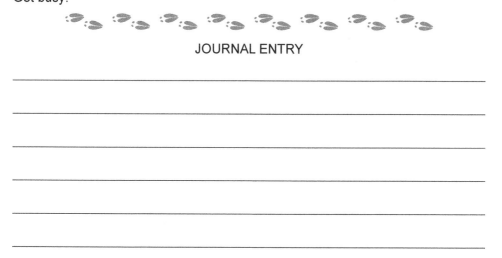

JOURNAL ENTRY

MARCH 15

WAIT PATIENTLY ON THE LORD

PSALM 40: 1-3

"I waited patiently for the Lord; he turned to me and heard my cry. He lifted me out of the slimy pit, out of the mud and mire; he set my feet on a rock and gave me a firm place to stand. He put a new song in my mouth, a hymn of praise to our God. Many will see and fear the Lord and put their trust in Him."

If there has been one major disappointment for me from childhood to adulthood it is that we don't deal with nearly as much quicksand as we were lead to believe. Most of us can remember the quicksand on Gilligan's Island, Johnny Quest and so many old westerns... But how many of us have ever come across quicksand in real life?

Well yesterday I came across quicksand, finally, right here in my basement! It's true! But it is figurative quicksand. I started the day out with replacing a jet pump for my well and everything went wrong. With guests coming today I HAD NO WATER... I struggled all day along with my friend Jim. Finally at 8 pm we stopped for dinner. I was full of mud, rust, sweat and even a little blood... I felt as though I was sinking in a figurative "quicksand". We stopped and I prayed and gave it to God... I was convinced that my well had silted in and I didn't have $10,000 for a new one. But I asked God to direct our work.

Within a minute or two after praying and giving this to the Lord and deciding to wait on Him, Jim said, "there is a little switch we have overlooked". We went one more time into the basement and dug into the new pump, flipped the switch and plugged the pump in. And it pumped!

Why is sincere prayer the last thing we try? Why do we, especially as men, tell ourselves, "I can handle this myself"? Our loving, caring God wants to help, all we have to do is, "wait patiently for the Lord" and "He will turn to us and hear our cry. He will lift us out of the slimy pit, out of the mud and mire"

We just need to "wait patiently on the Lord".

JOURNAL ENTRY

_____

_____

_____

_____

MARCH 16

FIGHT THE GOOD FIGHT

2 Timothy 4:7
"I have fought the good fight, I have finished the race, I have kept the faith."

This passage is quoted quite often and used in sermons and writing all the time... It is very significant in that it is the last letter that we have from the apostle Paul before he was martyred.

I have a friend bringing his dad, John, to my camp this week to hunt. His dad is not an old man, mid to late 60's... But recently has been diagnosed with Alzheimer's. John and his son want to spend as much quality time together as possible at this point in John's life. John got chances to sit with his son in stand and he even got a shot at a good buck. He didn't get a deer, but it didn't matter. It wasn't about the deer.

Back in Paul's letter he used the word "fought", the Greek word agonizomai, translated "fought," means literally "to engage in conflict."

John fought for the Lord (engaged satan and this world) much of his life. After working for many years he went to the mission field... After years there he decided to come home to spend his remaining years with his kids and grandkids... And then the news from the doctors... Why?

No one can answer why these things happen because of a sinful world. We do know that John loves the Lord and Romans 8:28 tells us that, "we know that in all things God works for the good of those who love him, who have been called according to his purpose." So as we come to places in our life like John is facing... We can be assured that God still has control. He knows the beginning and the end and has a plan. We are asked to continue to "fight a good fight".

In 1st Timothy 6:12 Paul wrote this to young Timothy... "Fight the good fight of the faith. Take hold of the eternal life to which you were called when you made your good confession in the presence of many witnesses."

No matter what we face today or tomorrow, continue to fight the good fight that God has called us to. We don't know what tomorrow brings... But we know who brings tomorrow and the fight we fight for the sake of Christ is never, EVER in vain.

Fight the good fight

JOURNAL ENTRY

March 17

NO OTHER GODS

Matthew 6:24
"No one can serve two masters, for either he will hate the one and love the other, or he will be devoted to the one and despise the other. You cannot serve God and money.

Yesterday I saw a friend's story that made me realize how we get off track, he wrote...

"A few years ago one of my younger children asked me "Dad do you love hunting more than God"?

Obviously my actions had been speaking louder than words. Remember to take the time to stay in tune with God. Don't allow our own selfish desires to consume us."

How often we allow "good things" to take over the top spot in our lives. It's so easy to allow these things, that are sometimes even godly things, to take the place of our "first love". But God tells us in Exodus 20, "You shall have no other gods before me."

Good things, bad things, godly things or earthly things, we are to put nothing before our God!

JOURNAL ENTRY

MARCH 18

HIS STRENGTH THROUGH MY WEAKNESS

2 Corinthians 12:9
But he said to me, "My grace is sufficient for you, for my power is made perfect in weakness." Therefore I will boast all the more gladly about my weaknesses, so that Christ's power may rest on me.

The apostle Paul had just written about the "thorn in his side" and then explains how Christ takes this weakness and uses it to perfect HIS power. We see this in our own lives all the time... As we feel we can't succeed and give it up to the Lord... He creates something beautiful.

This morning, on my way out to a hilltop to read and pray I came across dew covered spider webs. I stopped to take some photos and marveled at the strength in the miniscule threads that a tiny spider excretes.

One of these threads can do nothing, but woven together they are amazingly strong. The creator of that web supplies food for herself and her children. Just like our creator who took something like me, so weak, and made something so very strong in Him.

Do you feel weak today? Struggling? Give it to the Lord. He might not take the issue away... But he will show His mighty, loving power through your circumstance.

JOURNAL ENTRY

_____

_____

_____

_____

_____

_____

_____

_____

_____

MARCH 19

IS YOUR LIGHT SHINING?

Matthew 5:13-16

"You are the salt of the earth. But if the salt loses its saltiness, how can it be made salty again? It is no longer good for anything, except to be thrown out and trampled underfoot. 14 "You are the light of the world. A town built on a hill cannot be hidden. 15 Neither do people light a lamp and put it under a bowl. Instead they put it on its stand, and it gives light to everyone in the house. 16 In the same way, let your light shine before others, that they may see your good deeds and glorify your Father in heaven.

Sunday night we stood on our son's lawn and watched the lunar eclipse, the "blood moon". It struck me how the full moon that was so bright one moment and could show no light the next. I became aware then that moon's light only comes because of the sun. Without the relationship with the sun it is lost in the darkness... So it is with God's children.

The Moon has no light of its own. The light that shines is a reflection of the Sun. In and of ourselves, there is no light in us. Any light that shines from us is a reflection of the Son, the Light of the world!

If we are each truly one of God's children then we should be reflecting Christ to a dark world around us. Once we have that personal relationship with Him we have one main reason to be left here on this earth... That is to "let our light shine before others, that they may see your good deeds and glorify your Father in heaven."

Is your light shining? Are we walking in a way so others see God in and through us? If there is no light showing through us, then we need to examine our hearts, are we truly His child? Are we living the life that God has called us to?

Is your light shining for Him today?

JOURNAL ENTRY

MARCH 20

MORE THAN CONQUERORS...

Matthew 6:33
But seek ye first the kingdom of God, and his righteousness;
and all these things shall be added unto you.

Today there is so much, "name it and claim it" mentality in our culture... Too much. If you take this verse by itself you might think that by keeping God first we are promised, "all these things" that are "added unto" us... But what are "all these things"?

Matthew is talking about the fact that we don't need to worry... Verses 25-31 explain that we are not to worry about anything... But to know that if we observe God's creation, we can see that He is taking care of everything. Then in verse 32 Matthew writes, "For the pagans run after all these things, and your heavenly Father knows that you need them."

So what Father that is all-knowing, all-loving and all-powerful would not want to provide for His very own children? So we know that we need worry for nothing. And if we "seek first His kingdom" we no longer worry about our wants... Because our wants come in line with God's will for us.

Romans 8:37–39 answers the question of God's protection and provision, once and for all... 37 No, in all these things we are more than conquerors through him who loved us. 38 For I am sure that neither death nor life, nor angels nor rulers, nor things present nor things to come, nor powers, 39 nor height nor depth, nor anything else in all creation, will be able to separate us from the love of God in Christ Jesus our Lord.

We are more than conquerors...

JOURNAL ENTRY

MARCH 21

LOOK AROUND

Isaiah 55:12
You will go out in joy and be led forth in peace; the mountains and hills will burst into song before you, and all the trees of the field will clap their hands.

I've heard this verse so many times in my life I don't think I could count them all. And the song that was written from this verse sticks in my head from time to time. Tonight I realized that God's glory shows itself in so many ways. And we take them for granted. We were on the mountain and the elk were bugling at a deafening level. The mountains truly did "burst into song".

Our God is so amazing... He puts our lives into places and shows us things that we can't fathom... And yet, so many times we can't see His Majesty in the things around us.

Just this morning I was at 10,000 ft and there were dark clouds hanging on the mountain. Out 10 miles into the valley there is a butte and when the sun broke out it appeared to glow. It was a view that I can only describe as a "God sighting" (and I don't use that term). But God truly blessed me with a miraculous view.

Look around. Notice the things that our Lord shows you. He allows us to draw close to Him through His creation.

Some of these places take extra effort to get to. Some, like today's, are painful, but press in, dig deep. Discover God's great plan for your life. Discover God's special place that he wants you to experience. It won't necessarily be easy. There will be sacrifice. But it is worth it!

Corinthians 2:9 says it very well, "No eye has seen, no ear has heard, and no mind has imagined what God has prepared for those who love him."

Look around

JOURNAL ENTRY

_____

_____

_____

_____

MARCH 22

REMOVING THE SUCKERS

John 15:1-4

"I am the true vine, and my Father is the gardener. 2 He cuts off every branch in me that bears no fruit, while every branch that does bear fruit he prunes so that it will be even more fruitful. 3 You are already clean because of the word I have spoken to you. 4 Remain in me, as I also remain in you. No branch can bear fruit by itself; it must remain in the vine. Neither can you bear fruit unless you remain in me.

As a kid I hated gardening... At the time I didn't realize what it meant to our family. As I grew older and had my own family I learned to love the garden and the fresh vegetables. I had remembered much of what my dad had taught me all those years ago.

My wife loves tomatoes and I planted a lot, with a plan to have plenty for her to eat fresh, make salsa, can etc... After a short time my plants were getting out of hand. They were growing far bigger and bushier than the ones we grew back at home. I then remembered my dad removing suckers from his tomato plants years earlier. The suckers on the tomato plants literally sucked the energy needed for growth and fruit bearing of the rest of the plant. Often when a tomato plant's vine would grow and a new branch would split off, one of these suckers would grow in the crotch of the split. While your plants looked fuller, healthier and prettier, it kept the tomatoes from growing and ripening the way they should.

Such is life. As Christian men and women we often have a lot of things in our lives, that while they might look good and they might not really be harming us... They take away from the things that are important to what God has for us. These things really need to be removed so as to allow other parts of our lives to flourish and for our lives to produce fruit.

We need to allow God to prune back the things that are holding us back. He knows us better than we know ourselves and we need to allow Him to shape us into what is best.

John Trapp once said, "Better to be pruned to grow than cut up to burn."

Remove the suckers.

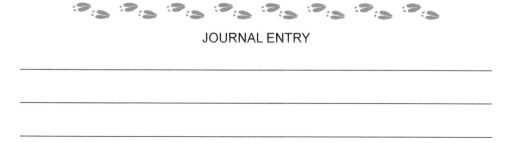

JOURNAL ENTRY

_____

_____

_____

MARCH 23

ACKNOWLEDGE HIM

Proverbs 16:9
A man's heart deviseth his way: but the Lord directeth his steps.
Another translation says it this way, "People do their best making plans for their lives, but the Eternal guides each step."

As a hunting guide we take on heavy responsibility at times. I have had hunts where I have searched at midnight for a lost hunter with temperatures well below zero. I've had to find my way out of dark woods miles from nowhere to save my hunter and I from an uncomfortable night outdoors. And, I've brought a boat full of hunters across 15 miles of northern Canadian lakes at midnight.

I know of hunters that have had their lives saved by a guide while hunting dangerous game. What would have become of those very people if it hadn't been for a guide? They would have wandered around aimlessly hoping to find their way in the darkness. Worst case, they might have died for not knowing how to get out of their situation.

God is our ultimate guide... We can plan and prepare for situations in life but in the end, God will direct us to where we need to be.

So often we wander through life when we have the best guide available at a moment's notice. Allow Him to hold your hand in the darkness, to carry your load when it gets too heavy. Just allow God to direct your path. We just have to "acknowledge Him"

Proverbs 3:6 In all your ways acknowledge Him, and He shall direct your paths.

JOURNAL ENTRY

_____

_____

_____

_____

_____

_____

_____

MARCH 24

FINISH STRONG... FINISH WELL

Hebrews 12:1-2

Therefore, since we are surrounded by such a great cloud of witnesses, let us throw off everything that hinders and the sin that so easily entangles. And let us run with perseverance the race marked out for us, 2 fixing our eyes on Jesus, the pioneer and perfecter of faith. For the joy set before him he endured the cross, scorning its shame, and sat down at the right hand of the throne of God.

When runners in ancient Greece would compete, there was a reward of laurel leaves waiting for the winners. They were running for the reward... going for the gold, so to speak. They didn't give up but pushed on to the end.

Keeping our eyes on Jesus keeps us going in life. It makes us move forward when the struggle gets too hard at times. Focusing on Him helps us to lean toward the ribbon at the end of the finish line.

It was Corrie ten boom that said, "Look without and be distressed. Look within and be depressed. Look at Jesus and be at rest." Keep our eye on Jesus, as the prize at the end of this earthly struggle makes it all worthwhile.

In a horserace some horses are strong starters and some are strong finishers... In life a strong finisher is what we need to be. It does us no good to lead until the homestretch just to fall short at the end. We want to run the race to win. We want to endure. We want to play by the rules... And we want to keep our eyes on Jesus.

Finish strong, finish well...

JOURNAL ENTRY

MARCH 25

TIE IT ON YOUR HEART

Deuteronomy 11:18-19
Fix these words of mine in your hearts and minds; tie them as symbols on your hands and bind them on your foreheads. 19 Teach them to your children, talking about them when you sit at home and when you walk along the road, when you lie down and when you get up.

All of us that hunt have heard the stories of someone pulling their bow or rifle up into a treestand and have the rope break or the knot come undone. I once watched my favorite rifle free fall 20' to the base of a large spruce tree. It is a sick feeling. I've got a friend that won't hunt one of my stands anymore because he saw his Mathews Bow clatter down the rungs of the tree stand.

Our hunting equipment is precious to many of us and we treat it like our babies at times. If only we were to treat our spiritual life with the same care and conviction all of the time. We passively live a "good life" and attend church on Sunday. We talk the talk on Sunday and maybe throughout the week... But do we walk the walk?

If we can just learn to cherish God's word like we do our "things" in this life. Verse 18 says to, "tie them as symbols on your hands and bind them on your foreheads". This is so we can never forget them or be without them.

Just as we are taught to do things as a child, we learn to do spiritual things by repetition and internalizing meanings... So it is with a close Christian walk. We need to continually surround ourselves with Godly people and Godly things.

Once when a skeptic expressed surprise to see him reading a Bible, Abraham Lincoln said, "Take all that you can of this book upon reason, and the balance on faith, and you will live and die a happier man."

Take all that is important and tie it on your heart.

JOURNAL ENTRY

MARCH 26

HOW DEEP IS YOUR LOVE?

Mark 8:29
"But what about you?" he asked. "Who do you say I am?"
Peter answered, "You are the Messiah."

There is little doubt in the world today that Jesus actually lived 2000+ years ago. Few would dispute that fact. Most, if not all, of these same people would agree that He was a very good man. (Few today in the world know Him as God). So what did this "good man" have to say? What were the most important points to His ministry?

John 15:13 tells us, "Greater love has no one than this: to lay down one's life for one's friends."

Jesus Himself was the greatest example of this. The one exception for Him was that He not only laid down His life for His friends, but He laid down His life for all the rest of us who's sins hung Him there on the cross.

So, can you, can I, lay down our lives for a friend? Do we show the love that Christ exemplified? Could you do it? Few of us will ever be called to show that kind of love, but if your loved ones know you love that deeply with a Christlike kind of love... It's enough.

How deep is your love?

JOURNAL ENTRY

MARCH 27

NEED WISDOM?

James 1:5.
If any of you lack of Wisdom, let him ask of God that giveth to all men liberally, and upbraideth not; and it shall be given him.

In 1 Kings 3:3, Solomon is described in the following positive terms: "Solomon loved the LORD, walking in the statutes of David his father." One night, the Lord appeared to Solomon and said, "Ask what I shall give you". In response, Solomon answered, "Give your servant therefore an understanding mind to govern your people, that I may discern between good and evil, for who is able to govern this, your great people?"

The passage notes, "It pleased the Lord that Solomon had asked this". God delights to give wisdom to those who truly seek it. God responds to Solomon's request for wisdom by promising three different gifts. The first is the wisdom Solomon had asked for: "I now do according to your word. Behold, I give you a wise and discerning mind, so that none like you has been before you and none like you shall arise after you".

There is no promise that if we ask for wisdom we will become wealthy or famous as Solomon did. However, God desires to give us wisdom and as James wrote, "let him ask of God that giveth to all men liberally".

So ask earnestly for wisdom, you might be surprised what you get along with it.

JOURNAL ENTRY

_____

_____

_____

_____

_____

_____

_____

MARCH 28

THE LEGACY WE LEAVE

John 17:1
"Father, the hour has come. Glorify your Son, that your Son may glorify you"

Yesterday, while walking on the mountain, I came across several quaking aspen trees that bears had climbed many years ago. The aspens show the claw marks where the bear gripped for climbing. Some of these trees were nearly 100 ft in height and probably 100 years old. The thought came to me that the impression of that bears claws were left for many generations to see. Then it came to me, all the "marks" that I leave in life will also be seen for generations to come.

I find it significant that in John 17:1 even the Son did not seek glory for Himself, but to glorify the Father? Jesus didn't want any credit; He wanted to point it all at the father. He just wanted to be obedient to His calling.

So what will your legacy be? We can build a building. We can plant a church. We can strive to be remembered for all kinds of good things... But what does God desire our legacy to be? It's obedience, pure and simple obedience.

Now that's a legacy worth living for. Not a building or an institution, but living men and women who carry on His mission for His glory. I cannot do this by myself, but I can focus my obedience so that Christ impacts others and they choose to live for Him. There is no glory for me, of course, but there is great glory for Him because only He can do this through me.

Leave your mark for generations to come. It is the LEGACY WE LEAVE

JOURNAL ENTRY

___

___

___

___

___

___

MARCH 29

IN ALL YOUR WAYS

Deuteronomy 6:11-12
11 The houses will be richly stocked with goods you did not produce. You will draw water from cisterns you did not dig, and you will eat from vineyards and olive trees you did not plant. When you have eaten your fill in this land, 12 be careful not to forget the Lord, who rescued you from slavery in the land of Egypt

I believe one of the biggest problems with people in this country is we've become too used to all the blessings the GOD has given us!!!!! We've become lazy and complainers just like the Israelites in the desert complaining about the food from heaven and all the blessings GOD gave them! When you start to count the blessings we have in this country it's like trying to count grains of sand on the beach! We were chosen to be born in this country instead of some poverty stricken land with not so much as a clean drink of water.

It is time as a nation and as individuals that we decide that we are a blessed people and turn back to God.

Proverbs 3:5-6 says Trust in the Lord with all your heart and lean not on your own understanding; in all you ways submit to Him and He will direct your paths.

Are you, am I, trusting in Him for everything? Are we submitting to Him?

Until we turn 100% to God and praise and thank Him for what we have... We will continue to struggle and eventually fall. This relates both to our personal lives and as a nation.

JOURNAL ENTRY

MARCH 30

WHAT IS LOVE?

1 John 3:14
We know that we have passed from death to life, because we love each other. Anyone who does not love remains in death.

Back in June while in Colorado, my brother Dave cut down some alder trees for use as an arbor that he built for his garden. These trees were "pronounced dead" when they were cut off... However, when we came back to Colorado last week those same trees have new limbs and green leaves growing beautifully. Where there was death in June there was life in August.

John goes on to tell us what the love looks like that brought us from death to life. In chapter 3 verses 16-18,

16 This is how we know what love is: Jesus Christ laid down his life for us. And we ought to lay down our lives for our brothers. 17 If anyone has material possessions and sees his brother in need but has no pity on him, how can the love of God be in him? 18 Dear children, let us not love with words or tongue but with actions and in truth.

When we work in Colorado we see terrible situations where there are two neighbors living side by side. One has a three year supply of firewood while the widow next door is nearly freezing to death with no wood. Verses 17&18 speak directly to that situation.

If we are truly part of Christ's family we have to love unconditionally. No matter what the other person has done to us or how they act. If they have a need and we have Christ, it's what we're called to do.

Today, I challenge us all to look for a chance to love, love where it isn't easy, where it isn't convenient just as Christ did for us.

Ephesians 5:2 tells us, "and walk in the way of love, just as Christ loved us and gave himself up for us as a fragrant offering and sacrifice to God."

JOURNAL ENTRY

MARCH 31

STRENGTH IN NUMBERS

Hebrews 10:24-25

And let us consider how we may spur one another on toward love and good deeds, 25 not giving up meeting together, as some are in the habit of doing, but encouraging one another—and all the more as you see the Day approaching.

Many times I've heard people say that they have quit attending church because they can sit home and watch preachers on TV. Or because of my outdoor connections I often hear, "the woods are my church, God speaks to me there". There are a ton of excuses for not going to church to fellowship with others.

God's word tells us over and over again of the importance of the fellowship of others. I think of a church family like a cyclone fence, sturdy, strong, faithfully connected to keep the wolves away. Each of us is interwoven with others on either side. If you try to do it on your own, you will eventually fall... With the support of others your "fence" can withstand many attacks and hold back the enemy.

N.T. Wright does a great job of why we are called to fellowship... "The church exists primarily for two closely correlated purposes: to worship God and to work for his kingdom in the world ... The church also exists for a third purpose, which serves the other two: to encourage one another, to build one another up in faith, to pray with and for one another, to learn from one another and teach one another, and to set one another examples to follow, challenges to take up, and urgent tasks to perform. This is all part of what is known loosely as fellowship."

There is strength in numbers

JOURNAL ENTRY

APRIL

John 10:10

The thief comes only to steal and kill and destroy; I have come that they may have life, and have it to the full.

APRIL 1

Proverbs 26:4-5
Do not answer a fool according to his folly, or you yourself will be just like him. ⁵Answer a fool according to his folly, or he will be wise in his own eyes.

I've had a few April Fools jokes pulled on me, and I must admit that I've pulled off a few pretty good ones myself. But I know that no one likes being called a fool, much less being made to look like a fool. We all like to think of ourselves as intelligent, witty and successful, not easily tricked or duped. However, when we hold ourselves against God's standards, we might be shocked at how much we've earned the title of fool.

In the book of Proverbs we can see that there are a lot of things that a fool does that most of us can relate to quite often. Proverbs 19:1 are perverse in speech, Proverbs 20:3 quarrel instead of keeping away from strife, Proverbs 29:11 always lose your temper, Proverbs 15:5 reject our father's discipline etc…

In Psalms 14:1, we see that, "*The fool says in his heart, 'There is no God'". Don't allow yourself to ever be this kind of a fool.* It's a matter of the hearts attitude. In fact it would be quite possible to say with your lips that there is a God but then to have your heart think and act as though God does not exist in your dreams and choices at all. When our heart says that there is a God, we readily obey Him and surrender to His in our lives. Though it's not always easy, a heart that honors God is willing to begin the process of forgiving those who have deeply hurt us, to think of others as more important than ourselves; to choose generosity over greed; and to be sensitive to the needs of the poor and oppressed.

Don't be foolish, live as though you know there is a God.

JOURNAL ENTRY

_____
_____
_____
_____
_____
_____

APRIL 2

THE TRUE CALL

John 6:44
No one can come to me unless the Father who sent me draws him.
And I will raise him up on the last day.

Turkey hunters are a devoted group... yet they are all a little off center. They are a group who will swear off sleep for weeks on end just to match wits with a bird with a brain the size of a small walnut, a group that will sit motionless for hours hoping to outsmart a stupid bird using calls and decoys.

When turkey hunting, most hunters utilize their calls of varying types as well as decoys to try to bring a gobbler into range. Some days it works and other days it doesn't. When it does work for the hunter, the turkey will be fooled by the call and the look of a "false" turkey... Coming close enough to be harvested and later eaten.

Then there are other hunts where the turkeys can discern that the calling isn't real and the decoy is just a substitute for the real thing.

Life is just like that, for every one of us. We will all be called to something. We will all make a decision in life to go to what is true and real or to go to a false calling. As in turkey hunting, going to a call that isn't true and from God can only lead to one thing, DEATH. This is an eternal death that damns us forever in the torment of hell.

Our other option is to go to the calling of the truth. In John 14 Jesus tells us who and what the truth is.

Verse 6 Jesus answered, "I am the way and the truth and the life. No one comes to the Father except through me.

While going to the false call brings eternal death and damnation, going to the true calling, that is Christ, gives you eternal life in heaven. Jesus is that truth, the life and the one and only way to heaven.

Don't be fooled by the false calls and pretty decoys of the world... Satan is an amazing hunter of men and women's souls...

1 Peter 5:8 tells us: Be alert and of sober mind. Your enemy the devil prowls around like a roaring lion looking for someone to devour.

Respond to the true call.

JOURNAL ENTRY

_____

_____

APRIL 3

MORE TIME IN THE GARDEN

1 Corinthians 3:6-7
I planted the seed in your hearts, and Apollos watered it, but it was God who made it grow. It's not important who does the planting, or who does the watering. What's important is that God makes the seed grow.

Today I was reminiscing of my childhood when I had to garden with my dad and the rest of the family. I recall before we had a rototiller we turned that whole big garden with shovels each spring... Then we raked it smooth, planted and waited for the weeds to grow. Then we weeded until the vegetables grew and then we picked. I hated gardening back then.

Now that dad is gone, I wish I had those times back, to have that wasted time again where I could share in that quality time. He so loved his garden. To have a successful garden someone has to plant while others have to water and so on. Our Christian life is like that, some of us will never see the harvest but we are all required/commanded to prepare the soil and plant the seeds for Christian lives.

We don't read of anyone in Scripture actually sharing the gospel with Saul (who later became the apostle Paul). But God used a number of people to prepare his heart to receive it. It was like the turning of the soil to prepare the seed bed... Someone has to do it.

As far back as I can remember in my life, I can remember many, many people that prepared the seed bed of my life and others that planted seeds and others that watered.

We all need to look for every opportunity to do our part in the garden of someone else's life. You see, we all have a part to play in God's kingdom. We all can do something.

Don't get to a point in your life wishing you had spent more time gardening

JOURNAL ENTRY

_____

_____

_____

_____

_____

APRIL 4

Ecclesiastes 3:11
He hath made everything beautiful in his time: also he hath set the world in their heart, so that no man can find out the work that God makes from the beginning to the end.

There are times that we realize that God's plans are far better than our own. When we think we've got everything perfectly planned and God shows us a different and ultimately better way.

What do we do when God changes our plans, goals, future etc? Sometimes we complain, sometimes we grumble, cry, or worry. But the right response is, "God you know what you are doing."

Romans 8:28 is a great example of how we can trust God's timing.

"And we know that all things work together for good to them that love God, to them who are the called according to His purpose."

Just today I had something happen that shook me a little. It really didn't affect me personally, but some great Christian friends. My first (second, third and fourth) thoughts were to worry about the situation. Their response to me was what God expects of us. "God has a plan and it will be fine".

Many of the conflicts in our world today come from not waiting on God's promises and His plan... Adam eating from the tree in the garden, Abraham not waiting on God and sleeping with Sarah's servant etc...

We know that God's timing is always best. Trust him

JOURNAL ENTRY

___

___

___

___

___

___

APRIL 5

A LIFE OF INTEGRITY

Titus 2:7-8
Show yourself in all respects to be a model of good works, and in your teaching show integrity, dignity, 8 and sound speech that cannot be condemned, so that an opponent may be put to shame, having nothing evil to say about us.

If you are going to claim to be a Christian today you will be watched closely. There are those that are just waiting to point out your failures... And we all fail at times. Even the apostle Paul said that among sinners, he was the "foremost of all".

This week I keep hearing about Josh Duggar and his spiritual failures. It shows that when we fail the world will jump on the chance to point it out. Integrity in our life is of the utmost importance.

Zig Ziglar wrote, "The most important persuasion tool you have in your entire arsenal is integrity."

As people watch you, give them nothing to point a finger towards. Let them see a Godly life... Make them want what you have.

Chuck Swindoll said it this way... "Few things are more infectious than a Godly lifestyle. The people you rub shoulders with everyday need that kind of challenge. Not prudish. Not preachy. Just crackerjack clean living. Just honest to goodness, bone-deep, non-hypocritical integrity."

There is a promise to those who live a lifestyle of integrity...

Proverbs 2:6-8 For the LORD gives wisdom; from his mouth come knowledge and understanding; 7 He stores up sound wisdom for the upright; he is a shield to those who walk in integrity, 8 guarding the paths of justice and watching over the way of his saints.

JOURNAL ENTRY

APRIL 6

MEET THEM WHERE THEY LIVE

Matthew 9:10-13
While Jesus was having dinner at Matthew's house, many tax collectors and sinners came and ate with him and his disciples. 11 When the Pharisees saw this, they asked his disciples, "Why does your teacher eat with tax collectors and sinners?" 12 On hearing this, Jesus said, "It is not the healthy who need a doctor, but the sick. 13 But go and learn what this means: 'I desire mercy, not sacrifice.' For I have not come to call the righteous, but sinners."

According to WORLD CHRISTIAN FELLOWSHIP MINISTRIES article entitled, "Relational Evangelism", Historical data shows that over 75% (three-fourths) of all Christian conversions occur in the context of a family or personal friendship suggesting lifestyle evangelism is the most effective method of evangelism for inviting people into a personal relationship with Christ.

Not every one of us will ever be an evangelist who will get up in front of crowds and proclaim the "Good News" about Jesus. Most just don't have a gift to do that. But all of us have something in common with many others in our circle of friends and acquaintances. We have shared passions with others.

I've found that I can talk hunting with anybody that hunts. Hunters are a passionate group. Fisherman are another group that shares a common bond.

We are called to share the story of Christ and what He did for all of us... It's a whole lot easier to do that with those who are like minded with similar interests. We need to meet them where they live when it comes to sharing in our world.

A friend in Colorado is an amazing Horseman. He has a true passion for his horses and sharing Christ through his horses. He has found the key to other's hearts. His signature line in his emails is: "As for me and my horse, we will serve the Lord ".

Find their passion and meet them where they live.

JOURNAL ENTRY

APRIL 7

SERVICE WITH A PROMISE

Hebrews 6:10
God is not unjust; He will not forget your work and the love you have shown Him as you have helped His people and continue to help them.

Service can be a great thing. At times it is completely draining and exhausting, both physically and emotionally... Yet at the same time it refills our heart in a way that little else can. To serve others in a loving way, expecting nothing in return is what Christians are called to do. To give selflessly, expecting nothing in return is true giving.

I believe that this is what I love most about guiding hunters. When I can call in an elk or turkey to a "first timer", especially a child, I am far more blessed than my hunter. The reward I get from the service that I am honored to give far outweighs doing it for myself.

However, as Hebrews 6:10 says above, "God will not forget your work or the love you have shown".... So there is a promise to serving. If God remembers, then surely, somewhere down the road, He will reward.

Arnold Schwarzenegger said it this way, "Help others and give something back. I guarantee you will discover that while public service improves the lives and the world around you, its greatest reward is the enrichment and new meaning it will bring your own life."

Matthew 25:40 says that in serving others we are really serving the Lord.

"The King will reply, 'Truly I tell you, whatever you did for one of the least of these brothers and sisters of mine, you did for me.'

"Test God and see that HE is good." Give it a try.

JOURNAL ENTRY

_____

_____

_____

_____

_____

APRIL 8

HIS LOVE, GRACE, AND MERCY ENDURE FOREVER

1 Thessalonians 5:16-18
Rejoice always, 17 pray continually, 18 give thanks in all circumstances; for this is God's will for you in Christ Jesus.

I woke early this morning and didn't want to bother my wife so I laid quietly and prayed. I prayed for some people I knew in need, jobs, health, fear etc. I prayed for safety in the travel that we had to do. I prayed for my children and grandchildren. But I mostly thanked God for the way that HE has blessed me.

I don't do that often enough, just taking the time to count my blessings. We are so blessed. If you too know Jesus in a personal way, you too are a child of the KING! Think about that today, not only a child of the KING, but a child of the KING OF KINGS

No matter what happens to you this day, this week, this month or this year... Give thanks to our almighty God. We can be thankful in every situation. Even in death, we can be thankful, for death does not have the final word... God has the final word and death is not the end but just the beginning of something far better, far greater and far sweeter than anything we've known to this point.

Psalm 118:1, "O give thanks unto the Lord; for he is good: because his mercy endures forever."

So, no matter what you face today, count the blessings you've received, if you can count that high.

JOURNAL ENTRY

_____

_____

_____

_____

_____

_____

_____

APRIL 9

A WORLD OF LIES

Romans 1:25
Who changed the truth of God into a lie, and worshipped and served the creature more than the Creator, who is blessed forever. Amen.

A well known senator, when recently confronted with his bare-faced lie during the 2011 presidential debates affirming that Governor Mitt Romney never paid taxes, simply responded with a smirking self-justificatory: "He didn't win, did he?" Why are so many "progressive" causes these days finally revealed as lies?

How is it that we've come from a country of respect to one of disgrace? How have we come from a proud nation to one of shame? I'm not talking about Republican or Democrat; I'm talking about the condition of the human heart. I'm talking about the lack of ability to speak the truth.

In this world we don't know what to believe anymore. We have literally "exchanged truth for lies"... As a nation we've learned that when a lie suits us better, it's fine to use it. In this world of lies and half-truths, what an amazing treasure it is to look into a person's face and know he or she is telling the truth!

Pilate, embodying the mega-power of Rome, saw truth in the face of the badly beaten prisoner, Jesus, who said, without apology: "I am the way, the truth and the life." Three days later resurrected life showed it was clearly true. This is truth we can count on.

Don't fall into the trap of relying on lies to cover your problems. Tell the truth in all cases. As Matthew 5:37 says: "Let your yes be yes and your no be no."

JOURNAL ENTRY

___

___

___

___

___

___

APRIL 10

LORD, LIAR OR LUNATIC

Matthew 16:15-17
He says unto them: But whom say ye that I am? 16 And Simon Peter answered and said, Thou art the Christ, the Son of the living God. 17 And Jesus answered and said unto him: Blessed art thou, Simon Bar-Jonah, for flesh and blood hath not revealed it unto thee, but my Father which is in heaven.

Recently my grandson posted online his feelings about a sin issue. A mutual friend of mine sent him a message telling him that he might be wrong and that you can interpret the bible in many ways and that it was just a bunch of men that had written down their feelings thousands of years ago....

When I first read this I got mad but then realized he has just been blinded to the truth. To the world the bible is either a bunch of stories, but to those that truly trust in the Lord, it is God's divine word.

The same is true of Christ... People say all the time that He was just a great man, or a great teacher. Really? So how could he be a great man or teacher if He claimed to be the "Son of God? First, that would make Him a liar and in today's world it makes Him a lunatic and we would look at locking Him in a padded cell for being crazy.

In his famous book Mere Christianity, C.S. Lewis makes this statement, "A man who was merely a man and said the sort of things Jesus said would not be a great moral teacher. He would either be a lunatic—on the level with a man who says he is a poached egg—or he would be the devil of hell. You must make your choice. Either this was, and is, the Son of God, or else a madman or something worse. You can shut him up for a fool or you can fall at his feet and call him Lord and God. But let us not come with any patronizing nonsense about his being a great human teacher. He has not left that open to us."

Wow! So today, who do you say He is? The One True Lord, a terrible liar, or just a complete lunatic... These are the only choices that we have.

Choose wisely.

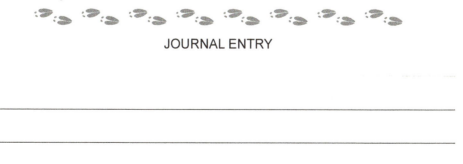

JOURNAL ENTRY

_____

_____

_____

APRIL 11

BEING WATCHED

Titus 2:12
Instructing us to deny ungodliness and worldly desires and to live sensibly, righteously and Godly in the present age,

A few years ago on Kodiak Island Linda and hunted black tail deer in an area that was covered with Brown Bear sign. There were tracks and droppings everywhere you looked. We had a feeling that we were being watched all the time. We got out safely, thank God, but it was a bad feeling that we were under the scrutiny of dangerous bears.

We need to realize that in our lives, we are always under the watchful eye of others. If we are going to claim to be something Godly then we had better live up to that. People are watching and waiting for Christians to screw up and if and when we do, we will be pounced upon. It is similar to the grizzlies in Alaska, in the dark waiting for something to devour.

This doesn't mean that we let people walk on us or try to hide who we are... It means we speak the truth in love and do our best always to lead Godly lives.

So what is the trick to staying in "the right place"?

Elizabeth George said, "When you cultivate a Godly thought life your soul will shine and you will exhibit the presence of the Lord in you."

Ephesians 5:15-17 Therefore be careful how you walk, not as unwise men but as wise, 16 making the most of your time, because the days are evil. 17 So then do not be foolish, but understand what the will of the Lord is.

JOURNAL ENTRY

APRIL 12

BELIEVE ON THE LORD JESUS CHRIST...

Acts 16:30
He then brought them out and asked, "Sirs, what must I do to be saved?"

We live in a world today that is far different than the one that many of us grew up in just 3-5 decades ago. To think of the changes that have taken place and how far from the God centered life we've drifted, it is discouraging.

So many people believe that because we live in a so called "Christian nation" and I'm not a Muslim or Atheist, I am a Christian... Right? Probably wrong. If you have to ask, then you don't know the answer.

The answer to the jailor in Acts 16:30, when he asked, "What must I do to be saved?" is a simple answer... "Believe on the Lord Jesus Christ, and thou shalt be saved..."

A simple answer, no. But many "believe" that there was a Jesus in history. They believe in God, but the Bible says in James 2:19 "Thou believeth that there is one God; thou doest well: the devils also believe, and tremble."

So if Satan and his demons believe that there is a God and "in" Jesus, are they Christians? I think not! We not only need to believe "in" Jesus, but also believe "on" Jesus. In a recent devotional I wrote about "spiritual training". I talked about working on my spiritual life. But let me make it clear, this work only comes after my salvation has been given to me as a totally free gift.

Ephesians 2:8-9 tells us, it is by faith, "For by grace are ye saved through faith; and that not of yourselves: it is the gift of God: 9 Not of works, lest any man should boast.

So our salvation comes from our faith in what Christ did for us and by accepting God's gift of salvation. Acknowledging that we are sinners and giving our life to Him.

There is NO other way. We can't earn it, and we can't buy it. It is a totally free gift. If we could earn it, why would Jesus have had to come to earth and die on a horrible cross?

So, today, right now... If I ask you... If today is your last day, if you don't make it until tomorrow, where will you spend eternity, do you know the answer with 100% confidence? If not, then don't go through another day without knowing. If you don't know, ask someone who does.

"Believe on the Lord Jesus Christ and you will be saved"

JOURNAL ENTRY

APRIL 13

SPIRITUAL "TRAINING"

Romans 8:16-18

The Spirit himself testifies with our spirit that we are God's children. 17 Now if we are children, then we are heirs—heirs of God and co-heirs with Christ, if indeed we share in his sufferings in order that we may also share in his glory. 18 I consider that our present sufferings are not worth comparing with the glory that will be revealed in us.

I've got a friend Ryan that has been in training for the last two years for hunting in the mountains. He pushes himself really hard every day. He climbs hundreds of stairs on Pine Mountain with a back pack, eats right and pushes himself to the limit. His reward is the glory of being in shape to reach places in the mountains that the rest of us can't reach and hopefully a trophy elk.

The Christian life is kind of like this; if we are truly living for Christ. We take beatings (mostly figuratively) and strain to do what Christ would have us do. We strive to grow and get our hearts in shape and in line with HIS. All to one day receive the crowning glory that awaits us. To hear the words, "well done my good and faithful servant"

John 16:33 tells us that we will pay a price... "These things I have spoken unto you, that in me you might have peace. In the world you shall have tribulation: but be of good cheer; I have overcome the world."

So if you are not, "sharing in His suffering" and not "having tribulations", start to examine your heart. In order to receive HIS glory we are told we must go through these things.

Ryan will probably see the glory of the back country and probably take another elk this year... Why, because he went through the sufferings. How about you? Will you get to experience the glory promised? Are you training to get to HIS glory?

JOURNAL ENTRY

_____

_____

_____

_____

_____

APRIL 14

DISCIPLE MAKING

Matthew 28:19-20

Go therefore and make disciples of all the nations, baptizing them in the name of the Father and of the Son and of the Holy Spirit, 20 teaching them to observe all things that I have commanded you; and lo, I am with you always, even to the end of the age." Amen.

D is·ci·ple, 1: one who accepts and assists in spreading the doctrines of another: as
- a: one of the twelve in the inner circle of Christ's followers according to the Gospel accounts
- b: a convinced adherent of a school or individual

Discipleship was Jesus' method of winning the world to Himself. In fact, Jesus converted very few people in a way that HE could say, "Here is how you win someone over". Instead, He literally staked His whole ministry on twelve men. As popular as He was during His earthly ministry, Jesus did not focus on the applause of men but quietly poured His life into those who would multiply His family. Jesus was not trying to impress the crowd, but usher in a kingdom. Christ expects His followers to be fruitful.

Jesus knew that He would have to equip His people to be able to lead the multitudes. This is not only what we need in our churches, but also in our personal lives. It is safe to say that discipleship was foundational to Jesus' ministry and it should be in each of our ministries as well.

We don't need to try to win the world over. Few of us have that capability. We need to "disciple" a few around us so that they can go and "disciple" a few and so on.

Oswald Chambers wrote in "My Utmost For His Highest"; "The "show business," which is so incorporated into our view of Christian work today, has caused us to drift far from our Lord's conception of discipleship. It is instilled in us to think that we have to do exceptional things for God; we have not. We have to be exceptional in ordinary things,"

Become exceptional at ordinary things and make disciples of a few close to you.

JOURNAL ENTRY

_____

_____

_____

APRIL 15

1 Samuel 13:13-14

"You have done a foolish thing," Samuel said. "You have not kept the command the Lord your God gave you; if you had, he would have established your kingdom over Israel for all time. 14 But now your kingdom will not endure; the Lord has sought out a man after his own heart and appointed him ruler of his people, because you have not kept the Lord's command."

Calling turkeys is a passion of mine. I love to get turkeys as well as elk, deer, owls even songbirds like cardinals and chickadees to come to me. When hunting elk and turkeys, calling is a huge part of the game, but patience is even bigger. Knowing the right time to move, to stalk, to call more or just to sit silently, these are the times of patience and discerning.

Our life is like this. We have goals and plans and God has given us promises and direction. Moving ahead of God will always cause hardship and disappointment. Consider Abraham, God promised him a son and Abraham and Sarah didn't wait on the Lord... They thought they knew better and the world is paying for their lack of patience and disobedience yet today.

Two of the hardest tests on the spiritual road are the patience to wait for the right moment and the courage to move forward when the right time comes.

Saul didn't wait as he was told and his family line was cut off as the kings of Israel. Now we might not pay that price but if we don't wait on the Lord, it will have huge effects.

Listen to God's word, look for the promises and most importantly, wait on Him.

JOURNAL ENTRY

_____

_____

_____

_____

_____

APRIL 16

Judges 7:2-3
The Lord said to Gideon, "The people who are with you are too many for Me to give Midian into their hands, for Israel would become boastful, saying, 'My own power has delivered me.' 3 Now therefore come, proclaim in the hearing of the people, saying, 'Whoever is afraid and trembling, let him return and depart from Mount Gilead.'" So 22,000 people returned, but 10,000 remained.

This chapter of judges goes on to tell how God lessened the number of Gideon's army to only 300 men. When they came to the camp of the Midianites and the Amalekites they were "as numerous as the locusts; and their camels were as numerous as the sand of the seashore".

But, what happened? God gave all of the 10's of thousands into the hands of Gideon's army of only 300 men that night, without a sword being drawn. God had it handled.

This shows us that God doesn't need our power and strength, He doesn't need our money or our gifts. God needs our trust and dedication to Him. He wants our love. God showed Gideon that even if he was afraid, HE had him covered.

We so often feel we "have to" do something great but God wants us to watch Him do something. We want to accomplish something for God, but He wants us to trust that He already has it taken care of.

When God asks you to do something for Him, just realize that He has already taken care of it... He just wants us to answer, "Here I am Lord, send me".

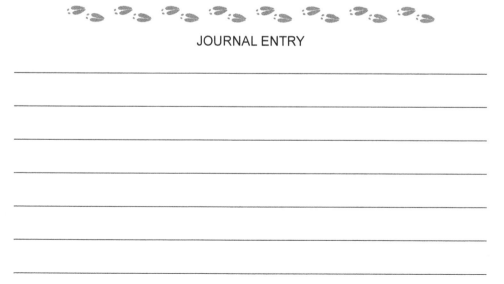

JOURNAL ENTRY

APRIL 17

NOT TO WORRY

Revelation 1:8
I am the Alpha and the Omega, the Beginning and the End, says the Lord,
Who is, and Who was, and Who is to come, the Almighty.

As things seem to get worse for all of mankind in our world we would appear to have opportunity to worry more and more. ISIS is marching across much of our world killing anybody they can that doesn't agree with them... Even now within our own country. This is only one threat of many that we have to face.

Yet, why should we be worried if we really believe that our God is the "Alpha and Omega, the beginning and the end"? This means that He has everything under His control and while He may be allowing things to happen right now, He will be in control until it's over as well.

Charles Spurgeon wrote, "Cheer up, Christian! Things are not left to chance: no blind fate rules the world. God hath purposes, and those purposes are fulfilled. God hath plans, and those plans are wise, and never can be dislocated."

So as we look around at our world and wonder, "WHAT IN THE WORLD IS GOING ON"... We can answer that with, God has got it covered.

He truly is the Alpha and Omega... No need to worry.

JOURNAL ENTRY

APRIL 18

A MUCH NEEDED REST

Mark 6:31
"Then, because so many people were coming and going that they did not even have a chance to eat, He said to them, "Come with Me by yourselves to a quiet place and get some rest.""

Ah rest... It seems as though there is never enough of this one thing in life. We struggle through life stretching and clawing and trying to please everyone else, and at the end of one project there awaits another.

Why is it that we fill our time with so many projects and programs that we can't get that much needed rest? Even when we come back from a "vacation" we are worn out. We have computers, tablets, smart phones and more gadgets to save us time yet we have less time every year... Which take way more of our much needed time to rest.

This Friday, prepare your mind like a Jr higher. Anticipate the weekend... Get excited for rest. Let your body and more importantly, your mind and heart go to a quiet place.

Take heed to what Jesus said to His disciples, "Come with Me by yourselves to a quiet place and get some rest."

We not only need physical rest, we need emotional and spiritual rest as well. Remember that we can't do it all on our own. Allow God to have control of our efforts and time. If we do that He will give us rest.

Psalm 127:1-2 "Unless the Lord builds the house, those who build it labor in vain. Unless the Lord guards the city, the guard keeps watch in vain. 2 It is in vain that you rise up early and go late to rest, eating the bread of anxious toil; for He gives sleep to His beloved."

JOURNAL ENTRY

___

___

___

___

___

___

APRIL 19

TRUE SUCCESS

Psalms 1:1-3

Blessed is the man who does not walk in the counsel of the wicked or stand in the way of sinners or sit in the seat of mockers. 2 But his delight is in the law of the LORD, and on His law he meditates day and night. 3 He is like a tree planted by streams of water, which yields its fruit in season and whose leaf does not wither. Whatever he does prospers.

I had someone ask how I felt about success and what it meant to me. After thinking about it for just a few minutes... Here are my thoughts. Please know that I believe that God blesses many Christians with great *financial" gain... But is that really what "success" is for those that love the Lord?

As we grow closer to the Lord the meaning of success changes. The old hymn "turn your eyes upon Jesus" says,

"Turn your eyes upon Jesus,
Look full in His wonderful face,
And the things of earth will grow strangely dim,
In the light of His glory and grace."

As God becomes a bigger part of our life, the things that marked success by the world become lesser and the true meaning of success change. We start to realize that the "stuff" of this world is just that, "stuff", it has no eternal value. Success might mean a loving family with grandkids in the yard. But unless that family loves the Lord even that can be a deterrent to true success.

The peace that only God can give us, is what true success is to me. As the apostle Paul wrote to the Philippian church in Philippians chapter 4. "I know what it is to be in need, and I know what it is to have plenty. I have learned the secret of being content in any and every situation, whether well fed or hungry, whether living in plenty or in want."

The "stuff" this world gives is not all bad in and of itself... But God provides for our needs and true success isn't in what we have or how much money is in our wallet. It is about our contentment in the place God has put us now.

JOURNAL ENTRY

APRIL 20

HUMBLE YOURSELF

1 Peter 5:5
In the same way, you who are younger, submit yourselves to your elders.
All of you, clothe yourselves with humility toward one another, because,
"God opposes the proud, but shows favor to the humble."

In our minds submission can be a wonderful thing... When others are submitting to us! But which of us really wants to submit to others or to anything? Who wants to lower them self?

A.W. Tozer once wrote, "The reason why many are still troubled, still seeking, still making little forward progress is because they haven't yet come to the end of themselves. We're still trying to give orders, and interfering with God's work within us."

So why do we find it so hard to give up of what we want, to give in to what God wants? SIN. We think we know best... We want what we want and that's all there is to it. God has put others around us that love us, to help "steer" us through life. Listen to those that give Godly advice, humble yourself, quite your heart and your mouth, read and absorb God's word and submit to the spiritual leadership of others.

The word submit is translated from the Greek word hupotasso. The hupo means "under" and the tasso means "to arrange." So we are to arrange ourselves under God and those that God has put over us.

I love the quote from Jesus in Matthew 23:12 "For those who exalt themselves will be humbled, and those who humble themselves will be exalted."

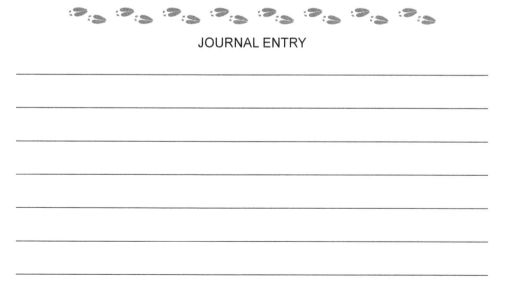

JOURNAL ENTRY

Trophies of Grace

APRIL 21

THE LEAST IN MANNASSEH

Judges 6:14-16

The Lord turned to him and said, "Go in the strength you have and save Israel out of Midian's hand. Am I not sending you?" 15 "Pardon me, my lord," Gideon replied, "but how can I save Israel? My clan is the weakest in Manasseh, and I am the least in my family." 16 The Lord answered, "I will be with you, and you will strike down all the Midianites, leaving none alive."

While riding the back roads of Colorado, we came to the small town of Manasseh and unknown to me; this was the hometown of Jack Dempsey, the world champion boxer. Dempsey was 6'1" and only 183 lbs., when he won the championship against Jess Willard, (the Pottawatomie Giant) who stood 6' 6 1/2 feet tall and weighed 240 pounds...

I don't know where Dempsey (the smaller fighter from Manasseh) stood with God, but I do know that Gideon (the smallest of his family from Manasseh) ended up trusting God and defeating the much stronger opponent.

If we hear a call from God, we don't need to be afraid; He is able to see us through. If we are living for Him we should have no fear of what we are called to do. Look at David when he was just a boy... He went out, with God at his side, and fought the biggest giant that the enemy could send against him.... And with God's help he overcame that giant.

There is an old saying that says... "If God calls us to it, He will bring you through it."

JOURNAL ENTRY

_____

_____

_____

_____

_____

_____

_____

_____

APRIL 22

DON'T WORRY... BUT PLAN

Matthew 6:33-34
But seek first his kingdom and his righteousness, and all these things will be given to you as well. 34 Therefore do not worry about tomorrow, for tomorrow will worry about itself. Each day has enough trouble of its own.

I love planning for a hunting trip... It is almost as much fun as the trip itself. I lay maps out on the table and study. I pack, unpack, repack and then add more. I meet with my travel companions to plan and plot a course. It is so exciting for me. A trip without a good plan can turn into a disaster in a hurry. Who's bringing the food, and the drinks, what will I bring for clothes to cover whatever the weather condition?

In life we often fail to look ahead. In Matthew it says not to worry about tomorrow, it doesn't say that we shouldn't plan for tomorrow. In our country, the chances of dying of thirst or hunger or going naked are slim... But if we don't plan we may run into some rough times in life.

God gives us a brain to think ahead. He gives us friends with wisdom to help direct us... We need to use that which God has given us.

Proverbs 15:22 explains it well. "Plans fail for lack of counsel, but with many advisers they succeed."

Don't worry... But plan

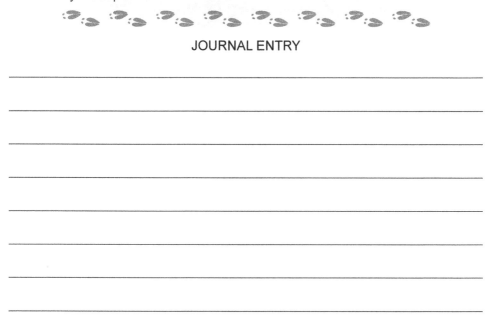

JOURNAL ENTRY

APRIL 23

TURN YOUR EYES UPON JESUS

Hebrews 12:2
Fixing our eyes on Jesus, the author and perfecter of faith, who for the joy set before Him endured the cross, despising the shame, and has sat down at the right hand of the throne of God.

A few days ago we took guests to two places on the ranch... The first was on a high point where you could look down on 10's of 1,000's of acres of land. God's Creation was laid out in front of us.

The second place we went was to a canyon that has steep walls that climbed to 13,000 ft above us. Here you had no choice but to look toward heaven and the God that created all that we saw. It is a humbling experience when you allow yourself to be put in that position. We become small and Christ becomes everything.

I love the old hymn, "Turn your eyes upon Jesus".

Turn your eyes upon Jesus,
Look full in His wonderful face
And the things of earth will grow strangely dim
In the light of His glory and grace.

Everything hinges on what you are looking at. Set your eyes on the Lord. Allow everything else to "grow strangely dim, in the light of His glory and grace".

JOURNAL ENTRY

APRIL 24

PRESCRIBED BURN

1 Peter 4:12-13
Beloved, do not be surprised at the fiery trial when it comes upon you to test you, as though something strange were happening to you. 13 But rejoice insofar as you share Christ's sufferings that you may also rejoice and be glad when his glory is revealed.

Wildlife habitat can become overgrown and the food that was once there is no longer useful. It is tough and the nutrition that was once abundant is now gone. As the plant life became tough it was of no use.

The same can be true of people. When we are young in our Christian walk we grow quickly and we are useful to Christ and to others. Some of us become toughened and bitter and the spiritual "nutrition" that we once shared goes away.

A habitat biologist will use prescribed burns that will bring back new growth to the plant life there. Peter writes that we shouldn't be surprised when "fiery trials comes upon us". Like the plants, these fiery trials produce new, tender growth in our lives, tender growth that is usable and is "nutritious" to us and to those around us.

So welcome trials as they come, stand firm in your faith. Look toward the coming glory that will be revealed.

JOURNAL ENTRY

APRIL 25

ONE BODY MANY PARTS

Romans 12:3-5
Do not think of yourself more highly than you ought, but rather think of yourself with sober judgment, in accordance with the faith God has distributed to each of you. 4 For just as each of us has one body with many members, and these members do not all have the same function, 5 so in Christ we, though many, form one body, and each member belongs to all the others.

There has to come a time in each life, when we realize that the world really doesn't revolve around "me". The sooner in life we learn that the more useful we become to others and to God, in His service, the sooner we're blessed by these actions.

As I took some new friends up near the top of the mountain. We were at 11,000+ ft in elevation. Yet even at that height all of the mountain ridges around us were from 12,500-13,000. From where we stood we could either look at our feet, or we could look toward heaven.

While looking up, it was then and there that I realized that I was very, VERY small in the overall scheme of things. I realized that in the face of all creation I was a miniscule piece in the puzzle. But like a puzzle I fit into God's big picture.

We all have to come to the place where we realize that we are a part of the plan, not in the plan itself, but God's plan. Find where you fit in God's plan. Then allow God to use you there.

1 Corinthians 12:27 You are the body of Christ. Each one of you is a part of it.

I challenge you to read verses 12-27 of 1 Corinthians chapter 12.

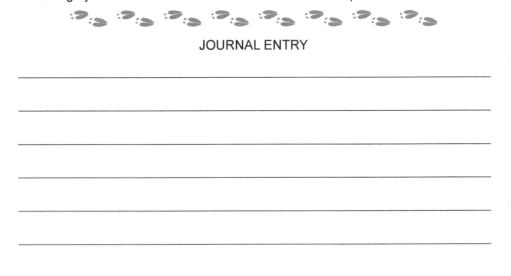

JOURNAL ENTRY

APRIL 26

DON'T HOLD BACK

Galatians 6:6
The one who is taught the word is to share all good things
with the one who teaches him.

According to Bo Lane in his article, "Why Do So Many Pastors Leave the Ministry, The Facts Will Shock You", 10% of people that start out as pastors retire as pastors? I can't imagine that there are many full-time jobs that are worse than that percentage.

What causes this? You would think that a person in a place that has dozens to hundreds of "loving" people around them all the time would be content in their work. Ha!

Let's look at some statistics... from the same article by Bo Lane; 97% of pastors have been betrayed, falsely accused or hurt by a trusted friend, 94% of pastors feel discouraged, 70%+ fight depression, 80% have NO close friends, 90% work on average of 65 hours per week and are on call 24/7 etc... Etc... Etc...

If you want to make your pastor successful in leading your church, love them. Make it a point to get to know them in a very personal way. Spend quality time with them. And never betray them.

Your pastor doesn't need your service as much as they really need your fellowship.

In Galatians 6:6 it says that we should share "ALL GOOD THINGS" with our pastors... Don't hold back.

JOURNAL ENTRY

APRIL 27

STOPPING THE SPREAD

Romans 5:12
Therefore, just as sin entered the world through one man, and death through sin, in this way death spread to all men, because all sinned.

The Rocky Mountain States have a problem, and its growing! There is a little beetle that can affect one tree in a stand of thousands of acres of evergreens and soon it spreads like wildfire until whole forests can become dead.

So it can be with sin in our lives... Romans 3:23 tells us that, "All have sinned and fallen short of the glory of God".

One seemingly small sin left unchecked can spread and multiply until you have the death of a useful spiritual life. We all sin, but it's when we don't turn from that sin that we stand the chance of losing the battle to that sinful pattern.

If those spruce beetles had been sprayed when they were first discovered, the forest could have been saved. So it is with our life... Kill the sin in your life by confessing it to God and turning from it.

1John 1:9 tells us, "If we confess our sins, He is faithful and just to forgive us our sins and cleanse us from all unrighteousness".

Don't let a life style of sinful patterns develop. Kill it before it spreads.

JOURNAL ENTRY

_____

_____

_____

_____

_____

_____

_____

APRIL 28

STRIVING TOGETHER

Philippians 1:27
Only conduct yourselves in a manner worthy of the gospel of Christ, so that whether I come and see you or remain absent, I will hear of you that you are standing firm in one spirit, with one mind striving together for the faith of the gospel

A while back I wrote about "standing strong together" as we work. That same day our supreme court made a decision that may forever change our country... For the better. Don't stop reading here...

While our court justices were redefining marriage, they were also figuratively signing gag orders and directives for our clergy and churches across the United States.

It is time for all Gospel teaching churches in all towns to come together to join their "roots" to make sure that one doesn't fall.

It's time to put away our petty differences and build God's church not our own congregation. If the Gospel is being preached and salvation is being taught through a relationship in Christ alone, then we need to join arms and fight these upcoming battles together.

Ecclesiastes 4:9-10 9 "Two are better than one because they have a good return for their labor. 10 For if either of them falls, the one will lift up his companion. But woe to the one who falls when there is not another to lift him up. Furthermore, if two lie down together they keep warm, but how can one be warm alone? And if one can overpower him who is alone, two can resist him. A cord of three strands is not quickly torn apart."

So, come together in one spirit, "striving together for the faith of the gospel"

JOURNAL ENTRY

_____

_____

_____

_____

_____

_____

APRIL 29

NOT TO CONDEMN BUT TO SAVE

John 3:17
For God did not send the Son into the world to condemn the world,
but that the world might be saved through Him.

What is the best known verse in the bible? John 3:16? We see it everywhere; football game end zones, semi trucks, banners, even Tim Tebo's cheeks. And I totally believe that my God did love me so much that He sent His only Son to die that I might live. But isn't it something to think that with all the pain we cause God, He came to save us and not condemn us?

In the song, "CAME TO SAVE" by Joshua Seller, the story of why Christ came is explained very well.

WHAT A WORD THAT WAS SPOKEN
THE VERY REASON THAT YOU CAME
NOT TO JUDGE OR CONDEMN US

YOU CAME TO SAVE
WHAT A LOVE THAT WAS LAVISHED
WHAT A PRICE FOR THOSE ENSLAVED
HOW YOU CHASED THE HEART
OF SINNERS
YOU CAME TO SAVE
OH, MERCY BEYOND MEASURE

THAT TO DIE IS NOW OUR GAIN
FROM YOUR HANDS WE CAN'T
BE SEVERED
FOR YOU CAME TO SAVE
AND WHEN ALL THE SAINTS ARE
GATHERED

AND WE WALK THROUGH
HEAVEN'S GATES
FOR ETERNITY WE'LL ECHO
THAT YOU CAME TO SAVE!

We are so blessed to have a God that would send His Son to die on our behalf... And not to condemn us but to save us. We can never repay... We can only accept.

JOURNAL ENTRY

APRIL 30

Hebrews 11:8-13

By faith Abraham, when called to go to a place he would later receive as his inheritance, obeyed and went, even though he did not know where he was going. 9 By faith he made his home in the Promised Land like a stranger in a foreign country; he lived in tents, as did Isaac and Jacob, who were heirs with him of the same promise. 10 For he was looking forward to the city with foundations, whose architect and builder is God. 11 And by faith even Sarah, who was past childbearing age, was enabled to bear children because she considered him faithful who had made the promise. 12 And so from this one man, and he as good as dead, came descendants as numerous as the stars in the sky and as countless as the sand on the seashore. 13 All these people were still living by faith when they died. They did not receive the things promised; they only saw them and welcomed them from a distance, admitting that they were foreigners and strangers on earth.

As I drove guests around the mountains we came to a very narrow passage across a rock slide. It was just barely wide enough for the truck... 1000 ft. straight up to our right, 500 ft. straight down to our left. The guest in my passenger seat exclaimed: "Whoa, now this is an exercise in faith".

It made me realize that I had 8 people in my truck and they had their lives in my hands. Their faith was in me! That was probably scarier than they knew.

I'm just a man and faith in a man can be a dangerous thing. But faith in a loving, all powerful God is different. We can always rely on His love and care for us.

Max Lucado, in his book, "He Still Moves Stones", wrote...

"Faith is not the belief that God will do what you want. It is the belief that God will do what is right."

Trust that God will always do right in our life... Have faith... Trust Him

JOURNAL ENTRY

___

___

___

___

MAY

Proverbs 3:5

Trust in the LORD with all your heart and lean not on your own understanding.

MAY 1

TODAY'S STRUGGLES

Genesis 50:19-20
But Joseph said to them, "Do not be afraid, for am I in God's place? 20 As for you, you meant evil against me, but God meant it for good in order to bring about this present result, to preserve many people alive.

Yesterday my grandson shared something he had seen online. It said, "The struggle you are in today is developing the strength you need for tomorrow".

In the book of Genesis, Joseph, would never have chosen to be sold into slavery by his brothers. In the book of Job, Job wouldn't have chosen to lose everything. The apostle Paul would not have chosen to lose his sight... But all of these painful situations were used by God to build these men into what God wanted for them in the future

What struggle are you dealing with today? What is it that it might be preparing for you tomorrow? Take note that, Joseph, Job and Paul all followed God, they trusted Him with their lives and their future... There is the key to Godly growth.

We may think that what we're dealing with now is a pretty big deal. It may be, but it could also be preparing you for something far bigger. God is always preparing us for greater work. It's up to us to cooperate with Him to see those results.

JOURNAL ENTRY

MAY 2

1 John 4:1-2
Beloved, do not believe every spirit, but test the spirits to see whether they are from God, because many false prophets have gone out into the world.
2 By this you know the Spirit of God: every spirit that confesses that Jesus Christ has come in the flesh is from God.

I carry and use decoys a lot when hunting. I started out with using turkey decoys then deer, antelope, elk, duck and goose. Why? Because they work. I have guided to and taken many game animals over the years because of decoys. They are so effective that some people think they should be illegal.

When an animal starts to believe what they see is real, or what they hear (a hunter calling) is authentic... It generally means death.

The same is true of people. When we start listening to things that are sounding good but not quite right, we need to turn and run away because someone is teaching "death". The best way to know if what you hear is false is to study what is true. Read and study the scriptures to know the truth.

There are people that are trained to spot counterfeit money... How are they trained? By studying the real stuff. The Bible tells us to be discerning about the false teachers. To know the difference between the truth and a lie.

Charles Spurgeon explained it this way. "DISCERNMENT is NOT knowing the difference between RIGHT and WRONG. It is knowing the difference between RIGHT and ALMOST RIGHT."

Don't get decoyed into what is almost right. Study the truth.

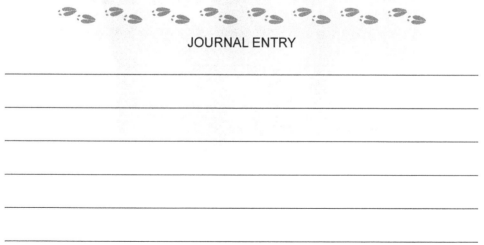

JOURNAL ENTRY

MAY 3

THE VALUE OF ONE LIFE

Psalm 8:3-4
When I consider your heavens, the work of your fingers, the moon and the stars, which you have set in place, 4 what is mankind that you are mindful of them, human beings that you care for them?

You are one person out of 7,125,000,000 people on earth right now. That's 7.125 BILLION... Any one of us is such a small piece of the overall universe. It truly is amazing that God even cares a little about our "insignificant" lives.

However, as an immeasurably small part of an immeasurably huge universe, God cares about each and every one of His children.

Like the shepherd that leaves his entire flock of sheep to search out one lost lamb, God won't allow even one to fall by the wayside.

The next time you think that you are insignificant, remember that even if you were the only one on earth, Christ would have come and died for just you.

Matthew 6:26 says, Look at the birds of the air; they do not sow or reap or store away in barns, and yet your heavenly Father feeds them. Are you not much more valuable than they?

God considered you worth allowing His son to die. Wow, that's value.

JOURNAL ENTRY

MAY 4

PATIENTLY WAITING

Galatians 6:9
Let us not become weary in doing good, for at the proper time
we will reap a harvest if we do not give up

God made a promise to Abraham that he would be the father of many nations. At the time he and Sarah were very old. After waiting a long time, they had a son, when Abraham was 100 years old.

Joseph was sold into slavery as a boy and ended up being thrown into prison for a long time. But Joseph never gave up hope and God raised him up into a great leader of both Egypt and God's people.

Job lost everything in his life and waited on God and God provided even more for Job than he had had before.

Whatever the task is that God has called us to; we need to continue doing the work even if we don't see the progress we would like to see. Even Jesus was teaching His disciples until the moment of His death. Jesus is an example of patience for us.

Patience is not just waiting for something, it's about how we wait, it's about our attitude while waiting. Trusting God that He will perfect in us His plans, no matter how long it takes... This is patience.

JOURNAL ENTRY

MAY 5

THY WORD HAVE I HID IN MY HEART

Deuteronomy 11:18
"You shall therefore lay up these words of mine in your heart and in your soul, and you shall bind them as a sign on your hand, and they shall be as frontlets between your eyes."

Ronald Reagan once said, "within the cover of the Bible are the answers for all the problems men face".

It doesn't matter if you are right wing, left wing or somewhere in between, this is so true.

God didn't inspire the writing of the Bible for His sake, it was to direct the lives of the billions of people that would come after. Even today it answers the questions of life. Those that say it has no meaning in today's world, aren't reading it.

I challenge you today. Consider what you are struggling with and Google those words with the word Bible... Then start reading.

All of the "self help" books, put all together, cannot answer the issues of our lives like the Word of God.

Ecclesiastes 1:9 says this, "What has been will be again, what has been done will be done again; there is nothing new under the sun."... God has already covered it.

Spending time in God's word will give you direction when you face tough situations. Check it out and make it a habit.

JOURNAL ENTRY

_____

_____

_____

_____

_____

_____

MAY 6

A LIGHT IN THE DARKNESS

Psalm 119:105
Your word is a lamp to my feet and a light to my path.

Before the time of GPS's, satellites, Lowrance systems or even compasses... Sailors had to navigate by night. How did they do it? They learned to follow the light of the stars in the sky. God placed these lights in the sky at the time of creation and even as far back as the early Old Testament the people had the constellations named. These are what guided the sailors through the darkness.

Today as we go through dark periods in our life we need to look to the light. Christ is the light that guides us through those dark times. If we take our eyes off of Him we lose our way. If we continue to look to Him we get through the periods of night and arrive again in times of light.

When in complete darkness of the night, the only thing that can get you through is the hope and promise of the morning light...

Martin Luther King Jr. wrote this "Darkness cannot drive out darkness: only light can do that."

Allow God's love to shine light in the darkness of your life

JOURNAL ENTRY

MAY 7

THE KING IS COMING

2 Timothy 3:1-5

But understand this, that in the last days difficult times will come. 2 For people will be lovers of themselves, lovers of money, boastful, arrogant, blasphemers, disobedient to parents, ungrateful, unholy, 3 unloving, irreconcilable, slanderers, without self-control, savage, opposed to what is good, 4 treacherous, reckless, conceited, loving pleasure rather than loving God. 5 They will maintain the outward appearance of religion but will have repudiated its power. So avoid people like these.

Is there ANY doubt that we are living in the time described in this passage? A time when not even the everyday citizen fit into this description but those we are supposed to look up to. Can we even imagine what would be left to our world in 100 years if the rate of decline remains at the pace it is at now? It can't go on...

There's good news... THE KING IS COMING!!!

When I was a boy my mom would bake on Saturday afternoons. The Suring, Wisconsin radio station, WRVM, would be playing on the counter. One day my sister Becky came running into the kitchen when she heard the Gaithers singing...

The King is coming, the King is coming
I just heard the trumpet sounding and soon His face I'll see
The King is coming, the King is coming
Praise God, He's coming for me

She excitedly said, "the King is coming momma, the King is coming!".

Are we that excited for His arrival? If He arrives today, do you know you're leaving with Him? Are those around you seeing something in you that makes them want to know the King too?

There's no doubt that the King is coming soon, coming for His people. Are you ready? Are you excited?

THE KING IS COMING VERY SOON. Spread the news.

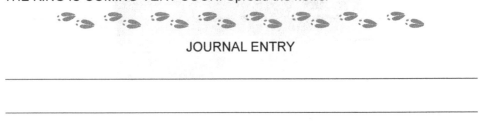

JOURNAL ENTRY

_____

_____

_____

MAY 8

IT'S NOT FOR ME TO UNDERSTAND

Matthew 26:36-46

Then Jesus went with them to a place called Gethsemane, and he said to his disciples, "Sit here, while I go over there and pray." 37 And taking with him Peter and the two sons of Zebedee, he began to be sorrowful and troubled. 38 Then he said to them, "My soul is very sorrowful, even to death; remain here, and watch with me." 39 And going a little farther he fell on his face and prayed, saying, "My Father, if it be possible, let this cup pass from me; nevertheless, not as I will, but as you will."

There is so much that happens in life we just can never explain; the death of a young person, handicapped children, natural disasters, etc...

We want to know the reasons why, but in our finite minds we have no way of understanding how these all fit together in a larger plan. And sometimes we have to realize that God's original plan was for a perfect spotless world... Then sin entered the picture. We live in a fallen sinful world and because of that, bad things will happen to good people.

All we can do is trust that God has control and loves us more than we can know. He has a plan that someday we will see in all its glory.

Willie Nelson wrote and sang a song called, "Not for me to understand" that speaks very well to this subject take a minute to listen to it... And realize that our God is in control and does have a plan for our lives.

It might not be for us to understand, but we can know that God does understand and we can trust Him.

JOURNAL ENTRY

___

___

___

___

___

___

___

MAY 9

TO GOD BE THE GLORY

Philippians 4:11-13

Not that I speak from want, for I have learned to be content in whatever circumstances I am. 12 I know how to get along with humble means, and I also know how to live in prosperity; in any and every circumstance I have learned the secret of being filled and going hungry, both of having abundance and suffering need. 13 I can do all things through Him who strengthens me.

The Apostle Paul's life was truly an example of a life that was set on glorifying God. In Acts 16, Paul and Silas were beaten and thrown in prison for serving God, by throwing out a demon from a girl. Yet, at midnight they weren't grumbling or crying... There they were, with their feet bound in the stocks, singing and praying.

Paul was confident that God would use all things—poverty as well as abundance, comfort as well as pain—for Paul's good and God's glory (Romans 8:28).

We as Christians, if we are discontented for any reason... job, spouse, finances... we are a terrible testimony about the goodness of our God. What kind of God do we have? Is He really in control? Can He really be trusted? Glorifying God means that we praise Him with absolute contentment, knowing that our situation is God's plan for us now

Charles Swindoll said it this way, "If your life is an example of glorifying God, others won't see your good works and glorify You, because they'll know what you are doing is for God's glory."

May your life bring glory to God.

JOURNAL ENTRY

MAY 10

A HOPE THAT THE WORLD CANNOT GIVE

Romans 15:13
May the God of hope fill you with all joy and peace as you trust in Him, so that you may overflow with hope by the power of the Holy Spirit.

While preparing my morning devotionals I quite often read a lot of quotes on the subject... This morning I did the same. I read so many quotes on hope it was dizzying. Almost every one of the quotes was an empty attempt to fill others with a sense that things might get better for them

Barbara Kingsolver wrote this on the subject, "Hope is a renewable option: If you run out of it at the end of the day, you get to start over in the morning."

Wow, what a shame. Our world's sad state of hope is a reminder of how lost we are without true hope. Over the last 6 years in our country we were told we should "hope" and that there would be "change"... What was the hope in?

There is only one way to truly have hope in this life. That is in knowing that we have the one true God that loves us. He loves us enough to allow His own Son to die a miserable death, nailed to a cross. (John 3:16) He loved us enough to give us an eternal hope as well as a day to day hope in this life. Where is your hope? If you know Christ, have you forgotten today what a great hope we have. And that joy and peace that God gives us comes through our hope. And today if you don't know Jesus personally, where is your hope for today or tomorrow? God knows each one of His children by name... And has a plan to give us all a hope.

Jeremiah 29:11 "For I know the plans I have for you," declares the Lord, "plans to prosper you and not to harm you, plans to give you hope and a future".

JOURNAL ENTRY

_____

_____

_____

_____

_____

_____

Trophies of Grace

MAY 11

CREATING BLESSING... FOR YOU AND OTHERS

Proverbs 11:24-25
One man gives freely, yet gains even more; another withholds unduly, but comes to poverty. 25 A generous man will prosper; he who refreshes others will himself be refreshed.

A while back I drove to Green Bay Wisconsin for a NATIONAL CHRISTIAN FOUNDATION breakfast. One of the speakers at the breakfast was Packer great "KGB" (Kabeer Gbaja-Biamila). KGB spoke of the joy of giving. I've been known to often say, "life is short" and this morning KGB quoted the bible when he said, "life is but a vapor". (James 4:14)

This life is so short and eternity is forever. What we do here in this life has eternal consequences, one way or the other... Generosity, with time, effort, money etc... has immediate, long term and eternal benefits, not only to those on the receiving end but as much or more so to the giver.

Do you believe that the bible is true and that it is inspired of God? Then contemplate this, Acts 20:35 says, "In everything I showed you that by working hard in this manner you must help the weak and remember the words of the Lord Jesus, that He Himself said, 'It is more blessed to give than to receive.'"

Do you want to be extraordinarily blessed in this life? Bless someone else. Written in Malachi 3:10, it say, "Bring the whole tithe into the storehouse, so that there may be food in My house, and test Me now in this," says the Lord of hosts, "if I will not open for you the windows of heaven and pour out for you a blessing until it overflows."

Test Him today, bless someone.

JOURNAL ENTRY

_____
_____
_____
_____
_____
_____

MAY 12

PROTECTING YOUR HEART

Psalms 19:14
Let the words of my mouth, and the meditation of my heart, be acceptable in thy sight, O LORD, my strength, and my redeemer.

ccording to the prophet Jeremiah, the condition of the human heart is deceitful above all things, and desperately wicked.

That is a pretty strong statement, "deceitful and wicked"... That's bad! But in the verse above makes it clear that we can control it with effort.

Satan, the very first terrorist, knows that if he can poison our heart, then he can corrupt our life! The quality of our life is determined by the condition of our heart. Whole ministries can be brought down by one poisoned heart being controlled by satan.

What does your heart meditate on when no one is around, what comes from your mouth? If we are filled with the Holy Spirit when we are in public, or on a Sunday morning, then this is the same person we will be when we are away from the people in church.

How do we protect our heart and control our mouth? By spending time with God, reading His Word and personal time in prayer. The word "Heart" is found 963 times in the bible. It would seem important enough to protect it.

JOURNAL ENTRY

MAY 13

STRENGTH IN NUMBERS

Ecclesiastes 4:9–12
Two are better than one, because they have a good reward for their toil. 10 For if they fall, one will lift up his fellow. But woe to him who is alone when he falls and has not another to lift him up! 11 Again, if two lie together, they keep warm, but how can one keep warm alone? 12 And though a man might prevail against one who is alone, two will withstand him—a threefold cord is not quickly broken.

I have always enjoyed archery. As a kid at bible camp I won trophies most years. I still love the curves and contours of a recurve bow. As children, most of us have bent a piece of wood and tied a string on and we were able to shoot an arrow a short way. But soon that bow breaks. A good bow builder will attach layers of lamination to support each other and strength the bow. So it is with people, if we surround ourselves with other like minded people we can stand up to so much more.

It's like a red hot ember in a fire. It will stay red and extremely hot if it remains in with the rest of the coals. But pull it out on its own and it soon turns cold and gray.

Hebrews 10:24–25 And let us consider how to stir up one another to love and good works, 25 not neglecting to meet together, as is the habit of some, but encouraging one another, and all the more as you see the Day drawing near.

So surround yourself with strong Christians. Hold each other up.

JOURNAL ENTRY

MAY 14

Mark 4:19
but the worries of this life, the deceitfulness of wealth and the desires for other things come in and choke the word, making it unfruitful.

There comes a time in life when we realize that we are too busy to fit one more thing into our day, our week, our month etc... We can't waiver from what we are doing or we won't get done all we've set out to do.

Unfortunately, the irony is that we are busy doing many things that don't matter and we have no time for things that do. Shouldn't we reverse it? Shouldn't we be looking at what's really important in life and cut some of the rest out?

Ahab was an evil king if Israel. He and his wife, Jezebel, are known as evil royalty. Ahab was extremely successful in battle... And God allowed him to be so. Ahab's life was full of business, yet none of it mattered for what was really important.

Being busy isn't bad, being busy with the "wrong" things is. Step back and look at where your time is spent. Who are you serving with your business? If you aren't serving God through these periods of being "too busy", then you are just that "too busy".

Reconsider your priorities.

JOURNAL ENTRY

MAY 15

Matthew 25:34-36

34 "Then the King will say to those on his right, 'Come, you who are blessed by my Father; take your inheritance, the kingdom prepared for you since the creation of the world. 35 For I was hungry and you gave me something to eat, I was thirsty and you gave me something to drink, I was a stranger and you invited me in, 36 I needed clothes and you clothed me, I was sick and you looked after me, I was in prison and you came to visit me.'

Mark Twain had an interesting way with words. He was given a way to explain men's thoughts that was different than most. He once said... "Kindness is the language the blind can see and the deaf can hear."

Kindness is one of the "fruits of the spirit" that Paul wrote about in his letter to the Galatians. You can't fake true kindness, you will be found out. It is a God-given trait.

In college you can major in hospitality... What is that? It is showing kindness to and serving others. It is hard to teach a heart to be kind.

Hebrews 13:2 says, Do not neglect to show hospitality to strangers, for by this some have entertained angels without knowing it.

God can change a heart toward kindness.

JOURNAL ENTRY

___

___

___

___

___

___

___

___

MAY 16

ALWAYS THERE!

Jeremiah 29:13-14
You will seek me and find me when you seek me with all your heart. 14 I will be found by you," declares the Lord, "and will bring you back from captivity...

During the darkest moments of our lives, there are times when God feels so far away, times of no hope in our small minds, think about the times when you struggled the most emotionally in your life. It felt like God wasn't there... Even King David had these feelings. David knew that no matter where he went, God was with him.

Psalm 39:7 Where can I go from Your Spirit? Or where can I flee from Your presence?

Not many in all of time struggled as David did with sorrow (much of itself inflicted). He went through terrible times of discouragement. But he also always came back to God, because he knew that no matter where he was God was right there alongside him.

No matter what you are facing today, or will face tomorrow, you can rest assured that God is with you. He is right there. It doesn't matter how far we run from Him or feel separated, the verses above assure us of that, "You will seek me and find me when you seek me with all your heart." These are promises to His children, those that have sought Him out and accepted His close relationship. Seek Him "with all your heart."

Just prior to verses 13 and 14 in Jeremiah 29 is a terrific reminder of God not only being close, but also, having plans for our benefit.

11 "For I know the plans I have for you," declares the Lord, "plans to prosper you and not to harm you, plans to give you hope and a future."

We have an awesome God that is ALWAYS there.

JOURNAL ENTRY

_____

_____

_____

_____

_____

MAY 17

HOW GREAT IS OUR GOD?

Psalm 14:1
14 The fool hath said in his heart, there is no God. They are corrupt, they have done abominable works, there is none that doeth good.

We spent yesterday at the Creation Museum in Kentucky... What an eye opener! I know what I believe and I have no doubts, however, yesterday taught me some amazing facts about why I believe what I believe.

We spent yesterday at the Creation Museum in Kentucky... What an eye opener! I know what I believe and I have no doubts, however, yesterday taught me some amazing facts about why I believe what I believe.

If scientists really looked at the proof of creation with an open mind, they would have to question secular sciences theories.

Did you know that the sun is shrinking at a rate that if the earth was really millions of years old, the sun would have been so big the heat would have made the earth uninhabitable by any life? Were you aware that a huge canyon was formed by the runoff of Mount St Helen and that scientist normally would have claimed it had taken millions of years? But they saw it happen in days, not centuries.

Dr. Louis Bounoure, a prominent Swiss scientist, summed it up rather succinctly when he stated, "Evolution is a fairy tale for grownups! The theory has helped nothing in the progress of science. It is useless." (undefined, SIGNS OF NATURE) The truth is that science disproves any theory of a slowly evolving earth, again confirming special creation.

There are countless signs that show us that life was created, it didn't just happen. We need to become familiar with God's truths so we can stand for God in the midst of the world views.

JOURNAL ENTRY

___

___

___

___

___

MAY 18

John 20:28-29
28 Thomas answered and said to Him, "My Lord and my God!" 29 Jesus said to him, "Because you have seen Me, have you believed? Blessed are they who did not see, and yet believed."

Good hunters are a faithful bunch. They will sit for days waiting in one spot hoping that their prey will come by. There was a time, and it wasn't too many generations back, where it was a matter of life and death. If you didn't harvest an animal, you didn't eat meat for a while. Today it's different. We don't have to count on game meat to survive. We also don't have to wonder if game is in or travels through our area. Some hunters use feeders & trail cameras, which will capture photos & video of the animals and their habits and send them to their phone. There isn't a big need anymore for a great amount of faith in most hunting.

The day after Christ's resurrection He appeared to the disciples. According to John's account, Thomas wasn't present at first and didn't believe it was really the Messiah that the others were seeing. He needed proof. I can't say that I would have had more faith than Thomas.

The Christian life, as in hunting requires a great deal of faith and trust. We can either doubt that He will come through when we need Him or we can wait patiently for Christ to show us He is real and we can count on Him.

Don't be a doubting Thomas. Trust that Christ is real and is always there beside His children. We don't need to see Him; we can see what He does and how He works.

JOURNAL ENTRY

MAY 19

STONG FENCES

Colossians 1:23
23 If ye continue in the faith grounded and settled, and be not moved away from the hope of the gospel, which ye have heard, and which was preached to every creature which is under heaven; whereof I Paul am made a minister

If you were to set out to build a straight fence you wouldn't be haphazardly setting poles in the ground without direction. You would dig one deep hole first to securely hold your post. Then as each post goes in you look back down the line of posts to make sure that they line up straight. Each post, like the first is buried deep to make sure it has a firm foundation, grounded well, then it has solid dirt or gravel packed around it to keep it from wavering back and forth.

As children of God we need to be well grounded on a firm foundation of faith and then be set in place by study of God's word so as not to waiver when pressures come against us.

If a fence is not secure it will topple over the first time that something applies pressure to it. It also is strengthened and tightened by being well connected to other fence posts of similar strength.

So it goes for God's people... We need to be bound to others with similar beliefs and strengths. We then are held up by those around us that are in turn held up by us. God's family, if it's to be strong, needs to be like a strong, straight fence. Holding each other up when the pressures of life push in on us.

Thank you to all of you like-minded fence posts that hold me up.

JOURNAL ENTRY

_____
_____
_____
_____
_____
_____
_____

MAY 20

DON'T SWIM IN THE PROP WASH

Romans 12:1-2

12 Therefore, I urge you, brothers and sisters, in view of God's mercy, to offer your bodies as a living sacrifice, holy and pleasing to God—this is your true and proper worship. 2 Do not conform to the pattern of this world, but be transformed by the renewing of your mind. Then you will be able to test and approve what God's will is—his good, pleasing and perfect will.

I've fished salmon a little around the great lakes and for one summer on Kodiak Island Alaska. When trolling on the ocean, off of Kodiak, we would run two lines down a little ways on the down riggers alongside the boat. We would troll along for a while and then look into the prop wash for fish. For those that don't know the prop wash is the area right behind the propeller.

Quite often there would be several salmon swimming right behind the boat's propeller. They would travel along following the boat blindly. When they were there you could drop a lure right in front of them and they would immediately bite and that salmon would become dinner.

In Romans 12, the Apostle Paul warned, "Do not conform to the pattern of this world" because it would certainly lead to death. Fitting in, or conforming, to the world will make it so you are not fitting in with Christ and His family. It's one or the other.

The problem with trying to fit in is, it's seeking pleasure in all the wrong places. You will never be satisfied when you do that. Find your joy or pleasure in Christ. Did Jesus find any joy in this world? No, and neither will those that are truly His followers. Why? Because the world doesn't want to hear about the Gospel message. The world is offended by God's word. The world gets excited about anything ungodly, God's family finds excitement in what God is doing in our world.

Don't follow the world blindly looking for an easy ride in the prop wash of the ungodly. Instead swim against the current of this earthly life and with Christ and His family.

The rewards are eternal.

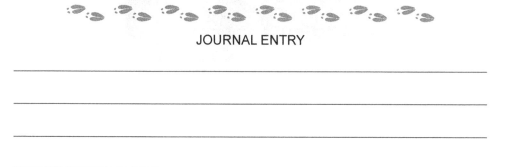

JOURNAL ENTRY

MAY 21

HE CALMS THE STORM...

Mark 4:35-41

35 That day when evening came, he said to his disciples, "Let us go over to the other side." 36 Leaving the crowd behind, they took him along, just as he was, in the boat. There were also other boats with him. 37 A furious squall came up, and the waves broke over the boat, so that it was nearly swamped. 38 Jesus was in the stern, sleeping on a cushion. The disciples woke him and said to him, "Teacher, don't you care if we drown?" 39 He got up, rebuked the wind and said to the waves, "Quiet! Be still!" Then the wind died down and it was completely calm. 40 He said to his disciples, "Why are you so afraid? Do you still have no faith?" 41 They were terrified and asked each other, "Who is this? Even the wind and the waves obey him!"

There is a song by Scott Krippayne called SOMETIMES HE CALMS THE STORM.

Part of the lyrics say this, "Sometimes He calms the storm and other times He calms His child"

Calming the storm was demonstrated in Mark 4:35-41. It's an impressive demonstration of Christ's power over nature and His ability to comfort us in the storm. It shows our need to call on Him in prayer and place our trust in Him and our total need to rely on him.

When the disciples cried out suggesting that He didn't care whether they perished or not, Christ showed His disappointment in their lack of faith. For Christ loves us all and wants for none to perish, but for all to have faith and go through the storm with Him. Each time we choose to trust Him in the storm the stronger our faith becomes.

But what we also see in this passage is the transformation from being afraid, to having the fear of God. The disciples just witnessed the power that He had over the sea and storm and realized the power that He had over them. They were now in awe, they were amazed at what they just observed and were filled with the fear of God, a godly fear of the power and grace of Christ during the calm, a fear of the Lord and all His goodness, a reverent awe that was full of honor and glorifying to Christ

So today, what do you fear? What needs "calming" in your life? There are so many things in life we can't control, but HE can... Ask God to calm your storms or to allow the storms to rage and to hold you close and calm you...

"SOMETIMES HE CALMS THE STORM AND OTHER TIMES HE CALMS HIS CHILD

JOURNAL ENTRY

MAY 22

CLEAN HEART AND A RENEWED SPIRIT

Psalm 51:6, 10-12
6 Behold, you delight in truth in the inward being, and you teach me wisdom in the secret heart.
10 Create in me a clean heart, O God, and renew a right spirit within me.
11 Cast me not away from your presence, and take not your Holy Spirit from me.
12 Restore to me the joy of your salvation, and uphold me with a willing spirit.

Last week a few of us went to the rifle range to do some shooting. When we left we evidently forgot a plastic ammo case on a bench. This case contained a lot of money in ammo. We never knew that it was left there until the owner of the box got a letter in his mail a week later. Rudy, a retired gentleman, had stopped by the range later in the day and seeing the box on the bench and finding a name and address, took it all home and wrote a letter to the owner, 250 miles away.

Rudy could have easily brought the case home and never said a word, he could have sold the ammo easy enough for a fair amount of money. Having talked to Rudy, I bet it didn't even cross his mind. His first and only thought was to do the right thing and return it to its rightful owner.

In verse 6 of Psalms 51 David writes, "Behold, you delight in truth in the inward being, and you teach me wisdom in the secret heart". The writer understood what God expects of us and how He is delighted when our lives are what they should be. In verse 10 then he asks for God to, "Create in me a clean heart, O God, and renew a right spirit within me". David wants what God wants for him.

How about you (and me)? Do we desire what God desires in us? Do we pray for a clean heart? Are we living out every day the, "truth in the inward being" that God not only wants, but also requires of us?

JOURNAL ENTRY

MAY 23

LOVE ONE ANOTHER

John 13:34-35
"A new command I give you: Love one another. As I have loved you, so you must love one another. 35 By this everyone will know that you are my disciples, if you love one another."

One day Thomas Edison came home and gave a paper to his mother. He told her, "My teacher gave this paper to me and told me to only give it to my mother."

His mother's eyes were tearful as she read the letter out loud to her child: Your son is a genius. This school is too small for him and doesn't have enough good teachers for training him. Please teach him yourself.

Many years later after Edison's mother died and he was now one of the greatest inventors of the century, he was looking through some old family things. Suddenly he saw a folded paper in the corner of a desk drawer. He took it and opened it up. On the paper was written: "Your son is addled [mentally ill]. We won't let him come to school any more."

Edison cried for hours and then he wrote in his diary: "Thomas Alva Edison was an addled (mentally I'll) child that, by a hero mother, became the genius of the century."

Young Edison's teacher was Reverend G. B. Engle... A pastor!! I'm not sure if this entire story is true, but if only part of it is true it is a shame.

This shows the impact we can have, good and/or bad, with one or two words. Christ said, "As I have loved you, so you must love one another." There are a lot of ways we can "love one another"... But just caring is the way that others will know that they are loved.

Start making a point to go out of your way to serve people. By "sincerely" serving the world others will know that we love them.

"By this everyone will know that you are my disciples, if you love one another."

JOURNAL ENTRY

___

___

___

___

MAY 24

PLANT AND WATER

1 Corinthians 3:6-9

I planted, Apollos watered, but God gave the growth. 7 So neither he who plants nor he who waters is anything, but only God who gives the growth. 8 He who plants and he who waters are one, and each will receive his wages according to his labor. 9 For we are God's fellow workers. You are God's field, God's building.

For the last two months there have been two potted shrubs sitting in my yard... My wife has "reminded" me many times that she would really "like" me to plant these for her. Her idea is that she would love to have these in front of the house for years to come. I'm sure that if I get them planted Linda will keep them watered and taken care of... One of these days I will get to it.

If I leave those plants in the pots on the deck they will never grow and they will eventually die. And if I plant those shrubs and no one waters them, they may live (maybe not) but they would never thrive...

The same is true as we plant seeds for God. God really does not "need" us to plant or water but He desires for us to do it. If we don't plant the seeds of God's love or if we don't water these seeds those that need God will certainly die. We have a responsibility, as Christ commanded, "go into all the world and preach the Gospel"...

Plant and water...

JOURNAL ENTRY

MAY 25

IMPOSSIBLE WITH MEN, POSSIBLE WITH GOD

Luke 18:27
"The things which are impossible with men are possible with God"

Abraham was sitting in the door of his tent during the heat of the day, when suddenly three men appeared before him, standing under a tree. Abraham went out to meet the men, prepared a meal for them and visited with them.

During their conversation, the Lord asked Abraham where his wife, Sarah, was. Then God said something incredible: "...lo, Sarah thy wife shall have a son" (Genesis 18:10).

At the time, Sarah was inside the tent, listening to their conversation. And when she heard this, she laughed at the idea. IMPOSSIBLE, she thought. She was way beyond the age of childbearing, and Abraham was too old to father a child. Yet when God heard Sarah's laughter, he said, "Then the LORD said to Abraham, "Why did Sarah laugh and say, 'Will I really have a child, now that I am old?' [14] Is anything too hard for the LORD? I will return to you at the appointed time next year, and Sarah will have a son." Genesis 18:13-14

God asks the same question of his children in these present times... Is anything too hard for the Lord? Each of us has to face our own difficult situations in life. And in the midst of them God asks, "Do you think your problem is too hard for me to fix? Or do you believe I can work it out for you, even though you think it's impossible?"

Again, Jesus told us in Luke 18:27 "The things which are impossible with men are possible with God". Do you believe this word from the Lord? Do you accept that he can perform the impossible in your marriage, in your family, on your job, for your future? We're quick to counsel others that he can. When we see our loved ones enduring difficult times, we tell them, "Hold on, and look up. The Lord is able. Don't stop trusting him. He's the God of the impossible." Yet, I wonder–do we believe these truths for ourselves?

Impossible with men, possible with God

JOURNAL ENTRY

___

___

___

___

MAY 26

A PAINFUL WORLD

John 16:33
"I have told you these things, so that in me you may have peace. In this world you will have trouble. But take heart! I have overcome the world."

Our world is a painful place. Everyday all of us feel pain of some sort or another; we might not be devastated by physical pain, but we might be emotionally hurt. So how do we get through life? We all experience troubles and need to learn to find our peace in Christ. On our own we wallow in our pain, through Christ we can be released from that.

But how? When we break a leg (or two as my friend Kirk did yesterday) we need the help of a doctor, someone who can start the healing process correctly. When we are suffering emotionally (and/or physically) we can experience healing through other people as well.

In 1 John 4:12 it tells us that by loving each other God's love is made complete... 12 "No one has ever seen God, but if we love each other, God lives in us and his love is made complete in us."

Christ suffered the ultimate pain and suffering in this world. He came to serve and to save His people... Giving up His place in heaven to come to a sinful earth. Then He was rejected and ridiculed while living here. Worse yet He was nailed on a cross with spikes driven through His feet and hands... what pain that must have been. But how did He respond? First He forgave those that were killing Him. Then He gave Himself to His father...

Luke 23:46, "Father, into Your hands I commit My spirit..."

Give your pain to God, allow Him to deal with it.

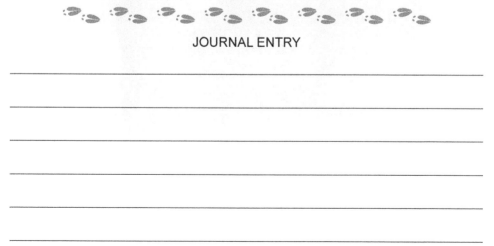

JOURNAL ENTRY

_____

_____

_____

_____

_____

_____

MAY 27

GIVING AND TAKING

1 John 4:8
Whoever does not love does not know God, because God is love.

How often we look at love by focusing on what we can get from it... But if our only view of love is based on what we can get from others, it will fail us every single time.

Romans 5:6-8 says... 6 You see, at just the right time, when we were still powerless, Christ died for the ungodly. 7 Very rarely will anyone die for a righteous person, though for a good person someone might possibly dare to die. 8 But God demonstrates his own love for us in this: While we were still sinners, Christ died for us.

What a great thought... We were considered "worthless" BUT, God loved us so much that he gave his only son to give us salvation. (John 3:16). That is true love, to give your son to die for someone else.

As hunters and fisherman most of learn to enjoy watching others succeed more than succeeding ourselves. Whether it is our kids, grandkids, spouse or others, the excitement of giving up of our own wants to give to others is what we are called to do.

So using the example of John 3:16; choose to remember that love isn't what we have the opportunity to get from this world. Love is what we have the opportunity to give.

Start each day deciding to give love to someone in Christ's name.

JOURNAL ENTRY

MAY 28

PATIENT PLANTING

Matthew 17:20
And He said to them, "Because of the littleness of your faith; for truly I say to you, if you have faith the size of a mustard seed, you will say to this mountain, 'Move from here to there,' and it will move; and nothing will be impossible to you.

I don't know many that are planting mustard seeds in the USA but I know land owners and managers that are planting oak trees from acorns and chestnut trees from chestnuts. It takes a lot of faith to be willing to plant a seed today that might not mature and produce fruit for a generation.

An oak tree from a planted acorn today might not bear fruit for 20 years, yet some land owners are planting. They know that someday those trees will grow more acorns and those acorns may again be planted and the family of oaks continues to grow.

This is the faith we should have in our life and testimony for Christ. We need to be bold in our dedication to planting seeds. Many of us might never see the new lives that come from the planted seeds about Christ's love, but we are all called to be planters.

Like planting an oak takes patience, so does planting seeds for Christ. We plant trusting God will provide the harvest, in His timing, not ours.

James 5:7-8 Be patient, therefore, brothers, until the coming of the Lord. See how the farmer waits for the precious fruit of the earth, being patient about it, until it receives the early and the late rains. 8 You also, be patient. Establish your hearts, for the coming of the Lord is at hand.

JOURNAL ENTRY

MAY 29

FRIEND OF SINNERS

John 8:7 says...
When they kept on questioning him, he straightened up and said to them, "Let any one of you who is without sin be the first to throw a stone at her."

The world has tagged us Christians with numerous titles: Evangelical, Conservative, Right-Winger, The Religious Right, and a host of others. But seldom do they call us ..."Friend of Sinners..."

Each of us is a sinner... Some of us have been chosen for and accepted forgiveness... Remember this next time you encounter someone that needs to be loved. There is an old saying, "there but for the grace of God go I". That is so true. Without God's grace we are in the same boat. I am no different, just forgiven.

Show true, real love to those you encounter, because they are no different than those that have been forgiven, they just haven't accepted God's free gift yet.

John 13:35 By this everyone will know that you are my disciples, if you love one another."

JOURNAL ENTRY

MAY 30

Romans 12:6-8
Having gifts that differ according to the grace given to us, let us use them: if prophecy, in proportion to our faith; if service, in our serving; the one who teaches, in his teaching; the one who exhorts, in his exhortation; the one who contributes, in generosity; the one who leads, with zeal; the one who does acts of mercy, with cheerfulness

Every one of God's children has gifts. We are equipped with gifts that are to serve each other and to serve the Lord. What are we doing with those gifts in service to God?

I've seen people that didn't put their gifts to use until later in life... Maybe they had been beaten down at an earlier time in life and afraid to step out in faith and use their gifts. What a shame. There are some of us that God will build our gifts through life. Some of us have gifts that stretch farther into our personal passions such as hunting and fishing than others. I know that my gifts are linked directly into the background that was given to me in the outdoors and I have now found better ways to use them.

Whatever your gift is in life, put it to use. Teach, preach, heal, encourage, serve etc... Whatever it is, wherever it is, use it, don't waste it. But use it with unending love as the apostle Paul wrote...

1 Corinthians 13:2 reminds us, And if I have prophetic powers, and understand all mysteries and all knowledge, and if I have all faith, so as to move mountains, but have not love, I am nothing.

All the God given gifts without love amount to nothing put your gifts to use... in love.

JOURNAL ENTRY

___

___

___

___

___

___

MAY 31

TRUE TROPHIES

Luke 15:4-6

"Suppose one of you has a hundred sheep and loses one of them. Doesn't he leave the ninety-nine in the open country and go after the lost sheep until he finds it? 5 And when he finds it, he joyfully puts it on his shoulders 6 and goes home. Then he calls his friends and neighbors together and says, 'Rejoice with me; I have found my lost sheep.'"

The end of the fall hunting season can be a depressing time. Many years we've spent a lot of effort for little to show for it. We wonder if all of the bucks or bulls that we had hoped to take are still alive or if someone else harvested them. Then in late winter there's hope again... The snow starts to melt and the antlers that were shed start to show up. In shed hunting, there's only one thing better than finding a big antler, that's finding the other side to go with it.

Shed hunters will search high and low for the matched set of antlers. When the first is found there are some that will devote days if not weeks to scouring brush and grass to find its match.

The parable above pictures God's desire to find sinners and bring them back into the fold. Thus the owner throws a party, asking his neighbors to celebrate with him since the lost sheep is found. In the same way, Jesus says, there will be more rejoicing in heaven over one sinner who repents than over ninety-nine righteous persons who do not need to repent. When a sinner turns to God, heaven throws a party. The prospect of such joy keeps Jesus associating with sinners.

If only we would search out those that are lost and headed for hell with the same zeal as we look for one lost shed antler or one trophy that was shot and lost. If only we considered the importance of bringing lost souls "home" in comparison to a chunk of mineral that grew on the head of an animal.

John 4:35 Don't you have a saying, 'It's still four months until harvest'? I tell you, open your eyes and look at the fields! They are ripe for harvest.

Search them out. They are ready to be found.

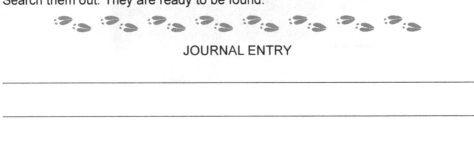

JOURNAL ENTRY

_____

_____

_____

JUNE

<u>Rom 8:28</u>

And we know that in all things God works for the good of those who love him,
who have been called according to his purpose.

JUNE 1

TRIALS WILL COME, "CONSIDER IT ALL JOY"

James 1:2-4
Consider it all joy, my brethren, when you encounter various trials, knowing that the testing of your faith produces endurance. And let endurance have its perfect result, so that you may be perfect and complete, lacking in nothing.

Training for a sporting event, a long race or a mountain climb can be very strenuous; it can also be painful and tedious. I'm not one that enjoys exercise for the sake of exercise...but put a goal at the end, a carrot hung in front of me, as it were, and I can put up with the discomfort...I can usually "endure".

God allows our faith to be tested, He allows us to face trials of many kinds. In the Old Testament, He allowed Job to lose everything he had except for his wife and a few friends (which weren't much help anyhow). God allows these things to come upon us for the strengthening of our faith and the building of our character.

Walt Disney said it like this... "All the adversity I've had in my life, all my troubles and obstacles have strengthened me...you may not realize it when it happens, but a kick in the teeth may be the best thing in the world for you."

God doesn't allow these things for a hardening of our hearts but to allow us to grow into a closer relationship with Him.

I read a small saying the other day and it struck me as not only being true but had a great lesson in it: "The same boiling water that softens potatoes hardens eggs. It's all about what you're made of, not your circumstances."

It's how we go into a trial or testing that determines how we come out. If we go in with our hearts set on God and in joy, we will come out stronger and closer to the Lord. If we go in already negative, we will only dig the hole deeper.

The trials will come, "consider it all joy"

JOURNAL ENTRY

_____

_____

_____

_____

_____

JUNE 2

WHY WORRY

Matthew 6:25-27

25 "Therefore I tell you, do not worry about your life, what you will eat or drink; or about your body, what you will wear. Is not life more than food, and the body more than clothes? 26 Look at the birds of the air; they do not sow or reap or store away in barns, and yet your heavenly Father feeds them. Are you not much more valuable than they? 27 Can any one of you by worrying add a single hour to your life?

Recently, while in the mountains, I lost radio contact for about 4 hours with my brother and the hunter that he was guiding. The last message I had was "we are half way down", which meant he should be to our meeting place in an hour. The two of them were tracking a bull elk and I had no idea where they were heading or at what speed. When it got to be two hours with no new messages I became concerned. Worry started to creep in. But what can we change by worrying?

Matthew wrote in verse 27, *Can any one of you by worrying add a single hour to your life?* The answer is clearly no. And we know that medical science now knows that it can actually take many days away.

Well, I decided to pray while reclining against a log, turning it over to God. Three hours later Dave and Tom came out off the mountain and they were just fine.

We can choose not to worry; it's easier than you think. Give it up to Him who truly has total control over all things.

JOURNAL ENTRY

JUNE 3

FACING UNCERTAIN FUTURES WITH PAIN AND SUFFERING

2 Corinthians 1:3-5
3 Praise be to the God and Father of our Lord Jesus Christ, the Father of compassion and the God of all comfort, 4 who comforts us in all our troubles, so that we can comfort those in any trouble with the comfort we ourselves receive from God. 5 For just as we share abundantly in the sufferings of Christ, so also our comfort abounds through Christ.

Do you wonder if God loves us, why do we suffer? Christian or not, it's a question that comes up over and over again during times of suffering and tragedy. In times of distress, we want to know that our suffering matters to God and that He cares about the pain we are going through.

God will take our suffering and use it to strengthen and purify us. In Isaiah 48:10 it says, "...I have refined you, though not as silver; I have tested you in the furnace of affliction."

This verse makes it clear that pain and suffering have a way of bringing our strengths and weaknesses up to the surface. God will make us "shine" if we allow him to.

If we look at this subject simply we seek God through His Word and prayer and we find Jesus. We need to remember, Jesus understands our pain because he also suffered a terrible amount of pain and death at a young age.

We read the words of Psalm 22:1: "My God, my God, why have you forsaken me? Why are you so far from saving me, so far from the words of my groaning?" David had others trying to kill him; he was running for his life.

Did God abandon His Son in His hour of need? We find the answer three days later—God raised Him from the dead! Because of this promise, we have hope for our future.

2 Corinthians 12:9 says, "My grace is sufficient for you, for my power is made perfect in weakness"

Allow God's love to be "sufficient for you" today. Whatever you are facing, whatever you are going through; God knows. Maybe he is waiting for you to rest on Him.

JOURNAL ENTRY

___

___

___

JUNE 4

A NEW BEGINNING

Ezekiel 36:26-37

I will give you a new heart and put a new spirit in you; I will remove from you your heart of stone and give you a heart of flesh. I will put My Spirit within you and cause you to walk in My statutes, and you will be careful to observe My ordinances.

In 2 Corinthians 5:17 the apostle Paul wrote: "Therefore if any man is in Christ, he is a new creature; the old things passed away; behold, new things have come".

Let the old things go, we don't need to carry them anymore. Receive your soft, warm heart (spirit) of flesh and use it. Don't hold onto the past hurts and pains. We fight to want to hold our feelings and not let them go. We think that we deserve to feel vindicated for a while, it makes us feel important.

God tells us that He will give us a new heart of flesh, that the old things will pass away and ALL things will be new.

Make a choice today to turn a positive slant to everything. When you think that you've been wronged, use it to grow. When you are under pressure, consider the diamond that was formed into purity by pressure. When things get really heated up, think of the refining fire that is used to purify the gold.

Use your soft heart and live a new life... Start today.

JOURNAL ENTRY

JUNE 5

ALLOW GOD TO CONTROL

John 11:43-44
Then Jesus shouted, "Lazarus, come out!" 44 And the dead man came out, his hands and feet bound in grave clothes, his face wrapped in a head cloth. Jesus told them, "Unwrap him and let him go!"

We often question our circumstances and whether we can get through them or not; whether we can even bear the load we are carrying for even another day.

In 2 Corinthians it says, "My grace is sufficient for you"... We can rest assured that our very lives are in God's hand. Our daily struggles are even HIS concern. Our burdens don't need to drag us down. We can give them up to Him. Even in death we (those that have truly given ourselves to Christ) are promised so much more than we have here.

I read a poem yesterday... They are good thoughts.

"The Bend in the Road"
Sometimes we come to life's crossroads
And we view what we think is the end.
But God has a much wider vision
And he knows that it's only a bend-

The road will go on and get smoother
And after we've stopped for a rest,
The path that lies hidden beyond us
Is often the path that is best.

So rest and relax and grow stronger,
Let go and let God share your load
And have faith in a brighter tomorrow-
You've just come to a bend in the road

Allow God to direct our paths this week and know that HE will direct us in HIS way if we let him.

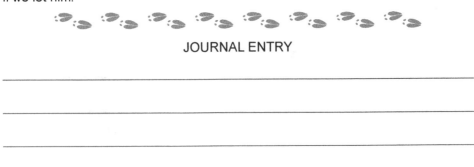

JOURNAL ENTRY

_____

_____

_____

_____

JUNE 6

SPIRITUAL TRAINING

1 Timothy 4:8
"8 For physical training is of some value, but godliness has value for all things, holding promise for both the present life and the life to come."

I think of how much time and effort that many people put into training for an event and it amazes me; I am actually a little jealous. I wish I had that drive to exercise to be in better shape. But many of us train and beat our bodies into shape and yet we never consider the poor shape that our heart is in. I have spent many hours walking and running on a treadmill or walking outside when preparing for a trip to hunt or guide in the mountains. Others spend as many hours in a day doing this as I spend in a week.

Timothy tells us that while the physical training is good for our bodies, training our hearts has a longer term benefit, from this life into eternity.

Spend time in God's word and in prayer as if training to compete for a prize...

Paul wrote in II Timothy 4:7-8 "7 I have fought the good fight, I have finished the race, I have kept the faith. 8 Now there is in store for me the crown of righteousness, which the Lord, the righteous Judge, will award to me on that day—and not only to me, but also to all who have longed for his appearing."

Train for that crown which the Lord awards.

JOURNAL ENTRY

JUNE 7

BE TRANSFORMED, NOT CONFORMED

Romans 12:2
"And be not conformed to this world: but be transformed by the renewing of your mind, that you may prove what is good, and acceptable, and perfect, will of God."

As believers, we ought to be different from the world. Our goal should be to act as Jesus did: forgiving, loving, and helping others yet knowing when to speak the truth in love or share our faith. When we sin, we should be quick to confess and repent.

A godly lifestyle will attract some people to you, and it will drive others away. But sometimes the same people who resist the gospel will seek out a Christian for help when life gets difficult.

Living out a transformed life will always bring attention to you. Once that attention is drawn it opens the door for relationships. Relationships turn into opportunities to serve brothers and sisters in Christ and reach others for Christ that don't know him. I've found that the best place for these relationships to build is in hunting camps and fishing boats. A hunting camp is a place of safety where people are generally free to share how they feel, therefore it is a great place to win souls for Christ. Be Bold.

We have some awesome responsibilities; first to God, second to those around us that are watching us and to our own heart.

So don't conform, but rather be transformed and be ready and willing to do the will of God.

JOURNAL ENTRY

JUNE 8

HOPE, JOY AND PEACE

Romans 15:13
"13 May the God of hope fill you with all joy and peace as you trust in him, so that you may overflow with hope by the power of the Holy Spirit."

If we can fully receive this hope, joy and peace what a difference it can make in our lives!

In "McLaren's Exposition" on these verses he writes, "Joy in the Lord and peace with God are the parents of all joy and peace that are worthy of the name."

So until we find "peace with God" and "Joy in the Lord" we will not find true Joy and Peace here in this life.

That would mean releasing all of the "stuff" we are holding in our hearts...the hurts, grudges, envy and pain; everything that we feel we need to "get even" with others for.

So first we need to truly trust God and know that He will provide ALL of what we need. And, that He will ALWAYS have our best interest at heart. Then pray for Him to fill you with the joy, peace and hope that we should all have as the very children of God.

JOURNAL ENTRY

JUNE 9

THE DESIRES OF OUR HEART

Psalm 37:4
"Delight yourself in the Lord, and he will give you the desires of your heart"

I doubt that there is one person anywhere that doesn't want all of "the desires of their hearts"...

In the midst of my turmoil I've often turned to Psalm 37:4 and thought about it. I love the idea of God giving me the desires of my heart, but that promise has a condition—delight myself in the Lord. That's the hard part of the verse—the place where I have to ask myself whether I am truly delighting myself in the Lord.

Today I wondered how the Bible defined "delighting" myself in the Lord. I knew it wasn't an abstract concept. Two verses that I found helped me to know if I was really delighting myself in the Lord or not:

Psalm 40:8 "I delight to do Your will, O my God, and Your law is within my heart".

Romans 7:22 "For in my inner being I delight in God's law."

How do we delight ourselves in the Lord? By doing what pleases him and putting his law in our hearts. Then, as we are sanctified, he gives us the desires of our heart.

This is when our desires come in line with His. That is when we truly are happy and filled with joy.

JOURNAL ENTRY

___

___

___

___

___

___

___

JUNE 10

IF GOD IS WITH US, WHO CAN BE AGAINST US

Psalm 125:1&2
"1 Those who trust in the Lord are like Mount Zion, which cannot be shaken but endures forever. 2 As the mountains surround Jerusalem, so the Lord surrounds his people both now and forevermore."

There are two great promises in the passage; first is that, "Those who trust in the Lord are like Mount Zion, which cannot be shaken".

Those that are truly God's people, totally dependent on Him and have given their lives over completely....will never be shaken, but will endure forever.

Secondly, we are surrounded by a great fortress, which is God himself. HE will protect us, "now and forever more".

Romans 8:31 asks the question, "What then shall we say to these things, if God is for us, who is against us?"

Is God really for us? How many times have we asked ourselves that question when things don't go our way or when we see things happen that we don't understand, especially after we've prayed about them?

The fact is, God is not only for us, He's reconciled to us. He's not against us, He's in covenant with us, and He's working for us on our behalf. All that He is and all that He has; all that He does and all that He plans to do is for us! Even when it seems that His acts are against us, you can be assured that they are for us.

So know that no one and nothing can come against us when we have God on our side.

JOURNAL ENTRY

___

___

___

___

___

___

JUNE 11

James 5:16
"Therefore confess your sins to each other and pray for each other so that you may be healed. The prayer of a righteous person is powerful and effective."

An elk herd will usually climb to a high mountain bench before lying down for the day. They will get to a safe place, generally with several other elk. While some sleep, others are alert and watching for danger. They work as a team protecting one another. So it should be with people.

In the first sentence of this verse, Christians are directed to confess their faults one to another, and so to join in their prayers with and for one another. It also indicates that there are some illnesses that are caused by our sins. Not all illness is a result of sin, but certainly some are.

So we are directed to have those around us that we can safely confess or sins and struggles to. Everyone needs someone that they can rely on to hold them up and hold them accountable. We need a safe place and a godly person to pray for us.

Then a great promise, "The prayer of a righteous person is powerful and effective." Like the elk, there is power in those around you who are always looking out for you.

Find that person that loves you enough to pray for you and allows you a safe haven. And go be that person for someone else.

JOURNAL ENTRY

_____

_____

_____

_____

_____

_____

_____

JUNE 12

1 Timothy 6:6-7 (NKJV)
16 Now godliness with contentment is great gain. 7 For we brought nothing into this world, and it is certain we can carry nothing out.

All of us are so blessed. I realize some are blessed more than others in one way or another, but we are very blessed. This past week I had the honor of visiting with some good friends and a hunting partner. This friend told me how wealthy that Linda and I are. He explained how he sees us as having an amazing life.

It's true that God has blessed us with opportunities to have friends all over the world and opportunities to hunt many places for many things. We get to travel and speak to groups and make new friends day after day, week after week, and year after year. And although our tax forms show little income our amazing God continues to bless us over and over again.

I told this friend that I hold these blessings with an open hand. God can put things in my hand and He can take them out. I believe that as soon as I close my hand around one of these blessing and try to grasp it, as if I own it, God could take it away.

Always keep your hand open when dealing with God's blessings. Even when he takes one out, we can be assured He will either make us content with what we still have or He will replace it with a new blessing.

JOURNAL ENTRY

JUNE 13

GOD'S TRUE WORD

2 Timothy 3:16
"All Scripture is breathed out by God and profitable for teaching,
for reproof, for correction, and for training in righteousness."

Do you ever feel like God has quit speaking to you? Sermons are losing their impact, times of genuine worship in life are growing more rare, and overall, you're just living out your life no longer looking for new revelation? We all go through times in life in which we feel alone and disconnected from God. If you feel this way, consider deeper study of your Bible. The Bible was given to many men by God's inspiration. He spoke directly to and through these men. He is still speaking this same way to people today.

It's when we quit looking for God's direction, deep within the pages of HIS word that we lose that direct contact with Him. However, the wonderful truth is that God hasn't moved and He is still speaking to us through the Bible. Remember; it's not just a book with worn-out phrases, rather, it's a treasure house of truth that's living and active. The Bible is a fountain of living water and is intended to be our prime source of strength. Pick it up, dust it off, and draw near to the God who speaks still.

We should approach scripture with the understanding that God still speaks to us every time we read His words.

JOURNAL ENTRY

JUNE 14

TO GOD BE ALL THE GLORY

Psalm 115:1
"Not to us, O Lord, not to us, but to your name give glory,
for the sake of your steadfast love and your faithfulness"

Each morning before we guide hunters on the Cielo Vista Ranch in Colorado, the guides come together for a short devotional and prayer. The main thing that we pray for is that whatever happens that day, that God would get all the glory. We want anyone that comes in contact with us, what God provides in the hunts, or in our lives…that all the glory is His and none of it is for men.

We train and prepare for a lot of things and when we succeed at what we train for it is easy to want to receive glory. But, my prayer is that all of the glory for the successes in my life will go to Him.

TO GOD BE THE GLORY

How can I say thanks
for all the things you have done for me
Things so undeserved
Yet you gave to prove your love for me
And the voices of a million angels
Could not express my gratitude
All that I am and ever hope to be
I owe it all to Thee

To God be the glory
To God be the glory
To God be the glory
For the things He has done
With His blood, He has saved me
With His power, He has raised me.
To God be the glory
For the things he has done

Just let me live my life
Let it be pleasing, Lord to Thee
Should I gain any praise,
Let it go to Calvary.
With His blood, He has saved me
With His power, He has raised me.
To God be the glory
For the things he has done.

Without God allowing any of us to succeed, we would fail. TO GOD BE ALL THE GLORY.

JUNE 15

HOLLOW AND DECEPTIVE PHILOSOPHIES

Colossians 2:6-8

"6 So then, just as you received Christ Jesus as Lord, continue to live your lives in him, 7 rooted and built up in him, strengthened in the faith as you were taught, and overflowing with thankfulness. 8 See to it that no one takes you captive through hollow and deceptive philosophy, which depends on human tradition and the elemental spiritual forces of this world rather than on Christ."

We hunters can be a gullible lot; we're always looking for the next best, latest and greatest thing that will make us successful. We might have 6 grunt calls in our backpack but when we see the newest one come on the market that promises to call in the big buck or big trophy gobbler, we are pulling out our credit card. The best example is when a well known scent company started to market a scent, "sure to bring in the biggest Tom turkeys" but when threatened with a law suit, "because turkeys don't have a sense of smell" the product was quickly pulled from the shelf.

The same is true today, we are overrun concerning our spiritual life. We are constantly seeing "deceptive philosophies, which depend on human tradition" in our world. But God has made it perfectly clear that we are not to follow lies. Christianity is being watered down and slowly the sacrifice that Christ made for us is being replaced by things that make us feel better.

Be on guard! Satan is moving through our world looking for who he can destroy. He is doing this by creating lies about what it takes to attain eternal life or to live a godly life here on earth.

The Bible is the true word of God, nothing else added to it is needed. Trust in what it says, live out the directives it gives.

JOURNAL ENTRY

JUNE 16

IT'S A CHOICE TO REJOICE

Mark 3:2-6

"2 Some of them were looking for a reason to accuse Jesus, so they watched him closely to see if he would heal him on the Sabbath. 3 Jesus said to the man with the shriveled hand, 'Stand up in front of everyone'. 4 Then Jesus asked them, 'Which is lawful on the Sabbath: to do good or to do evil, to save life or to kill?' But they remained silent. 5 He looked around at them in anger and, deeply distressed at their stubborn hearts, said to the man, "Stretch out your hand." He stretched it out, and his hand was completely restored. 6 Then the Pharisees went out and began to plot with the Herodians how they might kill Jesus."

What a shame, something so beautiful was preformed for someone and the Jewish leaders couldn't look past their negative, dark hearts. How many times are we knocked down, even by brothers and sisters in Christ because they don't understand your heart In Christ?

In our world today there are so many skeptical people that just look for the negative in everything. We all do it sometimes; we want to bring others down to our level of misery.

Let's try to look at the hand that was restored and not the manmade rule that we think was bent. Or we can rejoice in the life that was restored and not the sin that has already been forgiven. As God moves you to serve, don't worry about what others say or do, follow God's lead and then continue to rejoice in what God has called you to do.

We can love and encourage or we can live in the negative and destroy life and hope...it's really our choice. Choose wisely!

JOURNAL ENTRY

___

___

___

___

___

___

JUNE 17

TROPHIES OF GOD'S GRACE

Jude 1:24-25

"Now to Him who is able to protect you from stumbling and to make you stand in the presence of His glory, blameless and with great joy, 25 to the only God our Savior, through Jesus Christ our Lord, be glory, majesty, power, and authority before all time, now, and forever. Amen."

As a kid we all love to put a trophy on the shelf of our bedroom or in the family room of the house. It shows some sort of significant accomplishment in life. Then as hunters and fishermen we grow to hang mounts and photographs on the wall. These are not only accomplishments but memories of time spent in the field and with friends and family; memories that will always a bring smile when we see that trophy.

Did you ever think that we are a trophy of God or more accurately, of God's grace? Think about what God's grace is towards us. The most common definition of grace is, 'God's unmerited favor.' That is a great definition, but let's go a bit further.

God's grace is to offer each and every one of us a gift of eternal life and loving us enough to send His only Son when all the while not a single one of us is deserving in any way at all, totally without merit.

If you've accepted God's beautiful gift of grace, imagine your picture on God's wall and when He looks at it, He smiles knowing that you are His. If you haven't yet taken hold of that gift of a loving Father, do it now and forever be a Trophy Of God's Grace.

JOURNAL ENTRY

JUNE 18

FINDING REST

Matthew 11:28-30

"Come to Me, all who are weary and heavy-laden, and I will give you rest. 29 Take My yoke upon you and learn from Me, for I am gentle and humble in heart, and you will find rest for your souls. 30 for my yoke is easy and My burden is light."

There are times in life when we just don't know if we can get up one more morning. Or we look ahead on our calendar and tell ourselves, "There's no possible way I can get through this". Quite often we want to rely on our own strength but we can't.

I generally find that it is in these times of questioning, "How am I going to do this?" that I realize that I've been trying to do it on my own. I've not included God in my day and my planning.

But these verses were originally written to those that were under religious laws being enforced by the "spiritual" leaders of the day. The burden of trying to live up to the expectations of being seen as "good" is too heavy to bear. When Christ came He lifted that burden off of us and hung it on the cross, we just need to totally give ourselves to Him.

So today, whether you are burdened with trying to be good enough by man's standards to get to heaven or are overloaded with daily burdens...give them all to God... allow Him to carry those for you, and the ones that He sees as unnecessary, He will get rid of for you. Trust Him with all of it.

Through Christ we will find the rest we need.

JOURNAL ENTRY

JUNE 19

NO FEAR OF FAILING

Psalm 1:1-3

"Blessed is the man who walks not in the counsel of the ungodly, nor stands in the path of sinners, nor sits in the seat of the scornful; But his delight is in the law of the Lord; and in His law he meditates day and night. He shall be like a tree planted by the rivers of water, that brings forth its fruit in its season; whose leaf also shall not wither; and whatever he does shall prosper."

There is a great promise in these verses, the godly shall succeed. Perhaps you reply: "But I'm so afraid of failing ... failing to raise my children in the best way, failing to show my wife or husband how much I love them, failing to do for God the things He wants done." The promise from our unfailing God, however, is that our efforts will prosper.

In hunting we only get so many opportunities to "make the shot". We hunt with confidence and practice to be ready. If the time comes to finish the deal and harvest our quarry and we freeze up because of fear of failing…everything up to that point is wasted.

God assures us that we can be like a tree standing by a riverbank bearing beautiful fruit. Even in our deepest darkest moments, His Word restores us to green vegetation; offering shade to those we shelter, joy to those who watch us flower! We can have a fresh face and a happy heart. We can even know that our actions will provide a divine delight as He sees us in a prayerful posture!

The secret lies in meditating on His law...the word meditate means to chew things over. His nourishing Scriptures are ours for the "digesting", and will prosper our days.

Charles F. Glassman once said, "The fear of failure takes the joy out of living."

JOURNAL ENTRY

_____

_____

_____

_____

_____

JUNE 20

BLESSED THROUGH SERVING

Mark 9:35
"And he sat down and called the twelve. And he said to them, 'If anyone would be first, he must be last of all and servant of all.'"

It is not in my nature to want to be second...we always want to be first. And, just like most of Jesus' teachings, it goes against the grain of the world's thinking to not want to be first. To be first we must put ourselves last. The one who would be first must be the "servant of all" and this is certainly not the way of the world. Isn't it like God that His ways are in direct conflict with the ways most people think, even in the church?

It doesn't matter if you are a pastor, or you serve the church, or if you are the top salesman in your field...you serve your customers, a top guide, your clients or the owner or CEO of a company...you really just serve your workers. If you are not serving those around you, you will be either unsuccessful or unhappy.

Since the foot of the cross is level ground I am no better or no worse than anyone else in the church. I must serve Christ and by serving Christ I must serve others.

By serving others we allow ourselves to be open to so many blessings from God. Try it, put others first and step back and you might be amazed by what happens in your life.

Gordon B. Hinckley wrote about "Neglected Virtues", "One of the great ironies of life is this: He or she who serves almost always benefits more than he or she who is served."

JOURNAL ENTRY

JUNE 21

James 1:12
"Blessed is the one who perseveres under trial because, having stood the test, that person will receive the crown of life that the Lord has promised to those who love him."

It is hard to go through trials; death in the family, financial disaster, major health issues, abandonment, etc... And at the time we rarely feel blessed by the trial.

If and when we endure these trials and don't lose our focus on Christ, the one blessing we can have is peace in our lives. Linda and I always talk about how is it possible for people to go through major painful issues without God...it just doesn't seem possible.

The other promise and benefit is the ultimate sharing of glory with Christ. This vision is high enough for many to understand the possibility of joy in the midst of terrible trials.

The last part of the verse starts with, "He will receive the crown of life". Later, in Revelation 2:9-10, the Lord would affirm to the church in Smyrna, "I know your afflictions and your poverty," but this would not be his entire message to them. He would also encourage that persecuted church by adding, "Yet you are rich!" In what way could they possibly be called "rich" while knowing poverty, slander, imprisonment and other persecution "even to the point of death"? The Lord's answer would be his promise, "I will give you the crown of life." That promise of the Lord is the kind of encouragement James gives the suffering Christian in verse 12 promising with the same phrase that God will give the crown of life.

So today, this week, this month, this year, as you face struggles and trials... take heart! God knows your trial, endure it with His help and look forward to the coming Glory.

JOURNAL ENTRY

_____

_____

_____

_____

_____

JUNE 22

CROSS TRAINING

Matthew 16:24-26

24 Then Jesus told his disciples, "If anyone would come after me, let him deny himself and take up his cross and follow me. 25 For whoever would save his life will lose it, but whoever loses his life for my sake will find it. 26 For what will it profit a man if he gains the whole world and forfeits his soul? Or what shall a man give in return for his soul?

A few weeks back we were driving through a southern city and saw something I had only seen on TV before. There was a sixty-something bearded man in a white tunic crossing the street. Now his dress was eye catching enough, but that 16' foot cross that he was dragging, that really caught our attention.

We were in the middle of heavy traffic so we were not able to stop and talk to him so all we could do was use our imagination as to what is purpose was.

So my thought was this, what does it mean to "take up your cross" and follow Christ? It is a call to the life of daily obedience to Christ. A willingness to die to self, to put Christ and others in front of ourselves. To follow Jesus at all costs. Even to the point of death.

Following Jesus is easy when life runs smoothly; our true commitment to Him is revealed during trials. Jesus assured us that trials will come to His followers. Discipleship demands sacrifice, and Jesus never hid that cost.

John 16:33, tells us of the trials to come and the triumph as well. 33 "I have told you these things, so that in me you may have peace. In this world you will have trouble. But take heart! I have overcome the world."

Are you willing to lose everything for Christ's sake? He probably won't call you to that literally, but He might. He wants to know, are you willing to, "take up your cross and follow me?"

Now that is really, Cross Training.

JOURNAL ENTRY

JUNE 23

YOUR CITIZENSHIP

Philippians 3:20-21

"[20] But our citizenship is in heaven, and from it we await a Savior, the Lord Jesus Christ, [21] who will transform our lowly body to be like his glorious body, by the power that enables him even to subject all things to himself."

The thought/promise that "our citizenship is in heaven" is so great. When you are a citizen of a country you belong there and it is an honor or beneficial to the citizen. To be a citizen of heaven is something very special as normally when we change citizenship we have to change life drastically...with being a citizen of heaven we don't change at death...the only change is really going from an imperfect world to a perfect eternity.

So with this promise of continued citizenship we know that there should be no fear, there is nothing but joy and excitement for what lies ahead.

Henry Van Dyke once said, "Some People are so afraid to die that they never begin to live".

Begin to live today...don't fear what lies ahead; there is a promise that what is to come is much better than what we have here now.

JOURNAL ENTRY

JUNE 24

LORD, LIAR OR LUNATIC

1 Peter 3:15
"But in your hearts honor Christ the Lord as holy, always being prepared to make a defense to anyone who asks you for a reason for the hope that is in you; yet do it with gentleness and respect."

The world will tell you that Jesus Christ was a good teacher—a noble moral leader, but nothing more. They'll heap praise on Him, calling Him a religious revolutionary who changed the world with a philosophy of self-sacrifice and unconditional love. In fact, today almost any description of Christ is acceptable as long as it's not based in the actual words of Scripture. They will bunch him together with Buddha, Mohammed and others.

But this idea of Jesus as merely a good teacher is a complete lie, a lie created with a desire to undercut or discredit the truth of His life and ministry.

C.S. Lewis described the foolishness of claiming Christ as nothing more than a good teacher. He wrote: "I am trying here to prevent anyone saying the really foolish thing that people often say about Him: "I'm ready to accept Jesus as a great moral teacher, but I don't accept his claim to be God." That is the one thing we must not say. A man who was merely a man and said the sort of things Jesus said would not be a great moral teacher. He would either be a lunatic—on the level with the man who says he is a poached egg—or else he would be the Devil of Hell. You must make your choice. Either this man was, and is, the Son of God, or else a madman or something worse. You can shut him up for a fool, you can spit at him and kill him as a demon or you can fall at his feet and call him Lord and God. But let us not come with any patronizing nonsense about his being a great human teacher. He has not left that open to us. He did not intend to."

John 14:6 "Jesus answered, 'I am the way and the truth and the life. No one comes to the Father except through me.'"

Liar, lunatic or Lord? Those are the only options to consider when it comes to determining the truth about Christ. "...always being prepared to make a defense to anyone who asks you for a reason for the hope that is in you..."

JOURNAL ENTRY

JUNE 25

A HARD ROAD

Matthew 7:14
"For the gate is narrow and the road is hard that leads to life,
and those who find it are few."

I love the mountains, but my body and lungs hate climbing the mountains...however, you can't really appreciate the mountains without climbing. You look ahead at the hard road and keep trudging forward and it is tough. When you get to the summit you turn and look back to see where you've been it's generally very beautiful.

This is the life of one who knows the Lord. We've been promised that life will be hard, but the results are not only worth it, they are eternal.

So if you've chosen the narrow gate, keep "fighting the good fight"... in the future when you look back, you will see the blessings were well worth the struggle. If you don't know Christ and you are taking the easy road, consider the future and your eternity. Remember this, nothing worthwhile is ever easy.

Matthew 7:13-14 "13 Enter by the narrow gate. For the gate is wide and the way is easy that leads to destruction, and those who enter by it are many. 14 For the gate is narrow and the way is hard that leads to life, and those who find it are few."

JOURNAL ENTRY

JUNE 26

GOOD AND FAITHFUL SERVANT

Philippians 2:5-8
"In your relationships with one another, have the same mindset as Christ Jesus: Who, being in very nature God, did not consider equality with God something to be used to his own advantage; rather, he made himself nothing by taking the very nature of a servant, being made in human likeness. And being found in appearance as a man, he humbled himself by becoming obedient to death—even death on a cross!"

Can we make ourselves nothing? Can I personally lower myself and allow others to be raised up? That is a tough thing. No matter how humble a person might be, lowering yourself to a point of servanthood is not easy.

Yet, this is what Christ did for us. He not only lowered himself here on earth but came to earth from heaven. He gave up everything. This needs to be our ultimate goal, but first just putting others above ourselves is the starting point.

The servant attitude and action is contagious... others will see it and pass it along.

James Dobson was heard to say, "My legacy doesn't matter. It isn't important that I be remembered. It's important that when I stand before the Lord, he says, 'Well done, good and faithful servant.' I want to finish strong."

JOURNAL ENTRY

_____

_____

_____

_____

_____

_____

_____

_____

JUNE 27

I KNOW HE WATCHES ME

Psalm 121:1-8

"1 I lift up my eyes to the hills. From where does my help come? 2 My help comes from the Lord, who made heaven and earth. 3 He will not let your foot be moved; he who keeps you will not slumber. 4 Behold, he who keeps Israel will neither slumber nor sleep. 5 The Lord is your keeper; the Lord is your shade on your right hand. 6 The sun shall not strike you by day, nor the moon by night. 7 The Lord will keep you from all evil; he will keep your life. 8 The Lord will keep your going out and your coming in from this time forth and forevermore."

I get amazed at the amount of times in my life when I get depressed over something that I have no control over or something that is already past. I know without a shadow of a doubt that God has control over all things. The last few years I've been using the phrase, "What difference will it make in my life tomorrow?" So why do I get discouraged?

I hunt with a lot of people every year. I have so many friends that only get a few days to hunt each year. They come to camp and even when the animals aren't moving or the weather is bad, they head out because this is their time to be out, they are not going to allow little things get them down. Some of them sit day after day, never losing faith in that what they are there to harvest is going to show up at any second.

I want that kind of faith in know that God will never stop from providing His peace, comfort and love in my life.

I love the old hymn, "HIS EYE IS ON THE SPARROW". It begins like this:
Why should I feel discouraged, why should the shadows come,
Why should my heart be lonely, and long for heav'n and home,
When Jesus is my portion, My constant Friend is He:
His eye is on the sparrow, and I know He watches me;
His eye is on the sparrow, and I know He watches me.
I sing because I'm happy, I sing because I'm free,
For His eye is on the sparrow, and I know He watches me.

Sing and don't be discouraged...for "I know he watches me."

JOURNAL ENTRY

_____

_____

_____

JUNE 28

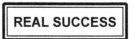

Psalm 1:1-3

"Blessed is the man who walks not in the counsel of the wicked, nor stands in the way of sinners, nor sits in the seat of scoffers; but his delight is in the law of the Lord, and on his law he meditates day and night. He is like a tree planted by streams of water that yields its fruit in its season, and its leaf does not wither. In all that he does, he prospers."

How do we define success? The world would say it's a financial level or professional achievement, etc. but this morning for me it was watching the sunrise and calling turkeys with a good friend. Day to day success is defined differently in our lives. Today it was enjoying the sunrise, tomorrow it might be making a good sale or time with my family. The Bible defines what it takes for success for those that love the Lord; you will see that it is different from what the world calls success.

If you are not walking with the counsel, taking advice from the wicked, standing in the way of sinners or the way that sinners are going and are also not sitting in the seat of scoffers (which means they scoff at God), then God will bless you. To be blessed means to literally "make happy". Your delight will naturally be in God's law and you will meditate day or night (all the time) and this means that like a tree planted by a stream of water, you will never whither or die but will always produce godly fruit and everything you do will prosper.

JOURNAL ENTRY

_____

_____

_____

_____

_____

_____

_____

_____

Trophies of Grace

JUNE 29

Proverbs 18:24
"One who has unreliable friends soon comes to ruin, but there is
a friend who sticks closer than a brother."

This morning I was driving through a small town and saw two little boys walking to school down the sidewalk. They must have been 6 or seven years old. The look on their faces was beautiful and it made me think of my great friends and how blessed I am. I've met some of my best friends over the years from being outdoors. There is something about sharing a passion for hunting or fishing that build bonds that can last a lifetime.

Sharing a bond of the outdoors with someone of like mind is a great basis for friendship. Even when we might only see a friend once a year, the ties that bind us together are strong. To share a mountain view, a sunrise in the bottoms of the south or a canoe ride down a river creates a lasting bond that is rarely broken in life.

Here are a few notes on friends...

"A friend is someone you can be yourself with. A friend is someone who knows your weakness and respect your strength. "

Abraham Lincoln said, "The better part of one's life consists of his friendships."

Ralph Waldo Emerson said, "The only way to have a friend is to be one."

A friend is one who is a source of sunshine when you are under the weather. A friend is one who believes in you, even when you stop believing in yourself. A friend is a source of celebration when you feel that there is nothing to celebrate.

So this week, be a friend to someone who needs one.

A brother may not be a friend, but a friend will always be a brother. Thank you my brothers and my friends.

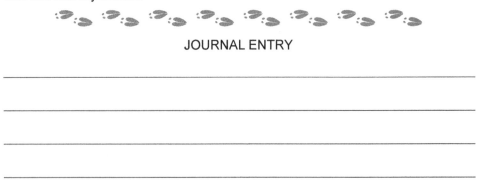

JOURNAL ENTRY

_____

_____

_____

_____

JUNE 30

ONE MORE DAY

Isaiah 53:5
"⁵ But He was wounded for our transgressions, He was bruised for our iniquities; The chastisement for our peace was upon Him, and by His stripes we are healed."

The day (June 30th, my 52nd birthday) started out innocent enough; the guys at camp decided to take a mule and horse ride into North Vallejos Basin and seeing it was my birthday, I was their special guest. It didn't seem to matter to any of them that I had not been on a horse for 10+ years and the ride might be a long one but more importantly, we didn't know if there was any kind of a trail to follow.

Well, my lack of riding was not a problem for the first couple of hours but the lack of trail and the distance caused major pain by the end of the day. As we rode I wondered why the others wore their sleeves down on such a warm day, I was soon to find out.

We busted through spruce timber and climbed over rock slides, across rushing streams and through aspen stands whose beauty couldn't be captured by a camera or paint brush. By the end of the day we had ridden 20 long, rough miles and when we arrived back at camp I had to be helped off the horse and into my bedroom where I promptly fell on the bed.

I suffered tremendous pain in my lower back and hips as well as my arms where it looked as though someone had taken a whip to me. As I looked at my arms and the blood that was flowing from the cuts I imagined what Christ had gone through in His last days on earth. My pain and suffering couldn't come close to comparing to what He did…and did for me. He was wounded for MY transgressions and He was bruised for MY iniquities. What a gift.

Christ doesn't expect us to repay Him for what He did on the cross, He just asks us to accept His gift of His death and resurrection offer.

Have you accepted this greatest gift from Christ? Have you thanked Him for what He went through for you? If not, do both today, don't put it off one more day.

Thank you Lord for what you have done for me, Amen!

JOURNAL ENTRY

JULY

John 3:16

For God so loved the world that he gave his one and only Son, that whoever believes in him shall not perish but have eternal life.

JULY 1

A BETTER PLAN

Genesis 50:20
You intended to harm me, but God intended it for good to accomplish what is now being done, the saving of many lives.

In the book of Job, we read that Job could have very easily, cursed God and died when he lost everything. In Genesis, Joseph could have felt sorry for himself or had his brothers put to death or imprisoned. Paul could have called on God to change his circumstances many times... But they all trusted God and knew that He had a plan for their lives.

On one evening's elk hunt we were above timber line and two to three rough miles from the truck. We were calling to a good bull elk for a friend. The excitement had built over a 45 minute calling sequence where the bull bugled continually. Finally the bull stepped out above the trees into the open. There were only a few stunted Alpine spruce scattered about.

When the bull finally turned broadside I was looking right over the hunters shoulder and right down his arrow. On release I watched as the arrow's flight. All looked good, but then a small branch was just an inch too long and the arrow sailed off over the bull's back and off the edge of the mountain. Turning to my brother Dave, who had been calling from behind me, he smiled and point way off in the distance towards the truck, then he said, "I've never been so happy to see an arrow fly over a bulls back".

We thought we had that bull, and we should have except for one small twig. We also thought we wanted the bull, and later found that we would have suffered badly to get him off the mountain. What we wanted wasn't what was best.

Sometimes God doesn't give us what we think we want. Sometimes it's because He has a better plan right away and sometimes it's because He is protecting us from something worse in the future. Rest assured He has a plan and we will be blessed because of it... If we trust Him.

JOURNAL ENTRY

_____

_____

_____

_____

_____

JULY 2

A LIGHT TO THE WORLD

John 8:12
When Jesus spoke again to the people, he said, "I am the light of the world. Whoever follows me will never walk in darkness, but will have the light of life."

I enjoy walking into the woods in the morning darkness... Not total darkness, but when there is just enough light to make out where I am going. Last year I tried to walk out on a high Colorado ridge in total darkness, I made it about 20 ft and dug out my flashlight. I was in a really dangerous situation without a light to shine my way.

In life, Christ is that light. He opens our eyes to the dangers around us and... If we allow Him, he illuminates the correct path. Once we have that true relationship with Christ, we then become light. We shine to show the world the difference between good and bad.

If you are not that light, take some time to consider where your heart is at this point in your life. The Bible doesn't say we "might" be or "can" be... It says if we know Him, we "are" the light. Be the light.

JOURNAL ENTRY

JULY 3

YOUR THOUGHTS SHOW THROUGH

Romans 8:6 (KJV)
For to be carnally minded is death, but to be spiritually minded is life and peace.

How many times do you ask your spouse, your kids, your coworkers or someone else, "what's wrong?" or "What's on your mind"? They don't have to say a word... You can just tell. Yet, we feel as though others can't tell what we are feeling and thinking.

We can bring "life" or "death" (positives or negatives) by our very thoughts. What we allow to control our minds comes out in our life, good or bad. It can't be hidden. Years ago I was, I thought I was hiding something from my wife that I didn't want known. I thought that I was doing a good job with it, but I was fooling myself. My heart showed through my words and actions.

Filling our minds with positive, godly things will bring life. Not only will it bring life to ourselves but eventually to those around us. And filling our minds with negative things will bring us down. It will make life miserable for us and those around us.

Guy de Maupassant, a popular 19th-century French writer said it this way, "A sick thought can devour the body's flesh more than fever or consumption."

JOURNAL ENTRY

_____

_____

_____

_____

_____

_____

_____

_____

JULY 4

WHAT A DAY THAT WILL BE

1 Thessalonians 4:16
For the Lord Himself shall descend from heaven with a shout, with the voice of the archangel, and with the trump of God: and the dead in Christ shall rise first:

Most Americans have at one time or another celebrated Independence Day. Just the thought of it brings back memories of hot dogs on the grill, the smell of sparklers burning, the sights of fireworks bursting overhead. But at the end of the day it has become a time of family picnics, big sales events and fireworks. Unfortunately it has become commonplace.

However, an Independence Day celebration approaches that will include and impress the whole world! We don't know the date and shouldn't believe anyone who tells us they do. But, **no one** on earth or in heaven will miss its importance, and it will mark a day of freedom from the greatest oppressor ever, Satan.

It is the day of the return of our Lord and Savior, Jesus Christ! It is the beginning of real freedom, like no one has ever had before (except Adam and Eve before they sinned). Those who have believed in Christ's atoning blood for their sins and have trusted and believed in Him, might have what some would call a Hallelujah Celebration.

The old hymn, "What A Day That Will Be" explains it well.

What a day that will be,
When my Jesus I shall see,
And I look upon His face,
The One who saved me by His grace;
When He takes me by the hand,
And leads me through the Promised Land,
What a day, glorious day that will be.

JOURNAL ENTRY

___

___

___

___

___

JULY 5

DEATH IS INEVITABLE, THEN WHAT?

Luke 12:20
But God told him, 'You fool! This very night your life will be demanded of you. Now who will get the things you've accumulated?'

Just about a year ago, one of my best friends was hunting and on his way home he was hit head on and killed... His mind wasn't even considering death that evening. He had just had a great evening and being killed was probably the furthest thing from his mind...

However, death is inevitable. The thief on the cross knew when his would occur, but most of us can't predict our own. Following his death, the crucified criminal went to live in paradise with Jesus. Some of us will also live in God's presence, forever, but others will experience everlasting torment, forever separated from Him.

If we trust Jesus as Savior, our penalty for sin is paid, we are adopted into God's family, and heaven is our eternal home. But if we reject Jesus, we remain removed from the Lord and under condemnation for our sin. God will not listen to any excuses, as there is no acceptable defense for unbelief

If your eternity is assured, share the Good News with others.

JOURNAL ENTRY

JULY 6

Psalm 62:5
My soul, wait silently for God alone, for my expectation is from Him.
He only is my rock and my salvation; He is my defense; I shall not be moved.

I've learned better to "wait on the Lord"... But waiting silently? Do I, can I, how should I?

As I've matured as a hunter, especially a turkey hunter, I've learned to wait a lot more patiently than I used to. When I was younger I would get up and move when I hadn't heard anything in a few minutes. Now, I understand that I have to wait patiently, sitting quietly at times and I am quite often rewarded for that quiet waiting.

To "wait silently on the Lord" is to put our trust totally and completely on Him, to not to look to our own strength at all. That is easier said than done. When we can finally do this, our hearts can honestly rest and the troubles of the day don't rock us like they used to.

When I can do it.... It brings amazing peace

Have a great and peaceful week, waiting patiently on the Lord.

JOURNAL ENTRY

JULY 7

Psalm 71:14
But I will hope continually and will praise you yet more and more.

Do you realize how important hope is to your mental, emotional, spiritual, and physical health? People without hope in their lives are destined to be miserable and depressed. They feel as if they are locked in the prison of their past. They can't see any way out. They are "hopeless".

But God gives us hope, if we allow him to do so. It is there just waiting for us to take it. He wants us to have a hopeful life, not a hopeless life. Hopeless people are afraid to believe anything good might happen in their life. They give up hope. They actually think they are protecting themselves from being hurt by not expecting anything good to happen.

When we really begin to study the Bible and trust God to restore us, we realize our negative attitudes have to go. We need to let go of our past and move into the future with hope, faith, and trust in God. We have to get rid of the heaviness of despair and discouragement.

God's word gives us great promises of hope.

Romans 5:2-5 Through him we have also obtained access by faith into this grace in which we stand, and we rejoice in hope of the glory of God. More than that, we rejoice in our sufferings, knowing that suffering produces endurance, and endurance produces character, and character produces hope, and hope does not put us to shame, because God's love has been poured into our hearts through the Holy Spirit who has been given to us.

JOURNAL ENTRY

___

___

___

___

___

JULY 8

REMOVING THE "CANCER"

Matthew 5:29-30

If your right eye causes you to stumble, gouge it out and throw it away. It is better for you to lose one part of your body than for your whole body to be thrown into hell. 30 And if your right hand causes you to stumble, cut it off and throw it away. It is better for you to lose one part of your body than for your whole body to go into hell.

Now, the idea of cutting off a body part to save the rest of the body is not a new one. We do this all the time with cancer. To stop the spread of cancer to the rest of the body, it's sometimes necessary to cut out the cancerous parts to save the rest of our body. From this perspective, what Jesus is saying makes perfect sense. If totally removing sin from our life was as "simple" as cutting off a hand, who wouldn't do that?

My wife has dealt with a lot of pain after having some cancer cut off her shoulder. It was hard to see her feeling miserable and hearing her whimper as she rolls over in bed at night... But while, like removing sin and cancer from our lives, it will save our lives in the long run. She will be better soon because she removed what was hurting her. If she hadn't had it removed eventually it would have killed her. It is the same with sin

If you have sin that is holding you, cut it out... Remove it... And then, RUN AWAY and never look back at it.

JOURNAL ENTRY

JULY 9

FORGETTING YOUR PAST

Philippines 3:13-14

Brothers and sisters, I do not consider myself yet to have taken hold of it. But one thing I do: Forgetting what is behind and straining toward what is ahead, 14 I press on toward the goal to win the prize for which God has called me heavenward in Christ Jesus.

It is sad to think how often we allow ourselves to live in the past. We spent countless, wasted, hours thinking of the bad decisions and actions that we've made. This only takes away from what we can do in our future.

For those that are hunters, if we allow past mistakes and choices to drag us down we never become a better hunter. Drawing our bow at the wrong time, setting up with the wrong wind, calling at the wrong time or moving when game is in sight can all spoil an otherwise successful hunt. We can't live in the past allowing these things to control our actions, however, we learn from those things to make our future more successful... The same is true with the rest of life.

The apostle Paul spent his young adult life killing the followers of Christ. Yet later in life, once he himself became a follower, he tells us, "forgetting what is behind and straining toward what is ahead"... He was free from his past.

This freedom can only come from Christ. Without Him we are bound to our past, with Him, our past is totally forgiven.

Move forward, leave your past behind, don't worry about what others think and "press on toward the goal to win the prize for which God has called me heavenward in Christ."

JOURNAL ENTRY

_____

_____

_____

_____

_____

JULY 10

2 Timothy 2:15
Be diligent to present yourself approved to God, a worker who does not need to be ashamed, rightly dividing the word of truth.

I have a friend who shared his testimony with me a while back... He told me about doing drugs as a young teenager and eventually dealing drugs and working with those that were doing far worse. I was amazed as he came from a strong Christian family.

After listening to his story, for a long time I asked how he got to that point when he had heard the truth his whole life. He not only heard it at home but also in Sunday school and other places. His answer was simple, "It was my parent's religion and God, not mine".

In Paul's letter to Timothy, he tells us to make Him "our God". How? By being "diligent" and by "dividing the word of truth". Study, live the life God has called you to live, know him...

When we've done all this, we will be prepared to pass our God and our belief on to others around us so they can have the same relationship.

JOURNAL ENTRY

JULY 11

GETTING COMFORTABLE

Romans 6:12-13

Do not, then, allow sin to establish any power over your mortal bodies in making you give way to your lusts. Nor hand over your bodily parts to be, as it were, weapons of evil for the devil's purposes. But, like men rescued from certain death, put yourselves in God's hands as weapons of good for his own purposes.

There are so many times in our lives that we allow sin to slowly creep in. We don't even know at times that we are doing it. And even worse, we allow it into our homes where it grows until it has consumed a life.

It starts innocent enough, but we forget to keep a check on it. We allow small things into our lives and home and before long we are trapped in something that is eroding away our walk with God.

There is a brand-new video game from a software company in Helsinki, Finland, called Lucius II The Prophecy. In a world that is filled with objectionable entertainment, this game is an evil standout. Not only does it invoke graphic images of violence and horror, it places the user in the role of Antichrist.

This isn't the only game that is evil and changes lives, just one of the worst. These "games" are dangerous...

Just one example of allowing Satan to get right into our homes. Don't allow him your time or the lives of your family.

JOURNAL ENTRY

JULY 12

1 Peter 5:6-7
Humble yourselves, therefore, under God's mighty hand that He may lift you up in due time. Cast all your anxiety on Him because He cares for you.

There are so many times in our lives where we hear of someone being caught in a crime and they say, "I'm glad I was finally caught "or "I wanted to get caught".

We get caught up in things in life, some big, some small, that we don't know how to get out. Well, God says to first humble ourselves before Him and then says to cast our worries, anxieties, and concerns on Him... Why? Because He cares for us.

If we do this, He will lift us up, not in our time, but in His time.

In Pilgrim's Progress, John Bunyan wrote, "Just as Christian came up to the Cross, his burden loosed from off his shoulders, fell from off his back, and began to tumble down the hill, and so it continued to do till it came to the mouth of the sepulcher. There it fell in, and I saw it no more!"

Don't carry the heavy loads alone, give them to God. Allow Him to take the worries of the day and carry it for you.

JOURNAL ENTRY

JULY 13

GOD GIVEN OPPORTUNITIES

Exodus 16:13-16

That evening quail came and covered the camp, and in the morning there was a layer of dew around the camp. 14 When the dew was gone, thin flakes like frost on the ground appeared on the desert floor. 15 When the Israelites saw it, they said to each other, "What is it?" For they did not know what it was. Moses said to them, "It is the bread the Lord has given you to eat. 16 This is what the Lord has commanded: 'Everyone is to gather as much as they need. Take an omer for each person you have in your tent.'"

At the beginning of a new year... it's a new start... Resolutions have been made (and most broken already).

God is so good. He provides our every need.

This year God will provide us all with opportunities, some great, and some small. Like the Israelites, God will give us what we need. He wants us to make use of these opportunities. Those opportunities that we don't grab a hold of and trust Him to see us through, will be pulled back. Like the manna that was there for the Israelites, what wasn't used disappeared. It was gone. The manna that they tried to take and hold on to without using it the way that God told them to... Spoiled and was useless.

So grab a hold of the opportunities that God sets before you. Go after them with confidence... But trust in God giving you direction. Don't waste what He's setting before you.

I pray you all have an amazing second half of the year ahead.

JOURNAL ENTRY

JULY 14

CHANGING LIVES, BY CHANGING YOURS

Romans 12:18-21

If it is possible, as far as it depends on you, live at peace with everyone. 19 Do not take revenge, my dear friends, but leave room for God's wrath, for it is written: "It is mine to avenge; I will repay," says the Lord. 20 On the contrary: "If your enemy is hungry, feed him; if he is thirsty, give him something to drink. In doing this, you will heap burning coals on his head." 21 Do not be overcome by evil, but overcome evil with good.

E very year at this time we get to reevaluate our direction. Sometimes we make big changes... Sometimes we don't.

These verses in Romans are a "hard pill to swallow" for most of us. But think of what difference they can make in a life, or a world. Can you imagine what our world would be like if we all lived by these verses? Or what your life would be like?

As we move into the second half of the year. Consider your relationships. Consider how others see us. Imagine what power we have to change lives... by a couple small acts of love.

Change your view of others. Look at them with the eyes of Jesus. Learn to treat the "unlovable" with respect. They will soon be lovable.

JOURNAL ENTRY

_____

_____

_____

_____

_____

_____

_____

_____

_____

JULY 15

TOO COMFORTABLE TO GROW

Joshua 1:9
Have I not commanded you? Be strong and courageous. Do not be frightened, and do not be dismayed, for the Lord your God is with you wherever you go."

Early yesterday morning I got a message from my good friend, James. He told me he was listening to a sermon by Pastor Steven Furtick and one point really stood out. "You can't fulfill your calling in your comfort zone"

Joshua went on to write, "God will allow you to go through trials and situations in your life that will cause you to come out of your comfort zone so you can fulfill your calling".

What's your calling? Are you resting in your comfort zone or are you ready to step out and trust God to take care of you while serving him?

If we continue to stay comfortable, we won't be used like God desires. Growth also comes with movement and trust.

Today, make it a point to allow God to stretch you and be ready to grow.

JOURNAL ENTRY

JULY 16

IT'S NOT OUR BATTLE BUT HIS

II Chronicles 20:15
...This is what the Lord says to you: 'Do not be afraid or discouraged because of this vast army. For the battle is not yours, but God's.

There are times where it seems like we fight a constant battle, sometimes for years on end. We struggle against evil people that want to bring us down. Sometimes these same people claim to be friends or even Christian brothers or sisters.

Why do we waste our energy on such things? God promises us that the battle isn't ours, but His. He has total control over what goes on in this huge world and what goes on in our little lives.

There is a great praise and worship song by Matt Redman's, "You Never Let Go"... He covers our fears...

Even though I walk through the valley of the shadow of death
Your perfect love is casting out fear
And even when I'm caught in the middle of the storms of this life
I won't turn back
I know You are near

And I will fear no evil
For my God is with me
And if my God is with me
Whom then shall I fear?
Whom then shall I fear?

Oh no, You never let go
Through the calm and through the storm
Oh no, You never let go
In every high and every low
Oh no, You never let go
Lord, You never let go of me

It's His battle and He NEVER, EVER let's go of me.

JOURNAL ENTRY

_____

_____

_____

_____

_____

JULY 17

Ephesians 5:1-2
Follow God's example, therefore, as dearly loved children and walk in the way of love, just as Christ loved us and gave Himself up for us as a fragrant offering and sacrifice to God.

In my basement and garage you will find several different kinds of decoys: duck, goose, deer, turkey and elk etc... I have more game calls than I could use in three lifetimes, bugles, box calls, tube calls, slate calls, diaphragm calls, grunt calls, owl calls etc...

I rarely go in the woods without imitating something; it's one of my favorite parts of hunting.

In our lives as Christians, we have but One to imitate, Jesus Christ. One of the ways Jesus taught us to imitate God is by loving those He came to seek and to save. He loved us, even to the point of death. That is being like God; and that is what is going to attract others and accept His gift of salvation.

John 13:35 says, "By this everyone will know that you are my disciples, if you love one another."

Being a Christian isn't all that complicated. The very word "Christian" means "Christ-like". We are to simply be like Jesus, and, therefore, imitate God's standards. To do that, we must love as Jesus loved–the Father above all else, and others as He loved them.

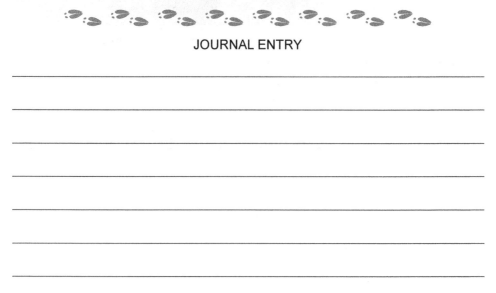

JOURNAL ENTRY

JULY 18

BEYOND THE FINISH LINE

Philippians 3:14
I press on toward the goal to win the prize for which God has called me heavenward in Christ Jesus.

As life grows harder and harder, it is so easy to fall into a pattern of "just getting by" it seems as no matter how much we put into it, we get the same results out of it.

I have a friend that always has a new "project" going on... I saw him this fall and he looked tired. He can buy whatever he wants; he has done very well for himself. Yet, even the wealthy get worn down by life. He is always telling me, "This is the last project". Yet he is always working on "one more"

But the writer of Philippians tells us to "press on towards the goal". I see a picture in my mind of a racer giving it his all and stretching his chest out to break the ribbon at the end of the race, to win the prize.

God has promised great reward for His children... Now is not the time to give up, but is the time to stretch forward towards what HE has set out in front, beyond that finish line. There is a purpose for the "pressing on", we have to believe God has a reason. The end of the verse says, "For which God has called me heavenward in Christ Jesus".

You've got more in you; give it all you've got. Finish well.

JOURNAL ENTRY

JULY 19

PROTECT YOUR HEART

Proverbs 5:18-19
May your fountain be blessed, and may you rejoice in the wife of your youth. 19 A loving doe, a graceful deer, may her breasts satisfy you always, may you ever be captivated by her love.

How is it possible that the divorce rate is higher in the church than out in the world? I believe it is solely because Satan targets Christians more than those he already has. If Satan has already lost our soul to God, he then wants to destroy our testimony to others.

God gave husbands their wives as their support. Likewise, He gave women their husbands for support as well. Together we stand, and "a house divided against itself cannot stand". Satan will take every opportunity he can to divide your house don't let him.

So men, protect your own heart, don't let Satan get a foothold in with thoughts of others, or hurtful thoughts of your wife... Pray that you will **ALWAYS** find her to be the very love of your life. Women, allow God to show you the man he has given you as a true soul mate. Pray that you will ALWAYS be his best friend.

If you truly pray for a strong marriage it will be the best thing in your life. Allow Satan in and it will fall apart.

Don't let Satan win.

JOURNAL ENTRY

_____

_____

_____

_____

_____

_____

_____

JULY 20

PUTTING OFF THE OLD

Ephesians 4:22-24

To put off your old self, which belongs to your former manner of life and is corrupt through deceitful desires, 23 and to be renewed in the spirit of your minds, 24 and to put on the new self, created after the likeness of God in true righteousness and holiness.

All through life we shed something old and start growing new. First and foremost, when we come to Christ He renews us in His image and then over and over again as we go through life.

Through my time in the outdoors, I've seen in God's creation examples of this. For instance, an elk's antlers are literally pushed off with new growth. In the spring when the new growth begins the old part weakens its grip on the elk and is shed away. When the old is gone, it allows for new, healthy and stronger growth.

In the same way, if we allow God to work in our lives the old "dead" and "dying" things in our lives will fall away and the new healthy parts will grow stronger.

God has a plan for us with that new growth.

JOURNAL ENTRY

JULY 21

GOD'S STRENGTH IN MY WEAKNESS

2 Corinthians 12:7-10

...Therefore, in order to keep me from becoming conceited, I was given a thorn in my flesh, a messenger of Satan, to torment me. 8 Three times I pleaded with the Lord to take it away from me. 9 But he said to me, "My grace is sufficient for you, for my power is made perfect in weakness." Therefore I will boast all the more gladly about my weaknesses, so that Christ's power may rest on me. 10 That is why, for Christ's sake, I delight in weaknesses, in insults, in hardships, in persecutions, in difficulties. For when I am weak, then I am strong.

Many of us know what it is like to feel on top of the world and we also know the feeling of being in the lowest of lows. We've had times of great pride and times where we just want to hide, because of our pain.

When we are so full of ourselves and how great everything is for us... Or how great we are, there is little room for God to work in and through us.

It is in our times of suffering that we have room to allow God to do work in and through us. As we hit those lows we need to be watching for the opportunities to allow Him to use our "thorn" to glorify Himself.

Matthew Henry put it this way... "This is a Christian paradox: when we are weak in ourselves, then we are strong in the grace of our Lord Jesus Christ; when we see ourselves weak in ourselves, then we go out of ourselves to Christ, and are qualified to receive strength from Him, and experience most of the supplies of divine strength and grace."

So when you find yourself weak, allow the great comfort and strength that God provides to fill you.

JOURNAL ENTRY

_____

_____

_____

_____

_____

_____

JULY 22

MIXED BLESSINGS

Exodus 4:10-13

Moses said to the Lord, "Pardon your servant, Lord. I have never been eloquent, neither in the past nor since you have spoken to your servant. I am slow of speech and tongue." 11 The Lord said to him, "Who gave human beings their mouths? Who makes them deaf or mute? Who gives them sight or makes them blind? Is it not I, the Lord? 12 Now go; I will help you speak and will teach you what to say." 13 But Moses said, "Pardon your servant, Lord. Please send someone else."

Throughout our lives we are called on to do things by people. Sometimes we feel capable, sometimes we don't. However, if God calls us to do something, He will ALWAYS make a way.

The first 17 verses of Exodus chapter 4 is God telling Moses what he should do... And Moses saying he can't do it. God showed Moses two miracles that he could show the Egyptians if they wouldn't listen, yet Moses didn't trust God and God sent Aaron to speak for Moses.

Believe that what God is calling you to do is possible, with Him. In Matthew 19:26 it comes right from the source...

Jesus looked at them intently and said, "Humanly speaking, it is impossible. But with God everything is possible."

Just think of the blessing Moses might have missed. The blessing God has in store for us, if we only follow His calling, could be beyond our imagination. If God is calling you to do something, know that He will provide what you need to do the job.

My challenge is for you to Read exodus 4:1-17

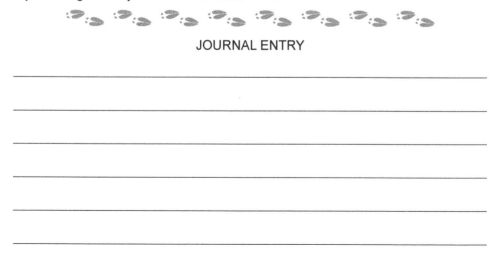

JOURNAL ENTRY

_____

_____

_____

_____

_____

JULY 23

THE JOY OF AN ARROW IN FLIGHT

1 John 3:7-8
Dear children, do not let anyone lead you astray. The one who does what is right is righteous, just as He is righteous. 8 The one who does what is sinful is of the devil, because the devil has been sinning from the beginning. The reason the Son of God appeared was to destroy the devil's work.

I love old movies where they show archery in medieval times. One of the Robin Hood movies showed men being taught to shoot longbows. I enjoy scenes where an entire company of men release arrows at once towards oncoming combatants. The sight of arrows flying high through the air is something of beauty to me.

Several years ago a good friend, David, built a small bamboo longbow for Micah, our grandson. It is beautiful with Osage orange and bamboo laminates and it shot like a dream, considering Micah was only about 3 at the time. On the back of the bow David wrote these words, "may you never lose the joy of an arrow in flight".

Our lives are very much like the flight of an arrow. We need stability to hit the mark that we are aiming for. The arrow has feathers or fletching to keep it stable. Without these feathers the arrow will fly off target after a short time. It might fly straight and true for a time, but it will very quickly lose its path.

Unless we spend time with God in His word and prayer, we are like a featherless arrow, sure to be quickly off course.

Stabilize your flight in life; hold tight to God in prayer and in reading His word so you "never lose the joy of an arrow in flight".

JOURNAL ENTRY

JULY 24

BROTHERS BUILDING BROTHERS

Psalms 133:1
Behold, how good and how pleasant it is for brothers to dwell together in unity!

There are few places that build strong relationships better than a hunting camp or a mountain. Some of the best friend/brotherly relationships were made and nurtured there. Once those brother to brother relationships are born it is so great to "dwell together in unity".

I've built some of my best friendships chasing elk, deer and turkeys around the mountains, plains and forests of the USA. Men of God have supported me because they know I support them. I can honestly say that I love these guys and I hold them up in their lives.

Relationships built with godly men are desperately needed in our world today. The pressures of standing alone will weaken or destroy many men. Seek out men of like mind and allow these friends to mold and support you.

Proverbs 27:17, as iron sharpens iron, so one person sharpens another.

Allow those relationships to build and sharpen you.

JOURNAL ENTRY

___
___
___
___
___
___
___
___
___

JULY 25

NOT OF WORKS

Ephesians 2:8-9
For it is by grace that you have been saved, through faith, not of works,
it is a gift of God so that no man may boast.

I've read these verses 1000 times and memorized them as a young boy... And I totally believe it. But, do I live it out in my daily life.

As hunters, we've learned that there are no "sure things". We believe that we have a buck located and patterned or a gobbler roosted and we figure that this is going to be a slam dunk. However, we can't control the weather, the animal or God's will. In the end we go out hunting with the faith that our part is done. The same is true of Salvation, out part is to have faith and accept God's gift. The rest is up to Him.

I can live out the "saved by grace, through faith" part. It's the "not of works" part that I mess up all the time. I allow Satan to convince me that I have to keep earning God's love. I forget that Christ died once for all.

1John 1:9 tells us that, if we confess our sins He is faithful and just to forgive our sins and cleanse us from ALL unrighteousness.

Not some of our unrighteousness but ALL of it! We can stop trying to earn God's favor; Christ paid the price for that on the cross.

We need to learn to live free.

JOURNAL ENTRY

JULY 26

NOT MY HOME

Hebrews 13:14
14 For this world is not our home; we are looking forward
to our city in heaven, which is yet to come.

The writer, Malcolm Muggeridge, once said, "The only disaster that can befall us is to feel ourselves at home on this earth."

In our lives, as we go through the day to day grind we forget what this Bible verse says. We are not at home here. If we know Christ personally, then we have no true home here. We need to live as if we are always preparing to leave here and go to our eternal home.

There is an old song that I remember from my youngest age. The title is, THE WORLD IS NOT MY HOME. The first verse and chorus tell a great story.

This world is not my home
I'm just a passing through
My treasures are laid up
Somewhere beyond the blue

The angels beckon me
From heaven's open door
And I don't feel at home
In this world anymore

Romans 12:2 makes this thought abundantly clear, do not conform to the pattern of this world, but be transformed by the renewing of your mind. Then you will be able to test and approve what God's will is—His good, pleasing and perfect will.

JOURNAL ENTRY

JULY 27

MUCH NEEDED REST

Genesis 2:1-3
Thus the heavens and the earth were completed in all their vast array. 2 By the seventh day God had finished the work he had been doing; so on the seventh day he rested from all his work. 3 Then God blessed the seventh day and made it holy, because on it He rested from all the work of creating that He had done.

I've often wondered why an "all powerful" God would need to rest. Certainly not from being tired. The original word translates not to rest but to "cease". But many believe that the verse was written as an example to us.

The original 7th day was the Sabbath under Old Testament law. A complete day of rest. Our bodies and our minds need rest. God designed us to need "down time". A time for "recreation". Look closer at this word... Re-Creation. It's a time that God can use to build us up.

So don't allow yourself to be worn down. Take some time to rest and recreate. Without that time we eventually break down and are of no use. Eventually anyone or anything, without proper rest breaks down.

Stop, allow God to give you rest and to rebuild what He needs in you.

JOURNAL ENTRY

JULY 28

THE GOOD THINGS IN LIFE

Philippians 4:8
Finally, brothers and sisters, whatever is true, whatever is noble, whatever is right, whatever is pure, whatever is lovely, whatever is admirable—if anything is excellent or praiseworthy—think about such things.

When I read these verses today I thought of where my thoughts take me day to day. While most of my day I know my hearts is right, there are times when I must confess that anger, jealousy, hurt feelings, envy and more drag my mind into places where my thoughts aren't all the things listed above.

The only way to keep thinking, "on such things", is through continued prayer, scripture and relying on true friends for accountability.

So surround yourself with Christian brothers and sisters that love you and expect the best from you. Keep your eyes on God's word and your head down in prayer.

Then lastly search out the; true, noble, right, pure, lovely, admirable, excellent and praiseworthy things in this world and work hard to build your life around those things.

JOURNAL ENTRY

JULY 29

Philippians 4:13
I can do all things through Christ who strengthens me.

In the several years following the diving accident that left her a quadriplegic, Joni Erickson Tada struggled with every imaginable emotion. She was helpless, but came to discover that God was not. The more she accepted her weakness and limitations, the greater her realization of God's strength in her. She has written, "Deny your weakness, and you will never realize God's strength in you."

When Paul wrote the often quoted words found in Philippians 4:13, he was in prison. "I can do all things through Christ" this is not a magic formula. It is not a promise that we can do anything we want. Rather, it is a promise that we can do anything God wants. Paul was confident that God was directing his life and was with him even in prison. He knew what God expected of him—faith, endurance, strength, boldness—he would be able to accomplish, not through his strength, but through the strength of the One who lived in him.

If God is asking something of you today for which you feel inadequate, it's okay to agree that you are! Confessing your weakness is the first step toward allowing Christ to show His strength in you.

D. L. Moody said, "Real true faith is man's weakness leaning on God's strength."

JOURNAL ENTRY

_____

_____

_____

_____

_____

_____

_____

_____

JULY 30

Matthew 7:7-8

"Ask and it will be given to you; seek and you will find; knock and the door will be opened to you. For everyone who asks receives; the one who seeks finds; and to the one who knocks, the door will be opened.

I wonder how many times in our lives we miss out on great opportunities or blessing, because we didn't ask. It is like being out to turkey hunt, we can have pockets full of calls, slate calls, box calls, wingbone calls etc, but if we never take them out and call to the turkeys; our chances of getting an answer are non-existent.

God gives us the greatest gift of all, eternal life with Him. This is totally a gift and we have to do nothing, just let Him give it and accept it in faith. The other blessings in the life that are God given need to be asked for. As the verses say ASK, SEEK, KNOCK. Not hard to do, but an action is required.

Think of it like this... What a great pleasure it is when one of our kids or grandkids crawls up into our laps and asks for something we can't wait to give them.

God has that same desire... To give us our deepest desires. All we have to do is ask.

JOURNAL ENTRY

_____
_____
_____
_____
_____
_____
_____
_____
_____
_____

JULY 31

IN GOD'S WILL, I CAN

Matthew 19:26
And looking at them Jesus said to them, "With people this is impossible, but with God all things are possible."

I've used this verse a few times lately in my devotionals and I truly believe that what it says is true. However, I think that it needs some clarification. "ALL THINGS are possible with God", but for God's children, those who honestly have a father/child relationship with Him, while it is possible, it has to be in His will for you to have it work.

When we start stepping outside of His will for us, we can try and try and even pray but we are wasting our breath and energy. That energy is much better spent seeking out what God wants for us. My granddaughter could have a true desire to become the starting quarterback for the Green Bay Packers next year. She can dream it, she can practice and train and do everything in her power to achieve it. However, if it isn't in God's plan for her (His will) it isn't going to happen.

Many are falling into the belief that is based on a popular saying, "If you can conceive it and believe it, you can achieve it!" The problem is, if we step outside what God's will is, we can plan and move forward all we want but our plans will fail. When we start conceiving thoughts and dreams, let's ALWAYS make sure that it's not what we want but what God wants for us.

John 5:30 30 I can do nothing on my own. I judge as God tells me. Therefore, my judgment is just, because I carry out the will of the one who sent me, not my own will.

JOURNAL ENTRY

_____

_____

_____

_____

_____

_____

_____

August

Ephesians 2:8&9

For it is by grace you have been saved, through faith and this is not from yourselves, it is the gift of God, ⁹ not by works, so that no one can boast.

Trophies of Grace

AUG 1

CARRYING THE LOAD

Matthew 11:28-30

"Come to me, all you who are weary and burdened, and I will give you rest. Take my yoke upon you and learn from me, for I am gentle and humble in heart, and you will find rest for your souls. For my yoke is easy and my burden is light."

I sit here writing this morning with a terribly sore back. I have been putting off some heavy lifting for two days. But it has to get done, and I have to do it myself. There are times when we carry an emotional load that weighs us down, beyond what we feel we can carry.

BUT, Matthew writes the words of Jesus when He said, "Come to me, all you who are weary and burdened, and I will give you rest". And then promises, "you will find rest for your souls. For my yoke is easy and my burden is light."

Trust God with the load you are carrying. Let Him carry you and the stress. The worry that you struggle with is NOTHING to Him.

Begin this new month with a trust in God, that whatever you deal with, it's an easy load for Him.

JOURNAL ENTRY

_____

_____

_____

_____

_____

_____

_____

_____

_____

AUG 2

TRUSTING GOD'S PLAN

Luke 1:46-47, 49
And Mary said: "My soul glorifies the Lord and my spirit rejoices in God my Savior, for the Mighty One has done great things for me— holy is his name.

In today's world becoming an unwed mother is commonplace. It is very sad that as a whole nearly 50% of the babies in our country are being born to unwed mothers. This was not the case at the time of Jesus' birth. These young women were to be put out, divorced or even stoned.

If a man marries a girl who is claimed to be a virgin, and then finds that she is not, "they shall bring the girl to the entrance of her father's house and there her townsmen shall stone her to death" (Deut. 22:20)

So consider Mary's response when she's told she will carry and give birth to Jesus. She doesn't say, "Not me" or "I don't want to face this". No she says, "*My soul glorifies the Lord and my spirit rejoices in God my Savior...*". WOW!

God isn't calling any of us today to play a part this big in history. But, He is calling us to serve Him in important ways. We need to be willing to daily say the same words that Mary did... "My soul glorifies the Lord and my spirit rejoices in God my Savior,"

JOURNAL ENTRY

AUG 3

WEARY AND BURDENED

Matthew 11:28-30
28 "Come to me, all you who are weary and burdened, and I will give you rest. 29 Take my yoke upon you and learn from me, for I am gentle and humble in heart , and you will find rest for your souls. 30 For my yoke is easy and my burden is light."

"Come to me," a tender call to intimacy with Christ for all those who are weary and burdened. "Weary" brings the image of persons exhausted from their work or journey. I think of what it is like at the end of a day of hard hunting in the mountains. I know that feeling of not being able to take one more step and literally falling into bed, completely weary. On the other hand, "burdened" makes us think of people weighted down with heavy loads. A pack being carrying that is overloaded to the point where the carrier is bent over forward, trying to keep moving. They are like the crowds that Jesus said earlier In Matthew 9 that were harassed and helpless, like sheep without a shepherd.

Yesterday I had a couple of hours when I felt spiritually burdened and weary. Later this brought on discouragement. I needed to turn to God and allow Him to carry that load for me. Once I gave the issues to Him, I was quickly lifted

Matthew 9:36 36 When he saw the crowds, he had compassion on them, because they were harassed and helpless, like sheep without a shepherd.

True rest and contentment can only come through a relationship with Christ. Then, when you have that relationship, allow Christ to give you the rest and help that you need. Trust all you are carrying to Christ's care.

JOURNAL ENTRY

_____

_____

_____

_____

_____

_____

August

AUG 4

RUSTING OUT FROM INACTIVITY

1 Peter 4:10-11

As each has received a gift, use it to serve one another, as good stewards of God's varied grace: whoever speaks, as one who speaks oracles of God; whoever serves, as one who serves by the strength that God supplies—in order that in everything God may be glorified through Jesus Christ. To him belong glory and dominion forever and ever. Amen.

Theodore Roosevelt once said, "Let us rather run the risk of wearing out than rusting out".

I've hunted and guided around the western states a fair amount. One thing that I have noticed in the prairies and mountains is in the past decades, people ran their vehicles until they just wouldn't go anymore. The vehicles were used until they had nothing left to give... then they were just left where they quit. They had nothing left to give, they owed their owners nothing at that point.

We all have been given gifts, some more visible than others. All are equally important in God's eyes. But they have no value at all if they are not put to use. It is dangerous to allow talents to sit idle because you can lose the ability to clearly see where and when they are valuable.

Alllowing your talents to sit idle is dangerous in that we can lose our ability to clearly see where and when it is valuable. We also stand the chance of have our gift pulled away. In Matthew 25 this is illustrated in a parable. The one servant that didn't use his talent lost it.

Put to use your God given gifts and talents... "Let us rather run the risk of wearing out than rusting out".

A good read Matthew 25:14-30

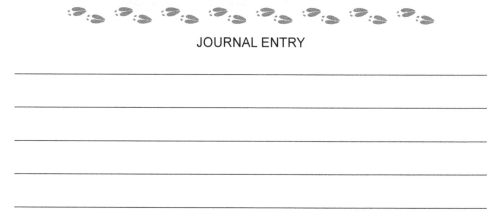

JOURNAL ENTRY

AUG 5

NEVER TOO LATE

Genesis 17:17
Then Abraham fell on his face and laughed, and said in his heart,
"Will a child be born to a man one hundred years old?
And will Sarah, who is ninety years old, bear a child?"

Now I can't imagine what was going through the heads of Abraham and Sarah at this time in their lives, but I'm sure the fact that they laughed at God gives us some indication. But while they doubted, God knew it wasn't too late.

The sadder part of the story is that they did not trust God and Abraham took another woman, a younger woman, and had a son with her. But even though they didn't trust God, He kept his promise and gave them a son.

This truth is found many places in the Bible. It is found in the story of David. God called David to be the political and moral leader of Israel, but David fell into sin. He stayed in Jerusalem instead of participating in a battle. While in Jerusalem he saw Bathsheba, enticed her, and made love to her. When he learned that she had become pregnant, he attempted to cover his sin by having her husband killed. And yet, God did not cast off King David but kept His promise.

So if we think we are too old, too weak, too unworthy, too sinful... We're wrong... It is never too late for God to use us. Abraham became the father of the great nation of Israel and David was later called, "a man after God's own heart".

Don't give up, God will use you yet.

JOURNAL ENTRY

AUG 6

Isaiah 41:10
10 Do not fear, for I am with you. Do not be afraid, for I am your God.
I will give you strength, and for sure I will help you.
Yes, I will hold you up with My right hand that is right and good.

I don't think that it's any coincidence that the number of times that the Bible says "do not fear" is 365, which matches the days of the year. God knows us so well that He knows we needed a daily reminder to "not fear".

We all struggle with some things that we are uncomfortable with; the dark, heights, being alone... But if you are a bow hunter, you go out in the dark, climb up in your tree stand all by yourself. How? You trust that God has all under control.

Author, Shannon L. Alder, wrote, "Fear is the glue that keeps you stuck. Faith is the solvent that sets you free."

Today when a situation arises that concerns you, have faith that God can and will handle it for you. and that the Faith in Him will keep you from fear of the known and the unknown. Give all situations over to Him and allow His power to overcome.

JOURNAL ENTRY

AUG 7

MOVING FORWARD

James 2:18
But someone will say, "You have faith and I have works." Show me your faith apart from your works, and I will show you my faith by my works.

There is a line in the movie, "FACING THE GIANTS" that explains this verse very well.

"I heard of a story of two farmers praying to God for rain to come. Both prayed, but only one prepared the land. Who do you think trusted God more to send the rain?"

God wants us to have faith that He will do all that He has promised, but He also wants us to move forward in faith. We can sit on the sidelines and watch to just see what God is going to do, or we can get in the game and go to work.

In the "Great Commission" God didn't say, I will bring all the world to you. Instead, in the Book of Mark "He said, unto them, Go ye into all the world, and preach the gospel to every creature." Mark 16:15-16

So then, move forward in faith and confidence to what God has shown you.

JOURNAL ENTRY

_____

_____

_____

_____

_____

_____

_____

_____

_____

_____

AUG 8

MEETING ALL OUR NEEDS

Philippians 4:19
And my God will supply every need of yours according to his riches in glory in Christ Jesus.

If we believe that our Bible is fully God inspired, thus being His word to us, then how or why do we worry about our needs being met? I don't mean our wants but our true needs. We have an assurance that "God will supply ALL our needs"

Charles Stanley has said, "Our heavenly Father understands our disappointment, suffering, pain, fear, and doubt. He is always there to encourage our hearts and help us understand that He's sufficient for all of our needs. When I accepted this as an absolute truth in my life, I found that my worrying stopped."

So if we can accept and believe that the Lord truly wants the best for us and wants our needs to be met, we can trust that things are taken care of for us.

Psalm 23:1 ...The LORD is my shepherd, I lack nothing.

Rest on that.

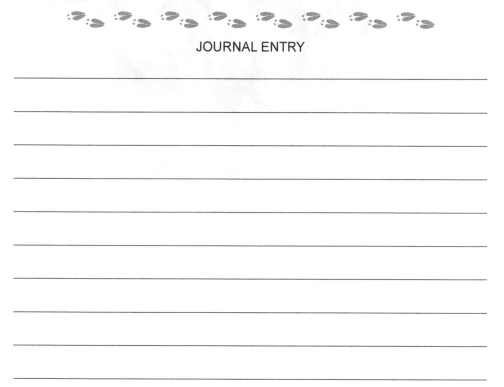

JOURNAL ENTRY

AUG 9

Philippians 2:1-3
Therefore if there is any encouragement in Christ, any comfort from love, any participation in the Spirit, any affection and sympathy, complete my joy by being of the same mind, having the same love, being in full accord and of one mind. Do nothing from selfish ambition or conceit, but in humility count others more significant than yourselves.

The "therefore" in verse one points back to verse 27 in chapter one, "that you stand fast in one spirit, with one mind striving together for the faith of the gospel."

This is a pretty big commandment to us. This means that quite often I have to look beyond what I want or feel is right for me. Instead I need to look at what God shows me is right for His family. This is a hard pill for me to swallow sometimes.

I think that we confuse unity with just plain union. We could tie two cats together by the tail and throw them over a close line. They are certainly in a "union" but by no means do they have unity. God wants His family to live and love together in such a way as the world only sees one body.

Mattie Stepaneck wrote the following, before he died at age 13. "Unity is strength... when there is teamwork and collaboration, wonderful things can be achieved."

I pray that I never EVER again cause any disunity in the family of God.

JOURNAL ENTRY

AUG 10

A REASON FOR YOUR HOPE

Peter 3:15-16

But sanctify the Lord God in your hearts: and be ready always to give an answer to every man that asks you a reason for the hope that is in you with meekness and fear: Having a good conscience; that, whereas they speak evil of you, as of evildoers, they may be ashamed that falsely accuse your good behavior in Christ.

Who would have believed 20 years ago that in our country today, Christianity would be under the attack like it is? But our world has changed drastically and it will get worse. "Our good behavior in Christ", is now considered evil. Sharing our beliefs is now an offense to those of the world.

But Peter writes to, " be ready always to give an answer to everyone that asks you a reason for the hope that is in you...". It doesn't matter what people say about us... Be ready with an answer.

Peter also writes to give your answer with, "meekness and fear". If we do it any other way the world will see it as adversarial and not love.

Charles Spurgeon made it clear that we don't need to sound "professional"... just willing. "Let eloquence be flung to the dogs rather than souls be lost. What we want is to win souls. They are not won by flowery speeches."

So, be ready with the answer for your hope in Christ and give it in love.

JOURNAL ENTRY

AUG 11

James 1:27
27 Religion that God our Father accepts as pure and faultless is this: to look after orphans and widows in their distress and to keep oneself from being polluted by the world.

The staff and volunteers at High Impact Family took care of the "looking after widows" love in San Francisco, Colorado. These two ladies had large piles of firewood in their yards that needed to be split and stacked.

A group of us went down and not only did this work but also moved furniture, fixed a stove, changed blades on a lawn mower etc.

Over the past few years, this same group has fed the locals with donated elk meat from the hunters that hunt the ranch, done maintenance projects for those in need, served the local children through the schools etc.

But who was really blessed? Those of us who served were as much (if not more) blessed than those who more that those that were served. The thankfulness on the faces of these widows was worth the effort alone.

T.W. Manson said... "In the Kingdom of God, service is not a stepping-stone to nobility: it is nobility, the only kind of nobility that is recognized."

There is no better blessing than serving others.

JOURNAL ENTRY

___

___

___

___

___

___

___

AUG 12

> **HE NEVER GIVES UP**

Psalm 144:3-4
3 Lord, what are human beings, that you should care about them, or mortals, that you should think about him? 4 The human person is a mere empty breath; one's days are like a fading shadow.

As people, in our own "infinite wisdom", we consider ourselves as being pretty intelligent and important. But David in this Psalm puts us in our rightful place. Compared to a loving God that has always existed and is all powerful and all knowing... What are we? In the scope of eternity, what are we? David says we are a "mere empty breath, his days are like a fading shadow".

In the Book of Job, Job came to realize that God was in charge and God has the answers. Job 40:1-4,

The LORD said to Job: ²"Will the one who contends with the Almighty correct Him? Let him who accuses God answer Him!" ³ Then Job answered the LORD: ⁴"I am unworthy—how can I reply to You? I put my hand over my mouth. ⁵ I spoke once, but I have no answer — Twice, but I will say no more."

God doesn't just doesn't think about us once in a while or just when we pray. He has the infinite ability to think about us all the time and loves us with no limit. We know that this all powerful God loved us (and still loves us) enough to let his own Son die on our behalf. We can rest assured that we are loved by this all powerful God.

Even though I don't deserve this love, He doesn't give up on me.

JOURNAL ENTRY

___

___

___

___

___

___

___

AUG 13

HE IS MY LIGHT

Psalm 27:1
The LORD is my light and my salvation; whom shall I fear?
The LORD is the strength of my life; of whom shall I be afraid?

What great thoughts, assurances and promise!

"The Lord is my light", in this world of darkness He is a light to show us a clear path. He makes things clear for us not to stumble or fall on our day to day travel through life.

"He is my salvation". That is He is my rescuer... David was under constant fear of being killed for much of his life. Yet, he writes, "He is my salvation. Whom shall I fear.". It's easy to read, hard to live out. We are amazingly blessed to have a Heavenly Father that cares about us, therefore enough that we really have no cause to fear. No one can lay a hand on us if we are His child, unless He allows it.

Our "LORD is the strength of my life; of whom shall I be afraid?"

God truly is our strength and without Him we can't live, He holds us up to withstand all that what the world throws at us. So, if we know that He is our strength, our light and our salvation... Then how or why would we ever be afraid?

As you go through your day remember this assurance and remember that David was under attack most of his life, but, because he loved the Lord and trusted totally in Him he was not only preserved, he was blessed beyond imagination.

JOURNAL ENTRY

August

AUG 14

Matthew 13:3-9

"A farmer went out to sow his seed. 4 As he was scattering the seed, some fell along the path, and the birds came and ate it up. 5 Some fell on rocky places, where it did not have much soil. It sprang up quickly, because the soil was shallow. 6 But when the sun came up, the plants were scorched, and they withered because they had no root. 7 Other seed fell among thorns, which grew up and choked the plants. 8 Still other seed fell on good soil, where it produced a crop—a hundred, sixty or thirty times what was sown. 9 Whoever has ears, let them hear."

I lease a farm that that we hunt for deer on each year. The farm has rolling fields and some wet swamps. The other day I checked a field, we call the slippery slope, located on the far back end of the farm. You can't see the field from anywhere else on the property so I was surprised to find the field had no crops planted and was all stones with very little soil exposed. The rest of the farm is growing great crops this year. It made me think of this passage.

Not only do we deal with rocky soils, but many times in our lives we allow things and circumstances to scorch what God is trying to do in and through us. We don't water and fertilize by times of prayer and scripture. We also deal with surrounding ourselves with "thorns", those people that intentionally or unintentionally choke out what God wants for us.

Whatever God plants in your life, water and care for it, remove the weeds from it and allow it to thrive. If you ever want to see growth or a harvest these things need to be done.

JOURNAL ENTRY

_____
_____
_____
_____
_____
_____
_____

AUG 15

HOW DEEP THE FATHER'S LOVE FOR US

1 John 3:1
3 See what great love the Father has lavished on us, that we should be called children of God! And that is what we are! The reason the world does not know us is that it did not know Him.

There is a great song by PHILLIPS, CRAIG & DEAN that speaks to me of how much God loves me/us and how unworthy we are on our own. The first and third verses are below. Read them slowly.

How deep the Father's love for us,	I will not boast in anything,
How vast beyond all measure,	No gifts, no power, no wisdom;
That He should give His only Son	But I will boast in Jesus Christ,
To make a wretch His treasure.	His death and resurrection.
How great the pain of searing loss -	Why should I gain from His reward?
The Father turns His face away,	I cannot give an answer;
As wounds which mar the Chosen One	But this I know with all my heart -
Bring many sons to glory.	His wounds have paid my ransom.

When we put ourselves into this verse as the "wretch" and the one causing Jesus' pain, we come to realize how much He loves us.

Thank you, Jesus, for loving even me, the wretch that I am, enough to die for me. My response needs to be that I live for Him.

JOURNAL ENTRY

AUG 16

WHEN I WALK THROUGH THE VALLEY

Psalms 23:4
Even though I walk through the valley of the shadow of death,
I fear no evil, for You are with me; Your rod and Your staff, they comfort me.

This passage is taken from the 23rd Psalm, which is probably quoted only second most after John 3:16.

The psalmist didn't say, "if" I walk through the valley but, "even though in I walk through the valley"... There WILL be valleys in life and some of those valleys will be deeper than we think we can dig out of, but God has promised to bring us out of those valleys and back to the mountain top where His glory shines.

The second half of verse 4 says, "I fear no evil, for You are with me; Your rod and Your staff, they comfort me.". We can rely on God to comfort and protect us in the valleys and darkness!

So, if today you are facing a deep, steep sided valley, remember God knows your situation and He sees your predicament. Call on Him, look for His light to get you through. He wants to help. Not only does God see you, He wants to help you.

Aristotle Onassis once said, "It is during our darkest moments that we must focus to see the light."

Remember, that the light is the shining presence of our loving God. Rest and rely on HIM.

JOURNAL ENTRY

_____

_____

_____

_____

_____

_____

_____

AUG 17

CARRYING BURDENS

Galatians 6:2
Carry each other's burdens, and in this way you will fulfill the law of Christ.

While guiding in the mountains I have had many occasions to pick up and carry my guests pack for them. (Not really a big deal)... But it freed them up to better do what they were there to do. There were times I felt a little like a pack mule, but it helped get the job done that we were there to do.

In the same way, as we carry the burden of someone, we free them up to be/do what they are called to be/do. AND, we are fulfilling Christ's law. God calls us to look for opportunities to serve and to lighten the load of others. In this way we are helping to fulfill what Christ came to do.

Here are a couple of verses that express the meaning of service in the life of those called by Christ.

Galatians 5:14 says For the entire law is fulfilled in keeping this one command: "Love your neighbor as yourself."

And Matthew 22:39 says, And the second is like it: 'Love your neighbor as yourself.'

So by carrying the burden of someone else, you are fulfilling what we are commanded to do and both parties will be blessed. There's one more thing... And it ain't easy...

Matthew 5:43-45 makes this tougher... 43 "You have heard that it was said, 'Love your neighbor and hate your enemy.' 44 But I tell you, love your enemies and pray for those who persecute you, 45 that you may be children of your Father in heaven.

So carry a burden whenever possible for those around you... It will bless them and you. And it will draw you closer to the Lord.

JOURNAL ENTRY

AUG 18

WHAT DOES LOVE LOOK LIKE?

1 Peter 3:8
Finally, all of you, be like-minded, be sympathetic, love one another,
be compassionate and humble.

As a Christian family we will never agree on everything. In fact in our personal lives, we may not agree on much. However in Peter's first letter, he directs us to love one another with sympathy and humility. How often we want our own way at the cost of others feelings.

The apostle Paul wrote in Galatians 5:22-23, "But the fruit of the spirit is love, joy, peace, patience, kindness, goodness, faithfulness, 23gentleness, self-control; against such things there is no law."

We will have disagreements, but the answer to this is not to argue or attack, it is to love and care for the other. When we can care more about a brother or sister's issues than we do our own we will fulfill what Christ taught us. Christ's example was to leave His home in heaven and to come to earth to live and die on a cross. Why? Because he loved us that much, it wasn't for His benefit but for ours.

What right do we have to treat a Christian family member with any less respect and honor?

John 13:34-35 A new commandment I give you. That you love one another, even as I have loved you that you also love one another. By this all men will know that you are my disciples; if you have love for one another.

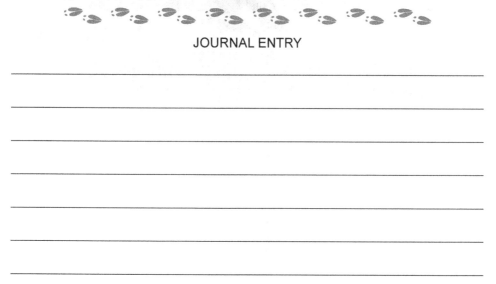

JOURNAL ENTRY

_____

_____

_____

_____

_____

_____

_____

AUG 19

THE JOY OF AN ARROW IN FLIGHT

1 John 3:7-8
7 Dear children, do not let anyone lead you astray. The one who does what is right is righteous, just as he is righteous. 8 The one who does what is sinful is of the devil, because the devil has been sinning from the beginning. The reason the Son of God appeared was to destroy the devil's work.

I love old movies where they show archery in medieval times. One of the Robin Hood movies showed men being taught to shoot longbows. I enjoy scenes where an entire company of men release arrows at once towards oncoming combatants. The sight of arrows flying high through the air is something of beauty to me.

Several years ago a good friend, David, built a small bamboo longbow for Micah our grandson who was 3 at the time. It is beautiful with Osage orange and bamboo laminates and it shot like a dream for him, considering Micah's age. On the back of the bow David wrote these words, "may you never lose the joy of an arrow in flight".

Our lives are very much like the flight of an arrow. We need stability to hit the mark that we are aiming for. The arrow has feathers or fletching to keep it stable. Without these feathers the arrow will fly off target after a short time. It might fly straight and true for a time, but it will lose its path very quickly.

Unless we spend time with God in His word and prayer, we are like a featherless arrow, sure to be off course quickly.

Stabilize your flight in life; hold tight to God in prayer and in reading His word so you "never lose the joy of an arrow in flight".

JOURNAL ENTRY

___

___

___

___

___

___

AUG 20

Jeremiah 10:13
When He thunders, the waters in the heavens roar; He makes clouds rise from the ends of the earth. He sends lightning with the rain and brings out the wind from His storehouses.

We have a tendency to always categorize God as love. We picture him as a "grandfather in the sky". What we tend to forget is God is ALL powerful!

I'm sitting this morning looking out the window, watching the flashes of lighting light up the trees in the yard. There's hail pounding on the metal roof and thunder shaking the house. He is a powerful force. I've seen His power in the swamps of Florida with the alligators and I've seen in the mountains of Alaska with grizzly bears. His power amazes me, it is beyond my understanding.

Today is a great reminder that God has more power than our human minds can comprehend. The most amazing thing to me is that all of this amazing power is available to us 100% of the time, we just have to call on Him. He is our Father.

Romans 8:17 And if children, then heirs; heirs of God, and joint-heirs with Christ; if indeed we share in His sufferings so that we may be also glorified together.

JOURNAL ENTRY

AUG 21

Psalm 18:1-2
1 I love you, Lord, my strength. 2 The Lord is my rock, my fortress and my deliverer; my God is my rock, in whom I take refuge, my shield and the horn of my salvation, my stronghold.

Many of us have heard or read these verses over and over in our lives. Even as I read them this morning, I read through them thinking in modern terms. The more I thought about it the more I realized that David could relate this to real life. Saul had hunted down David to kill him and he hid in the rocks to literally protect his life.

Most of us will never have to hide in the rocks to protect our lives. But the time may come (and it's coming quickly) where we will need a Rock to protect us. Isn't it great to know that we can rest on Him and rely on God's strength to protect us in our everyday struggles?

All we have to do is ask.

JOURNAL ENTRY

AUG 22

CHEERFUL GIVING

Malachi 3:8-12

"Will a mere mortal rob God? Yet you rob me. "But you ask, 'How are we robbing you?' "In tithes and offerings. 9 You are under a curse—your whole nation—because you are robbing me. 10 Bring the whole tithe into the storehouse, that there may be food in my house. Test me in this," says the Lord Almighty, "and see if I will not throw open the floodgates of heaven and pour out so much blessing that there will not be room enough to store it. 11 I will prevent pests from devouring your crops, and the vines in your fields will not drop their fruit before it is ripe," says the Lord almighty. 12 "Then all the nations will call you blessed, for yours will be a delightful land," says the Lord Almighty.

As a kid we had a lady in our church that loved the song "He owns the cattle on a thousand hills". Every Sunday we would sing it in Sunday school. To be honest, it got old week after week. But it had a great message. "Wonderful riches more than tongues can tell, He is my father so they're mine as well".

The Bible calls us to tithe, to give back to God. If everything in the world is really God's, then what we get is really His provision. We are called to give back. Not because God needs it, but because we need to come in line with God's heart. If everything is provided by God then in reality, it all is His, not ten percent, not twenty percent, but 100% of everything, our time, our money, our belongings, our everything. If you are a child of God, all of your life needs to be given back to God. Your life is no longer yours but His. This is a freeing thing, not a limiting thing.

If everything truly belongs to God in this world, what makes us think that God cannot or will not supply even more if we are faithful to Him.

2 Corinthians 9:7 Each of you should give what you have decided in your heart to give, not reluctantly or under compulsion, for God loves a cheerful giver.

JOURNAL ENTRY

AUG 23

1 Corinthians 13:1-3

If I speak in the tongues of men or of angels, but do not have love, I am only a resounding gong or a clanging cymbal. If I have the gift of prophecy and can fathom all mysteries and all knowledge, and if I have a faith that can move mountains, but do not have love, I am nothing. If I give all I possess to the poor and give over my body to hardship that I may boast, but do not have love, I gain nothing.

I have recently read somewhere that, "Love is when the other person's happiness is more important than your own."

I would go one step further and say, that the love Paul describes in 1 Corinthians is when you look out for another's happiness first and it fulfills you.

In John 13:34 Jesus said, "A new command I give you: Love one another. As I have loved you, so you must love one another". In John 15 He says it again... And in Ephesians 5 men are commanded to love their wives as Christ loved the church and gave Himself up for it.

So how do we love like that? That love is Agape love and is truly loving another more than yourself. This love is not emotion, its action. "As Christ loved the church and gave Himself up for it"... This is true love.

Read the rest of 1 Corinthians 13 and you will again see all that love is and is not.

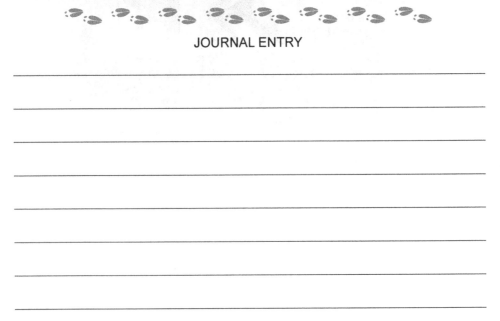

AUG 24

REFINERS FIRE

Zechariah 13:9
9 And I will put this third into the fire, and refine them as one refines silver, and test them as gold is tested. They will call upon my name, and I will answer them. I will say, 'They are my people'; and they will say, 'The Lord is my God.'"

I've always found it interesting just how a gold or silver refiner purifies the metals. The refiner heats the metal until the impurities rise to the top and the "dross" is skimmed off and thrown away. The process is repeated until the precious metal is pure (the refiners reflection is clearly seen). This process is not quick and often tedious.

This should be our lives in Christ. God allows us to be in the heat. He wants the impurities to be removed from us so in the end all He sees is the reflection of Himself in our lives.

Brian Doerksen wrote this song, REFINER'S FIRE, this would be my prayer for myself and you.

Purify my heart
Let me be as gold and precious silver
Purify my heart
Let me be as gold, pure gold
Refiner's fire
My heart's one desire
Is to be holy
Set apart for You, Lord
I choose to be holy

Set apart for You, my Master
Ready to do Your will
Purify my heart
Cleanse me from within
And make me holy
Purify my heart
Cleanse me from my sin
Deep within

May God refine you to His likeness.

JOURNAL ENTRY

_____

_____

_____

_____

_____

_____

AUG 25

A HEALTHY SPIRIT

Galatians 5:22-23
22 But the fruit of the Spirit is love, joy, peace, patience, kindness, goodness, faithfulness, 23 gentleness and self-control. Against such things there is no law.

I remember a while back hearing of a marathon runner that ran a complete marathon and when he crossed the finish line he fell over, dead from a heart attack. He looked perfectly healthy from the outside, but inside he was very different. I've hunted with men that looked as though they could be a model for a gym commercial, yet when it came time to do the hard work, they didn't have the heart to get it done.

These verses in Galatians give us a "check-up" of what we look like inside. These attributes of a spiritually healthy person are a measuring stick of where we need to be. Read them again carefully. How are you doing? Some of us look great on the outside, especially on Sunday morning. But how about the rest of the week, how do we look to the world?

I found myself reading them over and over again to check my own life. Great news, there are no laws against any of these things in verses 22 & 23. You are free to practice any and all of them at every opportunity.

JOURNAL ENTRY

AUG 26

KNOWING HIS WILL

Romans 12:2

"Do not conform any longer to the pattern of this world, but be transformed by the renewing of your mind. Then you will be able to test and approve what God's will is –his good, pleasing and perfect will."

How many times in our lives do we ask ourselves, "How do I know what God's will is for my life?" I know in my life I have asked it many times, usually when I am struggling with some situation. When I was young I asked a pastor this question. His answer... "Read your Bible". While this was a simple and obvious answer, it is only part of what's needed.

I believe that one of the main things required in finding God's will for our lives is being willing to follow His will when He reveals it to us. If we are deciding to follow His will based on our wants, we won't see God's true will for our lives. If we are just trying to find out if God's will matches ours, instead of the other way around, we'll never truly find where He wants us.

Desiring to follow God's will is the first step in knowing His will for us. The condition of our hearts will help reveal where we should be in life.

JOURNAL ENTRY

AUG 27

HITTING THE TARGET

Proverbs 13:20
Whoever walks with the wise becomes wise, but the companion of fools will suffer harm.

Our life is like an arrow flying through life. Somewhere out there is a target to shoot for but an arrow flying without stability rarely hits the target.

What adds stability to the arrow shaft? It is generally three fletching or feathers. The three fletching in our lives should be;

- The scripture- we need to be continually reading God's word to gain the wisdom on how we get through life.
- The Spirit- when we've come to Christ we are given the Holy Spirit to fill us and direct us in right and wrong.
- The saints- surround yourself with the saints or Christians that will hold you accountable. They will lead you and keep you going straight.

So for true stability in life allow these three things to help you to hit the "life target" that God has set before you; the scripture in front of you, the Spirit inside of you and the saints around you. Keep them all there, all the time and you will hit the target.

JOURNAL ENTRY

AUG 28

LET YOUR LIGHT SHINE

Matthew 5:15
In the same way, let your light shine before others, that they may see your good deeds and glorify your Father in heaven.

What does our life say about our relationship with Christ? Matthew 5:15 says that we let our light shine that others might see our good deeds and glorify our Father in heaven. This also means that we need to watch what we do so that our bad deeds don't tear down our witness of God's glory.

A good life is not our only responsibility in showing God's glory. We still have a responsibility to, "...Go into all the world and preach the gospel to all creation" Mark 16:15. Then once we've fulfilled this command, then we also live a life that shows others our good deeds.

So it doesn't matter if you are a clergy member, school teacher, construction worker, or you are enjoying retirement, you have a responsibility, once you have chosen to follow Jesus you are to fulfill the call in Mark 16 and Matthew 5.

Let your life always reflect God's glory.

JOURNAL ENTRY

_____

_____

_____

_____

_____

_____

_____

_____

_____

AUG 29

HEARING AND DOING

Mark 4:24
And He was saying to them, "Take care what you listen to. By your standard of measure it will be measured to you; and more will be given you besides."

I read a story this morning from a young man, John. that told of driving past a homeless man struggling with his belongings. He felt God tell him to stop and help this man get to where he was going. John thought he would be a blessing to this homeless man. As it turned out that John was extremely blessed by a wonderful person, that just happened to be homeless.

By the time they were done the man asked John, do you know Jesus? The whole time John was waiting to ask him that question. John was blessed because he listened to God telling him to stop and help a homeless man

If we will truly listen to God's prompting and calling, we will receive blessings beyond our expectations. We've been commanded to be doers, not just hearers... So choose to listen and do.

James 1:22 But be doers of the Word, and not hearers only, deceiving yourselves.

JOURNAL ENTRY

AUG 30

PREPARE TO STAND

Joshua 1:9
Have I not commanded you? Be strong and courageous. Do not be afraid; do not be discouraged, for the Lord your God will be with you wherever you go.

We are living in a world that seems to be going quickly downhill. Today I heard on NBC, YES NBC, that not only our country but the whole world is falling apart. I know that in my 1/2 century + I have never seen anything like we are seeing right now. ISIS is rolling across much of the world killing Christians and Jews in their path. What is happening is building intensity daily. Yet in Joshua, we are told to be strong and courageous and to not be afraid or discouraged. We can count on God to be with us always.

Twenty years ago we would hear, "someday we might face persecution here in the USA" but it was never real to us. But today we can see that we may soon have to stand for what we believe. We have to decide now if we will stand or fall... And falling really isn't an option.

Prepare your heart for the fight might be here soon. If we stand we are promised to have God alongside us and we are promised to be blessed.

Matthew 5:10 [10] "Blessed are those who have been persecuted for the sake of righteousness, for theirs is the kingdom of heaven.

JOURNAL ENTRY

AUG 31

IT IS WELL WITH MY SOUL

Psalm 46:1-2
"God is our refuge and strength, an ever-present help in trouble. Therefore we will not fear, though the earth give way and the mountains fall into the heart of the sea."

Horatio Spafford was a wealthy Chicago lawyer with a thriving legal practice, a beautiful home, a wife, four daughters and a son. He was also a devout Christian and faithful student of the Scriptures.

At the very height of his financial and professional success, Horatio and his wife Anna suffered the tragic loss of their 4 year old son to scarlet fever. Shortly thereafter on October 8, 1871, the Great Chicago Fire destroyed almost every real estate investment that Spafford had.

In 1873, Spafford scheduled a boat trip to Europe in order to give his wife and daughters a much needed vacation and time to recover from the tragedy. He also went to join D. L. Moody on an evangelistic campaign in England. Spafford sent his wife and daughters ahead of him while he remained in Chicago to take care of some unexpected last minute business. Several days later he received notice that his family's ship had encountered a collision. All four of his daughters drowned; only his wife had survived.

With a heavy heart, Spafford boarded a boat that would take him to his grieving Anna in England. It was on this trip that he penned those now famous words, when sorrow like sea billows roll; it is well, it is well with my soul...

There is no better way to face a terrible loss than to give it to God to handle, rest in His loving embrace. Call on Him for comfort.

God gives us our friends and family as gifts and support, God allows us time with all of them. We don't know when that time will end, but God knows and He wants us to call on Him in our time of sorrow. We can trust that He understands and loves us so much that we can go to Him with our grief.

There is only one way that the death of a loved one can be "Well With My Soul"... only through a reliance on Christ to carry the burden. If we know Christ, death is just a door opening to eternal life with God

JOURNAL ENTRY

___

___

___

September

Rom 10:9

That if you confess with your mouth, "Jesus is Lord," and believe in your heart that God raised him from the dead, you will be saved.

SEPT 1

Psalm 32:8
"I will guide you and teach you the way you should go.
I will give you good advice and watch over you."

GPS units have always fascinated me and I've owned three of them, but none have made it past the front door of the house. While I don't use mine, others have used their GPS to keep me from sleeping on the mountain.

One morning we watched a bunch of big bull elk above tree line and made a plan to get to them for the afternoon hunt. Well, afternoon turned into evening and evening turned into night. The hunting was so good we ended up a couple of long hard miles above and beyond the truck. Luckily Joe had his GPS in his pack and had the truck marked.

The best GPS that I have is imbedded in my heart; it's my "God Positioning System". In life when we start to stray too far from where we should be or we head into trouble, this GPS will warn us. There is always a signal and the battery never needs to be replaced. We just have to trust it and never doubt it will show you the best path or the safest place.

Because I don't totally understand how my three GPS units work I have an issue with totally trusting them. However, with God, we can always trust His "God Positioning System".

Jerry Bridges wrote about this subject... "God's plan and His ways of working out His plan are frequently beyond our ability to fathom and understand. We must learn to trust when we don't understand."

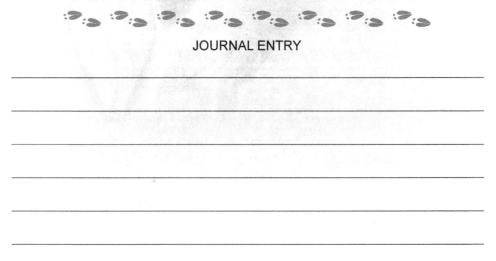

JOURNAL ENTRY

September

SEPT 2

WE ARE NEVER ABANDONED

John 10:11-13
"I am the good shepherd. The good shepherd lays down his life for the sheep. 12 The hired hand is not the shepherd and does not own the sheep. So when he sees the wolf coming, he abandons the sheep and runs away. Then the wolf attacks the flock and scatters it. 13 The man runs away because he is a hired hand and cares nothing for the sheep.

Do you ever find yourself wondering where God has gone? I admit that sometimes I wonder if He really is beside me. I put myself in a place where I cry out and all that comes back to me is my own echo, a place where I feel like I'm under constant attack and facing it all alone. My shield is pretty dinged up and scorched from fireballs coming at me. A place where I feel . . . lost.

And so I remind myself of whom Jesus is. He is the Good Shepherd. Not only does He lay down His life for His sheep, He would never abandon me when I'm under attack. This is no hired hand we're dealing with here. I also learned from the above verse that it is the sheep that scatter. I am the one who runs away, not my Savior. He is always there waiting to care for me.

So today when I cry out and hear my own voice echo back, I will also strain to hear the One who leaves the rest in order to find me and bring me safely home where I belong. How about you? Are you within hearing of your shepherd?

Then Jesus told them this parable: in Luke 15:3-6 "Suppose one of you has a hundred sheep and loses one of them. Doesn't he leave the ninety-nine in the open country and go after the lost sheep until he finds it? And when he finds it, he joyfully puts it on his shoulders and goes home. Then he calls his friends and neighbors together and says, 'Rejoice with me; I have found my lost sheep'".

WE ARE NEVER ABANDONED

JOURNAL ENTRY

_____

_____

_____

_____

_____

SEPT 3

THE CALL OF TEMPTATION

Proverbs 6:20-24

My son, keep your father's command and do not forsake your mother's teaching. 21 Bind them always on your heart; fasten them around your neck. 22 When you walk, they will guide you; when you sleep, they will watch over you; when you awake, they will speak to you. 23 For this command is a lamp, this teaching is a light, and correction and instruction are the way to life, 24 keeping you from your neighbor's wife, from the smooth talk of a wayward woman.

This fall I had the amazing opportunity to experience almost the entire elk rut on the Cielo Vista Ranch in Southern Colorado. We guided from the last of August through yesterday. The bulls bugled the entire month but the last week it was deafening with the screams, groans and bellows of mature bulls. The cow elk calls we used were very effective for calling in the bulls. There were times when the bulls were coming from several directions. Four of the big bulls we killed were taken when bulls lost their sense of normal caution and succumbed to the urge to breed.... Coming to the "smooth talk" that they thought was a cow elk, causing their demise.

How often this happens to people... We desire something so much it doesn't matter what the danger is, we are going to do whatever it takes to get it.

King David is a prime example of this very thing. He saw a beautiful woman bathing and allowed his desire for her to override his morality. To David, his actions on that fateful night seemed trivial, just a momentary pause in an otherwise steadfast life. The consequences, however, were devastating, not just for David, or for Uriah, but also for David's family and the entire nation. The whole nation paid a high price for David's immorality.

In 2 Samuel 12:14, the prophet Nathan passes the bad news on to David of what will happen because he has given in to the "call of sin". Verse 14 "But because by doing this you have shown utter contempt for the Lord, the son born to you will die."

Like the elk that runs to the call, we will pay a price if we give in to temptation. We must focus on our relationship with God and run from the call of temptation. Proverbs 14:12 tells us, "There is a way that seems right to a man, but its end is the way of death."

JOURNAL ENTRY

___

___

___

September

SEPT 4

I KNOW THE PLANS I HAVE FOR YOU...

Exodus 14:27-28
And Moses stretched forth his hand over the sea, and the sea returned to his strength when the morning appeared; and the Egyptians fled against it; and the LORD overthrew the Egyptians in the midst of the sea. And the waters returned, and covered the chariots, and the horsemen, and all the host of Pharaoh that came into the sea after them; there remained not so much as one of them."

Last night I watched the FOX GOP debate. I was encouraged by the fact that we have a few people standing up for what I believe God truly wants for this country... But I realize that God is the one that seats rulers and takes them out of power. God had allowed Egypt to become a great, yet godless nation. He allowed Pharaoh to rule, yet with one action God took Pharaoh and his army out.

Here in America we got our start with the Puritans who came over at the leading of God, and set up a brave, new nation. The first text book ever used in our schools and universities was the Holy Bible.

James Madison said this: "We have staked the whole future of American civilization, not upon the power of government, far from it. We have staked the future of all of our political institutions upon the capacity of mankind of self-government; upon the capacity of each and all of us to govern ourselves, to control ourselves, to sustain ourselves according to the Ten Commandments of God."

Wow, what a great start! A nation founded on submission to God and His commandments.

It's so sad to see how far we've come... Since 1973, 58,000,000 babies have been murdered! 58 MILLION and what is one of the top questions of Presidential candidates? "Are you going to allow America to continue to legally murder babies?". We elected a president largely because of this murderous belief. This is so sad.

But take heart, we are promised that God knows the beginning from the end and that He puts kings and rulers on the thrones and removes them to serve HIS purposes. No matter what we see going on around us, remember this, God has a plan and His plan is going to prevail.

Jeremiah 29:11-13 For I know the plans that I have for you,' declares the Lord, 'plans for welfare and not for calamity to give you a future and a hope. 12 Then you will call upon Me and come and pray to Me, and I will listen to you. 13 You will seek Me and find Me when you search for Me with all your heart.

JOURNAL ENTRY

SEPT 5

2 Corinthians 5:17
Therefore if anyone is in Christ, he is a new creature; the old things passed away; behold, new things have come.

Today we were cutting wood in a valley that's called wallow hollow. It's a place where the elk come down in the fall and the bulls roll around in the small puddles and cover themselves in mud. I've seen bulls, normally yellow in color, come out of a wallow jet black. There is no way to go into a wallow and come out clean. Also bull elk wallow to cool down when they get over heated. People also go into a wallowing mood when they get over heated by something. When they don't get their way and get upset they often shut down in self pity and wallow for a time.

So, why do we "wallow" in our past? Why do we continue to sin when we are, "a new creation" as Paul put it?

We don't need to continue in our old lifestyle... We can be free of the chains that have held us.

1 John 1:9 tells us that, "If we confess our sins, He is faithful and righteous to forgive us our sins and to cleanse us from all unrighteousness."

The mud from the wallowing is washed clean... We are that "new creation".

So stop wallowing in your sins. God made you Holy so that you can be holy...

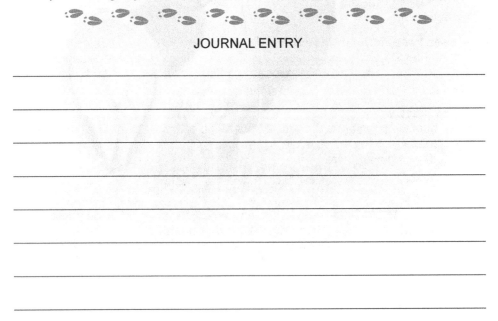

JOURNAL ENTRY

September

SEPT 6

LIKE AN ARROW IN FLIGHT

Proverbs 13:20
Whoever walks with the wise becomes wise, but the companion of fools will suffer harm.

I've loved archery since I was very little. My parents bought me a bright yellow fiberglass bow when I was about 8 years old and I loved shooting that bow. A few years ago a good friend made a beautiful little bow for Micah (our grandson). On the bow he wrote something like this, "May you never lose the joy of an arrow in flight".

What is it that keeps an arrow flying true? What makes it to fly straight toward its target and stabilizes it in flight? It is the fletching. Generally there are three of them.

And like the fletching of an arrow, we have things that stabilize us through life. I call them the three "S's". Allow these three S's to stabilize you through life. By dropping any one of them we lose stability. They are; The scripture, The Saints and The Spirit.

The Scriptures in front of us, daily reading of God's word gives us direction. 1 Timothy 4:13 says. Until I come, devote yourself to the public reading of Scripture, to exhortation, to teaching.

The Saints around us, surrounding ourselves with others that love the Lord will keep us "flying" a straight path. Proverbs 13:20

The Spirit inside us, once we've come to a saving relationship with Christ, the Holy Spirit indwells us and directs us by allowing us to see where we are going and speaks to us of right and wrong. 1 Timothy 4:13 tells us, "Until I come, devote yourself to the public reading of Scripture, to exhortation, to teaching."

Keep these three fletching, attached to your life at all times and you will fly straight. Try flying without them and you will drift off target... The longer you drift the harder it is to come back.

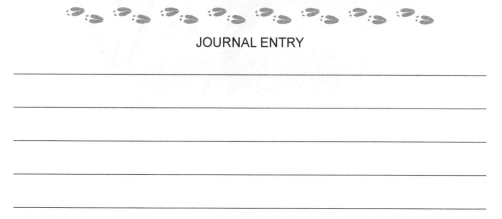

JOURNAL ENTRY

___

___

___

___

___

SEPT 7

Isaiah 32:17-18
The fruit of that righteousness will be peace; its effect will be quietness and confidence forever. 18 My people will live in peaceful dwelling places, in secure homes, in undisturbed places of rest.

I don't know about you but I don't see much peace, quietness and confidence in our world. Why not? It's because we've walked away from the righteousness from verses 16 and 17. The women of Jerusalem had become complacent; the people had become confident in their own plans and schemes and forgotten God's righteousness. Does this sound familiar? Are we there as a people? What's the future without a revival of our hearts?

Taylor, Hudson, an early missionary to China said – "If we could offer to the ungodly a worldly plan which would ensure their prospering in all that they undertake how eagerly they would embrace it! And yet when GOD Himself reveals an effectual plan to His people how few avail themselves of it".

This is so true, God's word has given us a plan for peace, quietness, confidence, to live in a secure and peaceful home. Yet, we choose human thinking and leave God behind.

Reconsider where you get your direction... God's already got the best plan.

JOURNAL ENTRY

SEPT 8

Ephesians 4:31-32
Let all bitterness, wrath, anger, clamor, and evil speaking be put away from you, with all malice. And be kind to one another, tenderhearted, forgiving one another, just as God in Christ forgave you.

Revenge seems to be in style today, forgiveness is not. We can see this in our society, with lawsuits running rampant for the stupidest things. We can see this in the media today, with talk shows like Jerry Springer and the like, and in movies like "Dirty Harry" where Clint Eastwood tells a criminal at gunpoint, "Go ahead. Make my day." We see that the world is drunk on wrath, and this is evidenced in road rage, drive by shootings, crimes of vengeance and shootings among teens.

So why do we forgive? First of all we read in Ephesians 4, we are commanded to do so.

Christ is our example and when we forgive we become most like Christ Himself. He took on all our sins and died so we might be forgiven. How many of us can say that? Yet we are called to forgive just the same. As Christ was hanging on the cross, having had nails driven through His hands and His feet, people standing below Him mocking Him... Did He strike out? No, He prayed and said, "Father forgive them". Could I do that? Could you? What an amazing example.

As we forgive, blessing and forgiveness flows from God to and through us.

Who has hurt you? Let it go... Christ has forgiven you...so forgive them.

JOURNAL ENTRY

_____

_____

_____

_____

_____

_____

_____

SEPT 9

CHANGE THROUGH AFFLICATION

Romans 8:28
And we know that God causes all things to work together for good to those who love God, to those who are called according to His purpose.

Charles H. Spurgeon once said, "The Lord's mercy often rides to the door of our heart upon the black horse of affliction."

If you think about this verse for a moment and then consider what Spurgeon said, so much more of life makes sense. There are so many times God allows things to happen in life that really changes us and shows us God's mercy and love.

This week I was talking to a friend about a terrible situation that has been going on in his life for 10 long years. He has been tormented by someone to the point where it would break most people. I said to him, "I can't comprehend the purpose of all this is... Why God has allowed it to happen to you and your family." His response was simple and delivered with a small smile, "I know what it is, it saved my life".

He knew that what he was going through was a refining process that has brought him into line with God's will. Oh that we would all have that faith.

The next time we are in adversity, instead of crying out, "Why am I being attacked?" Try instead to ask, "What is God having me grow into"

I know its cliché, but remember the beautiful butterfly that really came from the "death" of the caterpillar... This being a reflection of what Christ went through in His death and resurrection for us. God will stand by us as He refines us. Stand firm and know that nothing is out of God's control.

JOURNAL ENTRY

_____

_____

_____

_____

_____

SEPT 10

PROVISION OF WATER

Psalm 104:10
He makes springs pour water into the ravines; it flows between the mountains.

Psalm 104:6-16 speaks of God's awesome provision of water. He spoke and the waters listened. Every life on earth is dependent on earthly water to survive... And the Lord provides it in His timing.

If you have ever driven through parts of Kansas, Nebraska, Oklahoma and Texas in a period of drought you know what it is like to "need" water. The plants are either gone or stressed. Even the antlers of the deer are stunted from the need for water. In the worst of conditions the animals perish.

In the midst of mankind's drought, Christ came as "Living Water". Our souls cannot "survive" without this living water. Once we've trusted Christ to be our source of life, then God's word becomes our "water" and "food" so we continue to keep growing.

Without water and food we eventually weaken and die... Daily food and water is required. Don't let your spiritual life go dormant, feed and water it daily with God's word and with prayer.

JOURNAL ENTRY

SEPT 11

WHERE YOUR TREASURE IS

Luke 12:32-34

32 "Do not be afraid, for your Father has been pleased to give you the kingdom. 33 Sell your possessions and give to the poor. Provide purses for yourselves that will not wear out, a treasure in heaven that will never fail, where no thief comes near and no moth destroys. 34 For where your treasure is, there your heart will be also.

I have progressed over the years from a hunting fanatic to a scouting and guiding fanatic. I love to sit for hours staring at maps on my computer. I also love to discover new places to hunt or more likely to set someone else up to hunt. I could do this for weeks on end. I enjoy this to the point where I lose sleep over it, sometimes day after day. It sometimes becomes obsessive.

Fall is here, I want to spend every waking hour "seeing what's over the next hill". Now I have to question how much I love/treasure this desire. Is this where my true treasure is?

We all have things in our lives that we treasure, relationships, possessions, hobbies etc... Whatever it might be, we need to make sure that what we treasure more than anything on earth is the Lord. No matter how good something is, we need to ALWAYS keep God first in everything!

JOURNAL ENTRY

SEPT 12

A FIRM FOUNDATION

Matt. 7:24
Therefore whoever hears these sayings of mine, and does them,
I will liken him to a wise man who built his house on the rock.

We've all seen the news video of houses on beach front properties that get washed into the ocean. I've hunted out of many old hunting camps built just on logs sitting on the ground or on soft soils. I've always wondered why someone would build their house on such unstable soils. My dad, having been a builder, always stressed building on a firm foundation. Here in our area there are a lot of places where houses are built right on ledge rock. These houses never move.

Even though you might feel secure when you build on something less than a firm foundation it doesn't last. Putting your trust in anything but the solid rock is a disaster waiting to happen. This is all true for a hunting camp, a house or life in general.

Where do you have your foundation anchored? Christ is the ROCK, the solid place, where we can build our foundation that has eternal security... Anything else will fall away and has no true support for life.

JOURNAL ENTRY

SEPT 13

LOOKING OUT FOR OTHERS

Philippians 2:3-4
Do nothing out of selfish ambition or vain conceit. Rather, in humility value others above yourselves, not looking to your own interests but each of you to the interests of the others.

I am not against putting anyone else first, but the thought of "never" doing anything out of selfish ambition, seems unreachable. However, if we really looked out for "the interests of the others", what a fantastic world it would be.

I've learned through a life of guiding that if you don't put others first it is hard to get ahead in life. If you were to take up a guiding lifestyle you would soon learn that living life this way is so rewarding. I've learned that to watch someone else succeed, at times, is more fulfilling than succeeding myself. I see this in my brother Dave as he guides elk hunters. He has lost the need to hunt for himself because he gives so much to put others first.

Selfish ambition and vain conceit verses humility and the interests of others. Not only would my world be better, but like Zig Ziglar wrote, "you can get whatever you want out of life by helping enough other people get what they want."

So by looking out for others first it gets me what I want/need in the long run? This sounds good like a win/win to me. Besides it follows what we are commanded to do.

JOURNAL ENTRY

September

SEPT 14

SEEING CLEARLY

Psalms 119:18
Open my eyes that I may see wonderful things in your law.

I've been told that I can occasionally have selective hearing. That is to hear things with my ears but it doesn't register with my brain. There are times when my wife Linda watches TV and when I ask her what's happening she has no idea at all. She can sit for the longest time staring at the screen without a clue. She is evidently deep in thought on something else but her eyes are open and staring.

I think that this verse is talking about this same thing; but it is meaning your heart, not your brain. We might occasionally hear God but don't listen to Him.

I pray that you and I will always "hear" what God has to say and "see what He is showing us. Like this old hymn from the 1920's

Open my eyes that I may see
glimpses of truth thou hast for me.
Place in my hands the wonderful key; that shall
unclasp and set me free.

Silently now I wait for thee,
ready, my God, thy will to see.
Open my eyes; illumine me,
Spirit divine!

I pray the same for you.

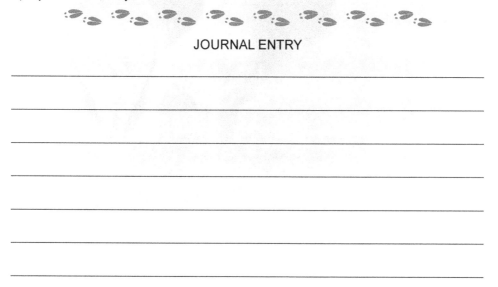

JOURNAL ENTRY

_____

_____

_____

_____

_____

_____

_____

SEPT 15

Psalm 33:4-6
4 For the word of the LORD is right and true; He is faithful in all He does. 5 The LORD loves righteousness and justice; the earth is full of his unfailing love. 6 By the word of the LORD were the heavens made, their starry host by the breath of his mouth.

As children of God, we need to believe that the Bible is God's spoken word. Once we believe that, then we need to trust what He has said and what He is can be trusted.

God said, "I will never leave you or forsake you" (Hebrews 13:5), "Ask whatever you wish and it will be done for you" (John 15:7), "no good thing does He withhold from those who walk uprightly." (Psalms 84:11)

So believe that our loving God can be trusted. Live day to day knowing that what He said He will do, will be done! Rest on this.

JOURNAL ENTRY

SEPT 16

Psalm 37:1-9

1 Do not fret because of those who are evil or be envious of those who do wrong; 2 for like the grass they will soon wither, like green plants they will soon die away. 3 Trust in the Lord and do good; dwell in the land and enjoy safe pasture. 4 Take delight in the Lord, and He will give you the desires of your heart. 5 Commit your way to the Lord; trust in Him and He will do this: 6 He will make your righteous reward shine like the dawn, your vindication like the noonday sun. 7 Be still before the Lord and wait patiently for Him; do not fret when people succeed in their ways, when they carry out their wicked schemes. 8 Refrain from anger and turn from wrath; do not fret—it leads only to evil. 9 For those who are evil will be destroyed, but those who hope in the Lord will inherit the land.

We can have complete peace in knowing that our loving, all powerful, all knowing God has complete control over everything in our lives, if we allow Him. We don't need to worry about others and their plans schemes and deeds... We are called to just "wait on Him". Those that do evil will be destroyed... Not by us, but by their own evil doings.

Verse 8 says "refrain from anger and turn from wrath; do not fret—it leads only to evil."

So lastly, don't fret... It not only leads to evil, but it only brings us down to a point where we are of no use to ourselves, to others, or to God.

JOURNAL ENTRY

SEPT 17

CLEANING HOUSE

Luke 11:24-26

"When an impure spirit comes out of a person, it goes through arid places seeking rest and does not find it. Then it says, 'I will return to the house I left.' 25 When it arrives, it finds the house swept clean and put in order. 26 Then it goes and takes seven other spirits more wicked than itself, and they go in and live there. And the final condition of that person is worse than the first."

Throughout our lives we continually deal with temptation and sin. There are times that we fall into sin, but 1 John 1:9 says, "If we confess our sin, He is faithful and just to forgive us our sins and cleanse us from all unrighteousness."

Over the span of the last 20 years I have put many food plots in for hunting. When I first started tilling land I assumed that if I tilled the land and turned the weeds and grasses under, I would have fresh clean soil. But what I found was that if I didn't kill the weeds first and then plant something that would combat the weeds they would come back heavier and healthier than before. Just tilling and allowing the soil to lay never works as the weeds and grasses will take back over very quickly.

The same is true of our life, once we've confessed and been forgiven we need to fill that space in our lives with more of God. If we don't fill that space with godly things, satan will come in stronger than before and consume us.

Protect your heart. Keep your eyes on God and fill your life with godly things.

JOURNAL ENTRY

SEPT 18

ON THE MOUNTAIN TOP

Mark 9:2-3
And after six days Jesus took with him Peter and James and John, and led them up a high mountain by themselves. And He was transfigured before them, and His clothes became radiant, intensely white, as no one on earth could bleach them.

All of us have had "mountain top" experiences in our Christian walk, times where the Lord has brought us to a place where we see Him more clearly and feel His presence more intensely. We come away wanting more of Him.

The other day I was in such a place both spiritually and physically. I had climbed up high looking for elk and was sitting on the rim of the Sangre de Christo Mountains looking over hundreds of miles of beauty. It was such a fulfilling place and time that I didn't want it to ever end. But eventually I had to come down to our hunting camp.

But as surely as we hit those mountain tops, we will also hit the valley floor. God lets us see those mountain tops so we know Him better. So we can best know HIS power, strength and love. That way when we hit the low spots in our .lives, we can remember how great our God is and hold on to Him/

Next time we hit the bottom remember that God has a plan to carry us to the top of the mountain again meant for a time of seeing Him work miracles in our lives.

JOURNAL ENTRY

SEPT 19

A GREAT GOD

Psalm 95:3-7
3 For the Lord is the great God, the great King above all gods.
4 In his hand are the depths of the earth, and the mountain peaks belong to him.
5 The sea is His, for He made it, and His hands formed the dry land.
6 Come, let us bow down in worship, let us kneel before the Lord our Maker;
7 for He is our God and we are the people of His pasture and the flock under His care.

If we believe the Bible (and I do) we should have absolutely no doubt that we have an awesome God. These verses show us His amazing power and control of everything.

Yet, like a shepherd that cares for his sheep and gives himself up for them, HE loves us unconditionally. A good shepherd the Bible says in Luke 15 will always do everything to bring a lost lamb back…

Luke 15:4-7 ⁴"Suppose one of you has a hundred sheep and loses one of them. Doesn't he leave the ninety-nine in the open country and go after the lost sheep until he finds it? ⁵ And when he finds it, he joyfully puts it on his shoulders ⁶ and goes home. Then he calls his friends and neighbors together and says, 'Rejoice with me; I have found my lost sheep.' ⁷ I tell you that in the same way there will be more rejoicing in heaven over one sinner who repents than over ninety-nine righteous persons who do not need to repent.

How can we not return that love? Like the sheep that trust totally in their shepherd, we can rest on God and rely totally on Him.

JOURNAL ENTRY

September

SEPT 20

Psalm 145:1-3
1 I will exalt you, my God the King; I will praise Your name forever and ever.
2 Every day I will praise You and extol Your name forever and ever.
3 Great is the Lord and most worthy of praise; His greatness no one can fathom.

Several years ago I was listening to a speaker talk about prayer. He talked about how often we come to God with a wish list and what we think we "need"... Instead we should be first praising God for what He is already doing in our lives. We are blessed beyond our imagination when we continually praise God in the good and bad times. Thanksgiving with the mouth will stir up thankfulness in the heart

In the Psalms the word praise is written 192 times, this, in the middle of terrible loss, persecution and pain. It is easier to praise Him when things are going well, but learning to praise him in every situation is where we need to be.

Amanda Penland "Life is not always what we expect. But, when we praise and trust God in the midst of it all, we can make it through anything."

It will make a difference not only in our own hearts but brings joy to an all-powerful God... Imagine, as insignificant as we are, we can bring joy to Him through our praise. Wow!

JOURNAL ENTRY

_____

_____

_____

_____

_____

_____

_____

_____

SEPT 21

Psalm 112:4
Unto the upright there arises light in the darkness: he is gracious, and full of compassion, and righteous.

I was up most of the night working on a presentation for a meeting today and when I tried to start a devotional I was totally blank. I was just about to send a note apologizing for no devotional this morning... That very second I read this verse... And just like that... God brought "a light into my darkness".

It is like sitting in a hunting blind in the darkness. We stare and eventually see shapes and we imagine things that look like deer, elk, bears etc. We try to make out the targets that we are hunting. The last 15 minutes is very frustrating, but when the light comes everything is clear.

Nora Roberts, Heaven and Earth "Evil cannot and will not be vanquished by evil. Dark will only swallow dark and deepen. The good and the light are the keenest weapons."

When we are feeling our lowest and darkest HE will lift us and enlighten us, all we have to do is ask.

JOURNAL ENTRY

_____
_____
_____
_____
_____
_____
_____
_____

SEPT 22

FOR ME TO LIVE IS CHRIST

Philippians 1:21
For to me, to live is Christ and to die is gain.

Several years ago Christian Pastor Hua Huiqi in Beijing, China was jailed for his faith and beaten into a coma. Before this happened he was quoted as saying... "It doesn't matter whether I live or die, as long as Christ shines in me and the gospel increases."

Dietrich Bonhoeffer wrote in his book, "The Cost of Discipleship", these very profound words. "When Christ calls a man, he bids him come and die."

Just a little perspective for those of us tempted to complain about our lives–OR about being ridiculed for speaking the truth about Jesus and the Bible.

We may come to a point here in our country where we pay for our faith... Even with our life. Let's make sure that our lives are lived for Christ's glory.

JOURNAL ENTRY

Trophies of Grace

SEPT 23

OVER ALL, PUT ON LOVE

Colossians 3:12-14
Therefore, as God's chosen people, holy and dearly loved, clothe yourselves with compassion, kindness, humility, gentleness and patience. Bear with each other and forgive one another if any of you has a grievance against someone. Forgive as the Lord forgave you. And over all these virtues put on love, which binds them all together in perfect unity.

These verses have an amazing message. There is not one word like, revenge, harm, pain etc... Just words like... compassion, kindness, humility, gentleness and patience. And over all these virtues put on love.

This sounds good but when someone is twisting the knife in your back, it is rough. But, we will be greatly blessed if we can strive to do these things. What a great world we would have if we all could treat each other this way.

Let's put it in practice this week.

JOURNAL ENTRY

_____

_____

_____

_____

_____

_____

_____

_____

_____

_____

_____

_____

September

SEPT 24

SERVANTHOOD

Philippians 2:5-7
Your attitude should be the same as that of Christ Jesus: Who, being in very nature God, did not consider equality with God something to be grasped, but made Himself nothing, taking the very nature of a servant, being made in human likeness.

Servant, in our day, in our minds, having a servant attitude towards someone sounds like a nice noble thing to do... And it is. "I get joy out of serving others". But in biblical times a servant was bound (figuratively) to their master. They were there most of all because they had to be not because they wanted to be.

We are told to serve joyfully. Easier said than done... But Christ was/is our example. He served us all the way to His death on the cross. Can we do that?

Life is short and we should be "building up treasures in heaven, where moths and rust cannot destroy, and thieves do not break in and steal." Matthew 6:20.

By serving we are not only lowering/humbling ourselves but we are lifting others and Christ up.

One more great promise is found in Mark 9:35, Sitting down, He called the twelve and said to them, "If anyone wants to be first, he shall be last of all and servant of all."

JOURNAL ENTRY

SEPT 25

I AM A BRANCH

John 15: 1-2
"I am the true vine, and my Father is the gardener. He cuts off every branch in me that bears no fruit, while every branch that does bear fruit He prunes so that it will be even more fruitful."

Christ is telling us that God, the Father, must remove some things from our lives to make us more fruitful. Even though we may not be a bad person and these branches might not be bad things, they can be things that suck "nutrition" from our lives as Christians. Anything that takes us away from God and serving Him are things that need to be pruned.

He must remove some things from our lives in order to discipline us and make us better disciples and instruments of His love. It may be painful for a while, but if we respond to His discipline in a positive way, we will be able to grow spiritually. When we are going through rough times, there is a choice, trust that God has control or be bitter. But if you choose Jesus, you can choose to be better.

Verse 4 goes on... 4 Remain in me, as I also remain in you. No branch can bear fruit by itself; it must remain in the vine. Neither can you bear fruit unless you remain in me.

So remain in that close fellowship with Christ, let him feed us as branches and we will flourish.

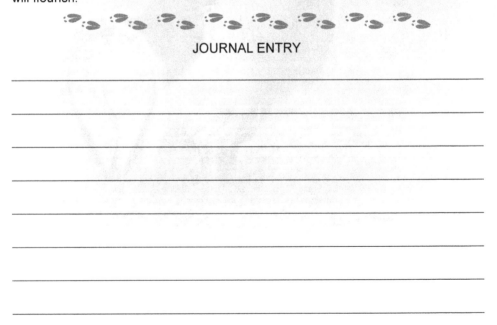

JOURNAL ENTRY

SEPT 26

Proverbs 31
A wife of noble character who can find? She is worth far more than rubies.
[11] Her husband has full confidence in her and lacks nothing of value.
[12] She brings him good, not harm, all the days of her life.

September 26th is my wedding anniversary. I have been blessed with a great wife who loves me and loves the Lord more. She has been a good mother and is a fantastic grandmother.

A very long time ago (35 years + or -) I made the mistake of saying something within ear shot of my wife. I kiddingly told a friend that I had learned that if I was going to be late getting home, I was better off being really late instead of just a little late. If I was really late Linda was worried instead of being mad, when I was just a little late she'd be mad. I was kidding but the one thing that I did learn over the years is that I can help my wife be the woman God called her to be, by serving her without reservation.

Ephesians 5:28-30 [28] So ought men to love their wives as their own bodies. He that loves his wife loves himself.
[29] For no man ever yet hated his own flesh; but nourished and cherished it, even as the Lord the church:
[30] For we are members of his body, of his flesh, and of his bones.

Loving your wife like this is a great long term investment and pays great dividends!

JOURNAL ENTRY

SEPT 27

PREPARED FOR ATTACK

Ephesians 3:10-16

10 Finally, be strong in the Lord and His mighty power. 11 Put on the full armor of God, so that you can take your stand against the devil's schemes. 12 For our struggle is not against flesh and blood, but against the rulers, against the authorities, against the powers of this dark world and against the spiritual forces of evil in the heavenly realms. 13 Therefore put on the full armor of God, so that when the day of evil comes, you may be able to stand your ground, and after you have done everything, to stand. 14 Stand firm then, with the belt of truth buckled around your waist, with the breastplate of righteousness in place, 15 and with your feet fitted with the readiness that comes from the gospel of peace. 16 In addition to all this, take up the shield of faith, with which you can extinguish all the flaming arrows of the evil one.

The Apostle Paul does not write "**IF** the day of evil comes" but "**WHEN** the day to evil comes". We **WILL** be attacked, be sure of that. It may come as a small voice of doubt or as a full out physical attack. These verses give us ways to be prepared.

Verse 16 says to "take up the shield of faith". If we continue to hold tight to this shield of faith it will help us to deflect the lies that Satan shoots at us. Satan will try to divide families, ministries, friendships, ANYTHING that is glorifying God. Do not fall for his lies of doubt and fear. Do not allow Satan to convince you that your worth is anything less than a child of the King.

Remember Philippians 4:13, I can do all things through Christ who strengths me.

Hold tight to the "shield of faith" today.

JOURNAL ENTRY

_____

_____

_____

_____

_____

_____

_____

SEPT 28

Ephesians 3:20-21
20 Now to Him who is able to do immeasurably more than all we ask or imagine, according to His power that is at work within us, 21 to Him be glory in the church and in Christ Jesus throughout all generations, for ever and ever! Amen.

The point here is not merely that God is able to do beyond what we expect. But more amazingly, this power is already at work in us. We don't have to wait for it... Just allow Him to work, in and through us.

What is truly mind blowing here is that God does not fit the limitations of our expectations. If we could only imagine and grasp not only His amazing power, but more importantly His immeasurable love, we would realize that we have a power source that will overcome any issue we face today, tomorrow and forever!

We can equate this to a loaded gun. We can have the most powerful gun in our hands and it can be loaded with powerful ammunition but until we put it to use, it really has no power at all.

God's ways and thoughts are exceedingly beyond our ways and thoughts. God is at work and eager to work in us to achieve His purposes. Allow Him to do this in and through you today... And be amazed.

Lastly, to Him be all the glory. Not me and not you.

JOURNAL ENTRY

SEPT 29

JESUS OUR LORD

Philippians 2:9-11

9 For this reason also, God highly exalted Him, and bestowed on Him the name which is above every name, 10 so that at the name of Jesus every knee will bow, of those who are in heaven and on earth and under the earth, 11 and that every tongue will confess that Jesus Christ is Lord, to the glory of God the Father.

"For this reason," signifies something that was just written. Christ had humbled Himself, to come to earth as a man. But He was also 100% God. There is no question that Jesus is part of the Trinity, our God. Jesus Christ is the Son of the Father. So united are the 3 Persons of the Godhead that when we worship the Son, this glorifies the Father.

Jesus left His place of total glory to come to this dirty, miserable earth to die for you and me. If there has been any question that Christ deservers our total worship, that question has been answered

Lift high the name of Jesus and glorify Him in your life today

JOURNAL ENTRY

SEPT 30

BLIND BUT NOW I SEE

John 9:24-25

So a second time they called the man who had been blind, and said to him, "Give glory to God; we know that this man is a sinner." 25 He then answered, "Whether He is a sinner, I do not know; one thing I do know, that though I was blind, now I see."

This passage is one most of us have heard many, many times. Last night I saw something here I've never seen before. Not only did this man, who was blind from birth receive his physical sight... He received his spiritual sight within minutes.

In verses 35-38 we see him have his eyes opened spiritually.

35 Jesus heard that they had put him out, and finding him, He said, "Do you believe in the Son of Man?" 36 He answered, "Who is He, Lord that I may believe in Him?" 37 Jesus said to him, "You have both seen Him, and He is the one who is talking with you." 38 And he said, "Lord, I believe." And he worshiped Him.

So many times we have our eyes open but we cannot see what God is showing us. Pray that God will clearly show us what He has for us.

JOURNAL ENTRY

OCTOBER

<u>2 Tim 1:7</u>

For God did not give us a spirit of timidity, but a spirit of power, of love and of self-discipline.

OCT 1

EMPTY YOURSELF

Acts 4:31
And when they had prayed, the place where they had gathered together was shaken, and they were all filled with the Holy Spirit and began to speak the word of God with boldness.

There is something special about a crisp fall morning. When you get into the woods for the first cold calm fall morning and take a deep breath the moist cool air completely fills your lungs and actually feels like it fills your whole being. It's a refreshing fulfilling experience that is hard to explain to someone that has never done it. There aren't many feelings like that... Accept to be filled with the Spirit of God.

The words, "to be filled with the Holy Spirit" have been explained differently by different people. But there is one thing that doesn't change... Like filling your lungs with crisp cold air takes emptying your body of the old air, to be filled with the Holy Spirit you need to completely empty yourself of you. There's no room for our own desires, needs or wants, just Gods Spirit.

We've often heard that someone feels empty... We are never empty, we cannot be empty. We are either filled with God's wonderful spirit or we are filled with selfish desires.

Empty yourself of what you desire and allow God to fill you with His sweet spirit

JOURNAL ENTRY

_____
_____
_____
_____
_____
_____
_____
_____

OCT 2

Proverbs 29:1
Whoever remains stiff-necked after many rebukes will suddenly be destroyed, without remedy.

Climbing mountains is hard work. And when you first start it can be very painful. But after time the pain of training your body makes you stronger. This past week my legs (especially my quads) are aching... But I know that the pain will bring future strength. So it is with life. We continually go through painful times. Some of this pain is brought on from sinful decisions. If we turn from that sin and straighten out we become stronger and grow.

Children make many mistakes and will have to be corrected along the way. How often does a child fall while learning to walk? They fall again and again, gathering bumps, bruises and even occasional stitches and maybe even a cast or a splint. Parents are continually correcting, instructing, and gently pushing, until we almost feel sorry for the kids. Growing up is tough! If kids are going to become mature, they have to keep going in spite of mistakes and rebukes. And hopefully someday they will look back on their own childish mistakes and just smile.

Some of the greatest Bible characters committed terrible errors (sins) and had to be rebuked.

* Moses made excuses when God called him to lead Israel out of bondage.
* David committed adultery with Bathsheba and had her husband killed and was rebuked by Nathan.
* Peter denied Jesus three times.
* Paul persecuted Christians before his conversion.
* Thomas doubted Jesus' resurrection.
* All the apostles forsook Jesus when He was arrested and crucified.

Yet all of these are remembered as some of God's greatest servants. Great servants are not people who live without ever sinning, but people who learn from their mistakes and go on to serve God faithfully.

Judas betrayed Jesus and is remembered as a traitor. Peter denied Jesus three times and is remembered as a great apostle. What is the difference? Judas, after betraying Jesus, hung himself. Peter, after denying Jesus, repented and went to work preaching the gospel, healing the sick and saving the lost. So, the pain you are feeling from bad decisions today can help you get to the top of that mountain you will face tomorrow. Learn from your mistakes, bad decisions, errors and sins. Grow from them and God can show you strength to make it to the summit.

Keep Climbing.

OCT 3

FORGIVE AND BE FORGIVEN

Mark 11:25-26
And when you stand praying, forgive, if you have anything against anyone; that your Father also, which is in heaven, may forgive you your trespasses. 26 But if you don't forgive, neither will your Father, which is in heaven, forgive your trespasses.

A few years ago I was driving across one of my leases and a half mile away I saw an orange jacket that wasn't supposed to be there. Driving fast, throwing mud as I went, I raced to cut off the interloper. As I approached the orange jacket that was filled with one of my neighbors, the first words I heard from him were, "you don't have much for brains do you? Driving out there in the mud isn't too smart." In the midst of arguing and more name calling on the trespasser's part, I lost my temper but was able to hold my tongue.

Someone had literally trespassed against me and I can say as my blood pressure stayed up for a long time I didn't forgive the trespass or the name calling right then. However, by the next morning, I had let it go. We all expect to be forgiven by someone else when we've done wrong or hurt them. We also know that Christ died to bring forgiveness to us for our sins. How much more should we forgive those that hurt us?

Christ literally died, not a peaceful death, be a painful, tortured, miserable death on a cross so we could be forgiven. For us to forgive is to "die to self", to give up of our desire to hold something against someone and allow God to take that away from us.

The Apostle Paul wrote to the Philippians in Chapter 3, verse 13, "Brothers and sister, I do not consider myself yet to have taken hold of it. But one thing I do: forgetting what is behind and straining toward what is ahead."

This is the answer, forgetting what is behind you and look to what is in front of you. Move on and press towards the mark for the price of the high calling of God in Christ Jesus. Allow God to take your feelings and holding on to how you've been hurt. Give it all to Him.

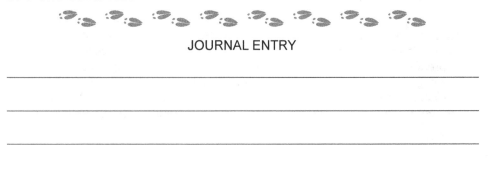

JOURNAL ENTRY

_____

_____

_____

_____

OCT 4

THERE'S POWER IN THE BLOOD

Hebrews 9:22
In fact under the Law almost everything is purified by means of blood, and without the shedding of blood there is neither forgiveness for sin.

To all of my friends it would come as no surprise that I love to hunt... I've spent much of my life hunting or more so taking others hunting. One of my favorite things to do in hunting is trailing/tracking an animal to harvest. A good "blood trail" is an exciting thing. The blood is what brings life to the animal. The "heavier" the trail the better chance for success... WITHOUT BLOOD THERE IS NO LIFE. Any hunter can relate to this.

More than anything else in the body, blood is essential to life. It's what carries the fuel and oxygen to the billions of cells in our bodies. Blood supplies the brain and the heart with the necessary nourishment to function. It also carries carbon dioxide and other waste materials to the digestive system, where they are then removed from the body. Without blood we couldn't keep warm or cool, fight infections, or get rid of our own waste products. Additionally, our very identity, our DNA, is located in our blood.

We must understand this: God is so obsessed with blood because He's so obsessed with life not death. The Israelites while in Egypt put the blood of a pure lamb on their door posts to preserve their lives. They also sacrificed pure animals, by shedding the blood, to receive forgiveness for their sins.

Thank God that today we don't have to do that. Jesus came and gave of himself so that we are cleansed by His blood. Christ's blood was shed to bring us life... He came for that purpose. Death didn't hold Him.

Romans 5:10 For if, while we were God's enemies, we were reconciled to him through the death of his Son, how much more, having been reconciled, shall we be saved through his life!

JOURNAL ENTRY

_____

_____

_____

_____

_____

OCT 5

Titus 2:2-5

Teach the older men to be temperate, worthy of respect, self-controlled, and sound in faith, in love and in endurance. 3 Likewise, teach the older women to be reverent in the way they live, not to be slanderers or addicted to much wine, but to teach what is good. 4 Then they can urge the younger women to love their husbands and children, 5 to be self-controlled and pure, to be busy at home, to be kind, and to be subject to their husbands, so that no one will malign the word of God.

So this morning I'm on my way in for medical tests... nothing of concern but they are a sign of the aging process. It's a point when we start to realize that we are no longer "young". Truly young people don't look at us as "one of them". They look at us in a new (old) light.

So what are we to do? Paul writes to Titus telling him to teach us to be an example to the younger generation. We have an amazing responsibility to teach those coming behind to love the Lord and to live a life worthy of His love.

Joanna Lumley has written, "I've looked forward to being older because you will have that many more miles covered. We mustn't be led into thinking getting old is bad. Growing old is good."

Don't allow your past years to go to waste... God has given you experiences that are only yours and there are younger people that need the knowledge that you've acquired.

I recently read this statement that hits it directly...

Look for someone that can learn from your past. All of us adults were once young. The young have not yet attained adulthood. The young must learn to appreciate the wisdom of elderly people and learn from their life experiences.

JOURNAL ENTRY

OCT 6

I KEEP FALLING IN LOVE WITH HIM

Acts 4:31
And when they had prayed, the place where they had gathered together was shaken, and they were all filled with the Holy Spirit and began to speak the word of God with boldness.

There's nothing like a fresh morning in the mountains. The air feels so great as you take a deep breath and it clears your lungs and somehow seems to clear your mind. That is what the Holy Spirit can do for us. He can work to completely fill us and refresh us.

D.L. Moody said it this way... "You might as well try to see without eyes, hear without ears, or breathe without lungs, as to try to live the Christian life without the Holy Spirit."

There's an old hymn that explains to me what happens when we're filled with the Holy Spirit...

I keep falling in love with Him
Over and over and over and over again

He gets sweeter and sweeter as the days go by
Oh what a love between my Lord and I
I keep falling in love with Him
Over and over and, over and over again

As we fall deeper in love with God, our entire life changes.

Act 1:8 "But ye shall receive power, after that the Holy Ghost is come upon you: and ye shall be witnesses unto me both in Jerusalem, and in all Judaea, and in Samaria, and unto the uttermost part of the earth."

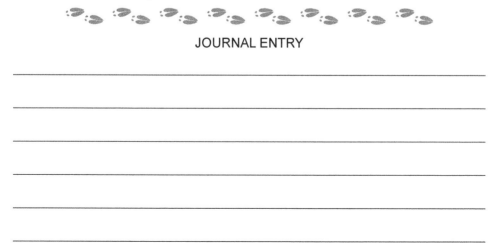

JOURNAL ENTRY

OCT 7

I WANT TO BE JUST LIKE HIM

Ephesians 5:1
Be imitators of God, therefore, as dearly loved children and live a life of love, just as Christ loved us and gave himself up for us as a fragrant offering and sacrifice to God.

Charles Caleb Colton once said "Imitation is the sincerest form of flattery".

That has never been truer than when we imitate God. It's not that God needs to be flattered but we flatter someone we show a desire to be like them. Our young children wear their parent's shoes, try their mother's makeup, and pretend to shave with their daddy... Why, because at a young, very tender age they want to be just like their parent.

Philips, Craig and Dean recorded a song a couple of years ago that tells the story well. The chorus alone is enough to show that they knew the truth.

"Lord I want to be just like you
Cause he wants to be just like me
I want to be a Holy example
For his innocent eyes to see

Help me be a living Bible, Lord
That my little boy can read
I want to be just like you
Cause he wants to be like me"

This is what God wants for us, to desire to be like Him, pure and Holy... Impossible in and of ourselves, but with Christ we can be that person.

Philippians 4:13 I can do all things through Christ who strengthens me.

JOURNAL ENTRY

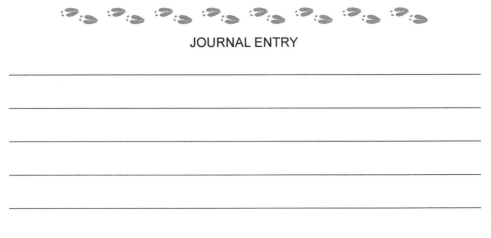

OCT 8

ALLOW GOD IN YOUR BOAT

John 6:18-21

A strong wind was blowing and the waters grew rough. 19 When they had rowed about three or four miles,[a] they saw Jesus approaching the boat, walking on the water; and they were frightened. 20 But he said to them, "It is I; don't be afraid." 21 Then they were willing to take him into the boat, and immediately the boat reached the shore where they were heading.

The disciples had been rowing to high winds and very rough seas and getting nowhere fast. It was dark, they were no doubt somewhat frightened and struggling to reach their destination, without success.

I find it interesting to think on this and compare it to my life. I'm sure those that have a personal relationship with Christ can understand that we so often struggle to achieve a goal or to accomplish something... But, we left God back on the shore, we didn't even invite Him in the boat with us. However, when we finally ask Him for help, to get into the boat with us, the "rowing" is easier and the goal is achieved. This is part of God's grace. I always wonder, why did I leave shore with Him in the first place?

Max Lucado wrote, "The meaning of life, the wasted years of life, the poor choices of life, God answers the mess of life with one word: 'grace'".

JOURNAL ENTRY

OCT 9

NO PROBLEM TOO BIG

Jeremiah 32:17
"Ah Lord GOD, behold, thou hast made the heaven and the earth by thy great power and stretched out arm, and there is nothing too hard for thee:"

I was driving in a pouring rain, the water was running like thin pudding down the road but so far my tires were holding to the mud. Just before heading downhill towards camp I went through a 20 yard long dip in the road. As I tried to come out of it, my tires started to not only spin but started to slide sideways as well. Two more feet and my truck along with Harris and I was going over the edge. I stopped and got out the passenger's side. We called for a ride and then got a come-along cable and attached my truck to the closest tree uphill. I fear that without that cable the truck would have gone over the edge and been destroyed.

Life is quite often like that, when we feel as though there is no way through our trouble and strife, we need to remember this verse. If HE made the heavens and the earth, then HE certainly controls it. "And there is nothing too hard for thee." God is the cable that keeps us from disaster.

Why do we ever doubt that God, in his infinite wisdom, couldn't handle a problem that is fairly meaningless in the face of eternity?

Maybe God is just waiting for us to fully surrender to His will for us.

JOURNAL ENTRY

OCT 10

BE ANXIOUS FOR NOTHING

Philippians 4:6-7
Do not be anxious about anything, but in everything by prayer and supplication with thanksgiving let your requests be made known to God. And the peace of God, which surpasses all understanding, will guard your hearts and your minds in Christ Jesus.

Whew... This can be tough, anxious about nothing? That is far easier said than done. But deep down inside we know that we are able to give our entire load to our Lord and he is more than capable to handle it.

Matthew 6:31-33 explains it very well... 31 So do not worry, saying, 'What shall we eat?' or 'What shall we drink?' or 'What shall we wear?' 32 For the pagans run after all these things, and your heavenly Father knows that you need them. 33 But seek first his kingdom and his righteousness, and all these things will be given to you as well.

King David in the Psalms prayed prayers of supplication all the time when in distress. Daniel, when in trouble with the king, prayed this way, "which one of us can add a day to our lives by worrying?" Actually, we all know that we lose days by worrying. Doctors tell us that worry and stress will shorten our lives.

Give it all over to Him... "And the peace of God, which surpasses all understanding, will guard your hearts and your minds in Christ Jesus."

JOURNAL ENTRY

OCT 11

GOD'S TIMING

Luke 18:1-8

18 Now He was telling them a parable to show that at all times they ought to pray and not to lose heart, 2 saying, "In a certain city there was a judge who did not fear God and did not respect man. 3 There was a widow in that city, and she kept coming to him, saying, 'Give me legal protection from my opponent.' 4 For a while he was unwilling; but afterward he said to himself, 'Even though I do not fear God nor respect man, 5 yet because this widow bothers me, I will give her legal protection, otherwise by continually coming she will wear me out.'" 6 And the Lord said, "Hear what the unrighteous judge said; 7 now, will not God bring about justice for His elect who cry to Him day and night, and will He delay long over them? 8 I tell you that He will bring about justice for them quickly. However, when the Son of Man comes, will He find faith on the earth?"

There are so many times that we feel that we are wronged and we cry out to God for justice. We wonder, "Why isn't God doing something?" These verses say that God will bring quick justice. But quick in our human thinking and quick in God's thinking are two different things... Remember, to God a day is like a 1000 years. Who are we to second guess the Lord's timing?

I once attended a Promise Keepers event where at the end of the first day several hundred men went forward to invite Christ into their lives. The next morning from the stage we were told a story of an 88 year old gentleman that had come forward was there because his son had invited him. He and his first wife had gotten divorced 40+ years earlier and yet his ex-wife had never quit praying for his salvation. She prayed daily for over 40 years and finally He turned his life over to Jesus. Now that is waiting on God.

What we really need to take from this passage is that God does care and He does listen and respond. He wants me to come to Him trusting and believing that He does love me and will take care of my needs... In His timing!

JOURNAL ENTRY

OCT 12

THE GOD OF ALL LIGHT AND ALL GOOD

Psalm 19:1-6

1 The heavens declare the glory of God; the skies proclaim the work of his hands. 2 Day after day they pour forth speech; night after night they reveal knowledge. 3 They have no speech, they use no words; no sound is heard from them. 4 Yet their voice goes out into all the earth, their words to the ends of the world. In the heavens God has pitched a tent for the sun. 5 It is like a bridegroom coming out of his chamber, like a champion rejoicing to run his course. 6 It rises at one end of the heavens and makes its circuit to the other; nothing is deprived of its warmth.

Not everyone gets to see such spectacular sights as I have in my life. I've gotten to see many mountain tops and seashores, fights between bull elk, grizzly bears and trophy whitetail bucks, tremendous storms come across the Bearing Sea with waves taller than most houses and many more glorious observations. We can all see the sun rise and set every day, we can see a rainbow, a lightning storm, etc. The Psalmist makes it clear here in this passage that the Glory of God is evident in everything that we see (and don't see) everyday. Our Heavenly Father is truly the Father of all light and all good. How blessed we are to know him and to be a part of His family.

His glory and majesty is evident in all His creation. Let's never forget how truly blessed we are and how good He is.

JOURNAL ENTRY

OCT 13

WE BELONG TO THE LORD

Romans 14:8
If we live, we live for the Lord; and if we die, we die for the Lord. So, whether we live or die, we belong to the Lord.

This is an extremely strong verse... No matter what happens in our lives, in our living or dying, we belong to the Lord.

But so many of us live like we don't trust him with our lives, we act like we are afraid that God is somehow wanting to use us like a big voodoo doll, for his own entertainment. Trust that He wants nothing but the best for us. Consider spending part of each day praising God for all that He has done for us, from the first breath in the morning to the last at the end of the day, the blessings are everywhere -we just have to look for them. If we truly praise Him day in and day out we will soon come to a place where we realize that God has our best in mind all the time. His blessings are never ending and we can fully trust in him.

Let's live as though we know this, all the time!

JOURNAL ENTRY

OCT 14

CALL OUT TO GOD

Psalm 86:4-7

4 Bring joy to your servant, Lord, for I put my trust in you. 5 You, Lord, are forgiving and good, abounding in love to all who call to you. 6 Hear my prayer, Lord; listen to my cry for mercy. 7 When I am in distress, I call to you, because you answer me.

I remember when I was younger and first married. We lived one and a half hours from my parents. After a visit they would always say, "Make sure you call as soon as you get home." When my kids grew up, I told them the same thing. That's what loving parents do.

The Lord is just like that with us, He wants to know that we are OK. He will always hear us and answer our call, he loves us that much.

When we are in distress and we call to him, he answers. Like a father to their child that has fallen and gotten hurt, He comes to our aid.

Use the privilege of that most loved child... Call to Him and He will be there to comfort and love.

JOURNAL ENTRY

Trophies of Grace

OCT 15

EVERYTHING UNDER HIS CONTROL

Ecclesiastes 3:1-11

1 There is a time for everything, and a season for every activity under the heavens: 2 a time to be born and a time to die, a time to plant and a time to uproot, 3 a time to kill and a time to heal, a time to tear down and a time to build, 4 a time to weep and a time to laugh, a time to mourn and a time to dance, 5 a time to scatter stones and a time to gather them, a time to embrace and a time to refrain from embracing, 6 a time to search and a time to give up, a time to keep and a time to throw away, 7 a time to tear and a time to mend, a time to be silent and a time to speak, 8 a time to love and a time to hate, a time for war and a time for peace. 9 What do workers gain from their toil? 10 I have seen the burden God has laid on the human race. 11 He has made everything beautiful in its time. He has also set eternity in the human heart; yet no one can fathom what God has done from beginning to end.

I often wonder why God created things such as ticks, mosquitoes or biting flies. Why does He allow all these things to exist that mess with our fun while hunting or fishing. Life would seem to be so much better without the hardships of life. I'm sure he had a reason... But I still wonder. However, I need not worry because I can trust that all that God has done has a reason and a season. He speaks and everything falls into place just as He pleases.

God, thank you that we can trust that you have everything under your control and that we can trust that you love us enough to make sure that everything good is from you.

JOURNAL ENTRY

OCT 16

THE LOVE OF CHRIST

John 21:15-17

15 When they had finished eating, Jesus said to Simon Peter, "Simon son of John, do you love me more than these?" "Yes, Lord," he said, "you know that I love you." Jesus said, "Feed my lambs." 16 Again Jesus said, "Simon son of John, do you love me?" He answered, "Yes, Lord, you know that I love you." Jesus said, "Take care of my sheep." 17 The third time he said to him, "Simon son of John, do you love me?" Peter was hurt because Jesus asked him the third time, "Do you love me?" He said, "Lord, you know all things; you know that I love you." Jesus said, "Feed my sheep.

This was the first time that Peter talked to Christ after the resurrection. Peter had climbed out of the boat and ran to Jesus. It had only been a few days since Peter had denied he even knew Christ.

First, Peter had confidence that Jesus loved him enough to take him back. Second, Jesus loved Peter so much that He wanted him to run back to Him.

When we sin and move away from God, He is longing for us to run back to Him. Instead of running away and hiding when we've messed things up, God longs for us to come back into His arms for His comfort.

Next time you fall into sin don't go into hiding, go into God's love.

JOURNAL ENTRY

_____

_____

_____

_____

_____

_____

_____

_____

OCT 17

IN SEASON AND OUT

2 Timothy 4:2
Preach the word; be prepared in season and out of season; correct, rebuke and encourage—with great patience and careful instruction.

As hunters we all know of the armies of guys that pull into an area the night before season and hunt a few days and go back home, generally without success. Then there are those of us that live the hunt year round. If we aren't hunting were studying maps, hanging stands, searching for shed antlers etc... It is a year-long endeavor. We're all in.

Can you imagine how God could use us if our spiritual life was as intense as our hunting or fishing life, if we were all in for Him? If we were "prepared in season and out of season", imagine what God could do through each of us.

God probably isn't going to call you to leave the outdoors, but He might. More likely God is calling you to give Him more passion, more dedication and more love for Him and His work than you do for anything and everything else in your life.

In Psalm 37:4 the writer tells us this... 4 Delight thyself also in the Lord: and he shall give thee the desires of thine heart.

There's a great promise in that verse. If we delight in the Lord, He will give us the desires of our heart. When our hearts align with His, our desires become His desires. Go all in.

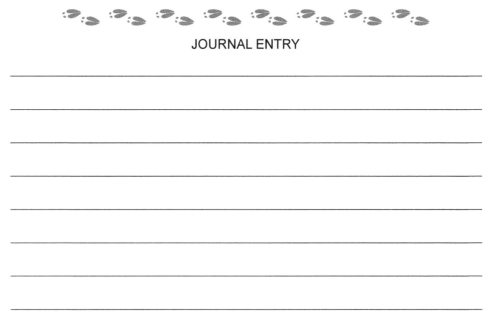

JOURNAL ENTRY

_____

_____

_____

_____

_____

_____

_____

OCT 18

John 16:33
These things I have spoken unto you, that in me ye might have peace.
In the world ye shall have tribulation: but be of good cheer;
I have overcome the world.

God makes it clear that we can be sure that we will face tribulation, nothing new. The church has been living through tribulation since its birth. The second thing is that Jesus does not want us to focus on tribulation, but on Him. Jesus has overcome the world, but if we put our focus on tribulation, the world can easily overcome us with worry and fear.

The third and fourth things are major points for us. HE tells us that even though we will have tribulation we can have His perfect peace; HE also tells us that we are to be of good cheer. These two things, perfect peace and good cheer, should dominate our thinking, our speech, and our attitudes... Always!

Nothing in this world has the power to take from you what Jesus wants to give you.....Peace. It is Jesus who is working out His plan in our lives. He alone has all the power, all the peace, and all the good cheer you will ever need.

One last thing... The verse doesn't say I will overcome the world... But "I have overcome the world", it's already done. So take his perfect peace and live victoriously.

JOURNAL ENTRY

___

___

___

___

___

___

___

___

OCT 19

HE KNOWS MY HEART AND KNOWS MY NAME

Isaiah 65:24
I will answer them before they even call to me. While they are still talking about their needs, I will go ahead and answer their prayers!

When I was very young I was taught that attributes of God. It is a pretty impressive list. But as humans, how do we fully understand the "all" in things like all-knowing, all-powerful, all-knowing, all-loving, etc?

If we truly believe God and believe that He is what He says He is, then we know that we have a God that can know what our heart is and respond before we even think to ask. He knows our hurts and our joys, our wishes, our needs and our love. Without speaking a word, He knows.

FRANCESCA BATTISTELLI sings a song, HE KNOWS MY NAME. You can use HEART in place of NAME.

Spent today in a conversation
In the mirror face to face with
somebody less than perfect
I wouldn't choose me first if
I was looking for a champion
In fact I'd understand if

You picked everyone before me
But that's just not my story
True to who You are
You saw my heart
and made
Something out of nothing

This doesn't let us off the hook for coming to him, but when we have a need, He is there for us. Let your heart cry out to Him... He will hear it and answer. He knows your name and He knows your heart!

JOURNAL ENTRY

___

___

___

___

OCT 20

HE DOES THE IMPOSSIBLE... ALL THE TIME

Jeremiah 18:14
Does the snow of Lebanon ever vanish from its rocky slopes?
Do its cool waters from distant sources ever stop flowing?

Our God is a God of wonders. Who can really understand how our world or our universe works? We hear fools try to explain how or why certain things within our world do what they do... But I don't think we can answer the question, why.

There are rivers on the Cielo Vista Ranch that if you follow them to their source, you will find water pouring out of a rock... Not just any rock, but a rock at 12,000 ft + in elevation. There is no normal water table at that elevation, no snow pack above it to melt down into the rocks. To the human mind this cannot happen.

I took a friend to see this a year ago; this friend runs a water system for a small town. We drove up to a place where we could glass to the water springing from the rocks. His words were, "that isn't possible". To the human mind it is impossible, but to God this is like child play.

I love having a relationship with a God who is in the business of doing the impossible. It gives me hope every day.

JOURNAL ENTRY

OCT 21

A GREAT HOPE

Proverbs 24:19-20
19 Do not fret because of evildoers or be envious of the wicked,
20 for the evildoer has no future hope, and the lamp of the wicked will be snuffed out.

I know that I struggle when I see someone that is apparently succeeding in life that is doing it by ungodly means. I want to ask God, "Why do you let this happen"?

Then I remember verse 20 "for the evildoer has no future hope". There are times that God allows us to struggle as He knows that this will build us into what He wants us to be. Those that don't know Him don't have a hope beyond this life.

MATTHEW 5:45 45 so that you may be sons of your Father who is in heaven; for He causes His sun to rise on the evil and the good, and sends rain on the righteous and the unrighteous.

Our God is a fair and just God... He gives everyone the same chance to know Him in a very personal way. For those that have that relationship, there is tremendous hope... For those that don't know Him, there is just today.

Do you have this hope?

JOURNAL ENTRY

OCT 22

WE'RE WATCHED

1 Peter 3:17-18
17 For it is better, if it is God's will, to suffer for doing good than for doing evil.
18 For Christ also suffered once for sins, the righteous for the unrighteous,
to bring you to God. He was put to death in the body but made alive in the Spirit.

Back in high school and since, I was, at times, ridiculed for not attending the parties that others were throwing on the weekends. Or for not talking the way that others talked. I was somewhat of a joke to many others in our school. At the time I felt bothered a little by this. However, I was also proud of what I was representing.

Verse 17 confirms that it was better to suffer for making this stand. It wasn't fun, but it was right.

Many years after high school, while at a class reunion, a woman started up a conversation with my wife. She told her that she had always respected me for standing for what I thought was right.

If you believe it or not, people are watching... They notice when you stand up and suffer for what you believe. We are all called to make a stand.... Do it humbly as if you are being watched and judged for Christ.

JOURNAL ENTRY

OCT 23

WHERE IS YOUR DELIGHT

Psalm 119:143
Trouble and distress have come upon me, but your commands give me delight.

I find it funny that David writes that trouble and distress have "come upon me"... We don't have to go looking for trouble; it will come to us without looking for it. We double our "trouble and distress" when we move away from the Lord and dabble on the edge of sin.

Romans 6:6, tells us, "We should no longer be slaves to sin".

Charles Spurgeon wrote about this... "Dear Christian, why are you flirting with sin? Hasn't it cost you enough already? Will you continue to play with fire even after you've been burn? After having been caught in the jaws of the lion, will you now step a second time into his den? Don't be so foolish."

I've always wondered how, in the world of hunting, that poachers found any enjoyment, any pride in taking an illegal animal. How do they brag about a trophy or thrill in the harvest of any animal? I can't imagine delighting in anything that was done illegally.

There is an old saying, "they are good who delight in good things, and they are evil who delight in evil things."

Where is your delight today?

JOURNAL ENTRY

OCT 24

GOING ON A WALKABOUT

Colossians 2:6-7
⁶ So then, just as you received Christ Jesus as Lord, continue to live your lives in him, ⁷ rooted and built up in him, strengthened in the faith as you were taught, and overflowing with thankfulness.

In the aboriginal people in Australia, males go on a "walk-about" as part of their rite of passage into manhood. They travel alone across their land to become familiar with it and thus a part of it... The Greek word for live (peripateo) literally means to "walk about." According to Paul, our trust in the gospel of God's grace through Christ results in a "walk about" in him; we become familiar with him and a part of him.

So as we experience God's love and explore His relationship with us, we learn more and more about our lives in Him. This is a lifetime thing, not just a one-time thing.

Go on a spiritual "WALK ABOUT"

JOURNAL ENTRY

OCT 25

WHEN YOU ARE LOW, GET LOWER

Matthew 15:25
But she came and began to bow down before Him, saying, "Lord, help me!"

This woman that came to ask Jesus for help had a daughter that was seriously demon possessed. The bible doesn't say how old the daughter or the woman was but no matter how old they were any mother would be severely distressed and down in that situation. What she did was to bow down before Christ and ask for His help.

John 15:7 says, "If you remain in me and my words remain in you, ask whatever you wish, and it will be done for you."

If we "remain in Christ", that is keeping Him first in our lives and giving Him "Lordship" over our lives, He will answer us in our time of need.

Remain in Him and when we are low and need help, lower ourselves further and ask and it will be given.

JOURNAL ENTRY

OCT 26

Hebrews 12:28
Therefore, since we are receiving a kingdom that cannot be shaken, let us be thankful, and so worship God acceptably with reverence and awe,

We live in a world that is constantly changing... Countries fall, new ones rise up. Thinking back on Sept 11th, this was the first time since 1918 that an actual "military" attack was brought against the US on our mainland, so few if any of those living remember that. In 2011 we were shaken as a country... It was frightening.

God has given His children a kingdom that will never be shaken. We can be assured of that. What an amazing gift... No worries for the future.

Daniel 2:24 tells it again of what is to come... 24 "In the time of those kings, the God of heaven will set up a kingdom that will never be destroyed, nor will it be left to another people. It will crush all those kingdoms and bring them to an end, but it will itself endure forever.

JOURNAL ENTRY

OCT 27

1 Chronicles 16:15-17

15 He remembers his covenant forever, the promise he made, for a thousand generations, 16 the covenant he made with Abraham, the oath he swore to Isaac. 17 He confirmed it to Jacob as a decree, to Israel as an everlasting covenant:

It's hard to find loyalty in today's world. Businesses aren't built on loyalty like they used to be. Good friendships are hard to find and hold... No matter how hard you try life isn't the same and we've learned that people can't be counted on, (With exceptions of course).

But we know that God can always be counted on. No matter what we do, God will always keep His promise. His promise to protect and bless the Israelites has been held for thousands of years. And in Jeremiah 29:11 He promises loyalty to us what He said, "I know the thoughts that I think toward you, saith the Lord, thoughts of peace, and not of evil, to give you an expected end.

When we find that we can't count on anyone or anything else 100% of the time, we know that we can count on Him.

JOURNAL ENTRY

OCT 28

Romans 8:9
"You, however, are controlled not by the sinful nature but by the Spirit, if the Spirit of God lives in you. And if anyone does not have the Spirit of Christ, he does not belong to Christ".

There's a strange ailment that falls on men, women and children of ages old enough to hunt. I've seen it take grown men that are as strong as an ox and turn them into Jello. Men have been known to draw their bows and hold at full draw while a bull elk walks by at under 20 yards and then do it again when the bull is called back past, forgetting the whole time to release the arrow.

This ailment is known as "Buck Fever". Most everyone that hunts has some level of this debilitating sickness at one time or another. It generally leaves you sick to your stomach, babbling incoherently, shaking uncontrollably and with an inability to stand.

Nevertheless, as powerful as "buck fever" is, there is something much stronger at work in us. This power occasionally erupts and injures anyone that is close to us. The power that I am talking about doesn't just affect hunters but unfortunately comes for all of us.

The power that is in all of us is our sin nature. Occasionally we allow it to get out of control and when it does it can do considerable damage to our life and the lives of those close to us.

But, there is great news, God didn't leave us without hope to defeat the sin nature within us. He sent the Holy Spirit to fight within and alongside us to defeat that nature. Once we have the Holy Spirit, the Apostle Paul tells us that we, "however, are controlled not by the sinful nature but by the Spirit, if the Spirit of God lives in us".

Take control, allow God's Holy Spirit to drive out the sinful nature.

JOURNAL ENTRY

_____

_____

_____

_____

_____

OCT 29

YOU ARE IMPORTANT TO SOMEONE

John 3:16
For God so loved the world that he gave his one and only Son,
that whoever believes in him shall not perish but have eternal life.

Many of us have wanted to be a TV personality, rock star, pro athlete etc... For me it was professional hunter. We all want to be important, to be loved, needed and admired. But I want to tell you, if you are a parent, a grandparent or a son or daughter you are already the most important person in the world to someone. More importantly, you mean so much to God that he gave his only son to die for you.

Think about it for a second, if you were the only person here on earth, God would have given his son to be tortured and put to death to give you a chance to live... You are worth that much. There are over fifteen billion stars in the Milky Way galaxy, which is one of million if not billions of galaxies, which also have billions of stars. If we think about how small we are compared to all of this, yet we are loved enough for God to send His Son to die just for any one of us.

If you don't know Jesus in a very personal way, He is waiting for you. Remember, He gave up His life just for you. Make a choice to live for Him. The eternal benefits are amazing.

JOURNAL ENTRY

October

OCT 30

2 Peter 1:3-4

3 His divine power has given us everything we need for a godly life through our knowledge of him who called us by his own glory and goodness. 4 Through these he has given us his very great and precious promises, so that through them you may participate in the divine nature, having escaped the corruption in the world caused by evil desires.

I read a story about Crowfoot, the chief of the Blackfoot Indians in southern Alberta, Canada. Crowfoot gave the Canadian Pacific Railroad permission to cross the Blackfoot land from Medicine Hat to Calgary. In return, the railroad gave Crowfoot a lifetime pass to ride on the railway. He put it in a leather case and wore it around his neck for the rest of his life. But there is no evidence that he ever used it to travel anywhere on the Canadian Pacific trains.

We may think that the neglect to use his pass is a terrible waste, but many Christians are just like him, they don't take advantage for themselves of the unlimited promises of God. They may put them up on display, but they practically never actually use God's promises in their daily lives.

We are God's children; we need to call on Him when we have needs not just when we feel we can't do it on our own — for all needs, always. He is available 24/7 to care for us in any situation.

This is a great promise made to His children. Are you His child? Then put it in to practice. If you're not His child, then make that right first.

JOURNAL ENTRY

Trophies of Grace

OCT 31

BEHIND THE MASK

Proverbs 12:22
The Lord detests lying lips, but he delights in men who are truthful.

The doorbell sounded and I faked a fearful scream as I opened the door. There in front of me was a little person, maybe three feet tall with a rubber mask with an eye half out, broken teeth and a big nose. The mask was surrounded by black and purple hair. I exclaimed that I really was scared and I dropped a couple of Tootsie Rolls in the plastic orange pumpkin.

The mask reminded me of how we often hide behind a mask with a smile on it. We do our best to conceal our pain and emotional suffering by wearing a mask that entertains others. When we are asked how are we doing, we answer ok, great or fine, yet inside we are often miserable.

Masks are stuffy, binding and often ugly. It is hard to breathe when the mask is on. When we decided to slip the mask off the air is fresher and the view is clearer. God has put others around us to support us when we are in need of help.

Spencer Johnson has been quoted as saying,

"Integrity is telling myself the truth. And honesty is telling the truth to other people."

Speak the truth with honesty

JOURNAL ENTRY

_____

_____

_____

_____

_____

_____

_____

_____

NOVEMBER

Ephesians 3:20

Now to him who is able to do immeasurably more than all we ask or imagine, according to his power that is at work within us,

NOV 1

SET APART

1 Peter 2:9
But you are a chosen race, a royal priesthood, a holy nation, a people for his own possession, that you may proclaim the Excellencies of him who called you out of darkness into his marvelous light.

Yesterday morning I was blessed with the chance of a lifetime... Linda and I were hunting deer in South Dakota with great friends. In the area we were hunting others had been seeing a drop tine whitetail and I was hoping to bump into him. The first morning of the season was great, with deer moving all around. Two hours after daylight the drop tine buck showed up and I was so blessed to harvested him. So what? For most deer hunters a buck with drop tine antlers is a type of "Holy Grail". These deer are estimated to be 1 in a 1000. They truly are "set apart" in the world of trophy bucks.

Those of us that are Christians are "set apart" from the rest of the world. We are, as Peter said it, "a royal priesthood." How many of us live up to this title in life. When the world sees us, do we look like we are different and a part of God's family? Or can they not see anything special in us? Are we like everyone else or are we seen as just "one of the guys or girls." We need to be "in this world but not of this world."

The apostle Paul declared himself, "special" in Romans 1:1, when he introduced himself as,

"Paul, a servant of Christ Jesus, called to be an apostle, set apart for the gospel of God."

Are you just a "typical" worldly person, or are you set apart as a trophy for your Lord?

Be set apart

JOURNAL ENTRY

___

___

___

___

___

November

NOV 2

Romans 8:23
...we ourselves, who have the first fruits of the Spirit, groan inwardly as we wait eagerly for our adoption as sons, the redemption of our bodies"

The last few days have been miserable... I've got one of the worst colds I've ever experienced. REALLY SICK, yet I had a lot of work to do prior to going hunting this week. I pushed through with the anticipation of two of my favorite hunts coming up. This morning we are heading west to spend time with some great friends in South Dakota for a hunt and then back home for the opener of Michigan's gun season.

While getting excited about this time I started to consider how much I anticipate the Second coming of Jesus Christ, I realized that my longing for these hunts should pale in comparison to my eagerness for the return of my Savior. I wondered how I could spend so much time looking forward to earthly joys and give little thought to the event that represents the culmination of human history.

When Jesus returns to the earth, he will avenge evil, free the oppressed, and reward his followers. His coming will eventually bring an end to all suffering, death, and even the presence of sin. And we will come face to face with the One our soul has been longing for, the One who died for us.

John wrote Jesus' words when HE talked about what to anticipate... John 14:2-3 In my Father's house are many mansions: if it were not so, I would have told you. I go to prepare a place for you. (3) And if I go and prepare a place for you, I will come again, and receive you unto myself; that where I am, there ye may be also.

God wants us to live each day in anticipation of the event that will mean the exchange of my earthly body for a new imperishable one, and our removal from a temporary fallen world to an eternal home. All of my struggles and trials seem small when compared to the glory of my future as God's child.

I can't wait!

JOURNAL ENTRY

_____

_____

_____

_____

NOV 3

2 Corinthians 5:17
Therefore if any man be in Christ, he is a new creature:
old things are passed away; behold, all things are become new.

"There's fresh snow this morning" I said to Linda, as I glanced out the window into the predawn gray today. Linda moaned and rolled over. I guess growing up in the UP of Michigan you might assume that we would be a cold weather, winter type people. In reality, winter is something I have never looked forward to.

It seems like all the life and energy of the summer dwindles away as birds fly south, and insects disappear. The days become shorter, and even the bright sun doesn't seem as bright or as warm. Instead, with every second you stay outside you grow colder and colder.

Yet today, something else crossed my mind. There really isn't anything like the first snowfall, which leaves the ground a fluffy pure white, free from any dirt or debris. Immediately, my mood shifted from one of coldness and bitterness, to one of awe for what God can do with any situation.

While the winter may not be as warm as the summer, or have the same characteristics, God makes it special and wonderful in its own way. The same way He does with all of us. But regardless, God makes all things anew, clean and beautiful in His (and our) site. In Romans 8:28 we see that He takes our past situation, and makes it work out for His glory.

Today, remember how God has changed and improved your life. Remember the power that He holds, power to take any situation and make it good. And when you see someone who needs God, think just that... and then share His love story with them.

Godly change (like the season) is always good.

JOURNAL ENTRY

NOV 4

LET YOUR YES BE YES

Matthew 5:37
But let your 'Yes' be 'Yes,' and your 'No' be 'No.' For whatever is more than these is from the evil one.

Last night we sat around the table with a couple of friends. Somehow the conversation turned to politics. I mentioned that I felt that what we are seeing in our world and country today has been foretold and leading to what many call the "end times." One friend didn't understand what I was saying and questioned at length. He said he just didn't know how you can believe all that is written in the Bible.

We talked about the Bible being God's word. He said, "but it was written by men." I tried to explain that I believe 100% that it was inspired by God. This went on for quite some time.

Early this morning he mentioned to me that his real problem that makes him question the Bible is this; "if the Bible is written by men, then I can't believe all of it, I know too many "Christians" (his quotation marks) that have said one thing to me and done the opposite ".

This made me realize that the world is watching us more than ever. We have to continue to be diligent in our walk both in public and in private. To be a "Christian" literally means to be "Christ-like." So how Christ-like are you while in the world? How are your business dealings? If you commit to somebody for something, do you follow through? Can people trust you 100% of the time?

In the Book of Numbers chapter 30 it talks of keeping your word... Verse 2,

"If a man vows a vow to the Lord, or swears an oath to bind himself by a pledge, he shall not break his word. He shall do according to all that proceeds out of his mouth."

The world is watching, let your "yes be yes."

JOURNAL ENTRY

_____

_____

_____

_____

_____

NOV 5

SPEAKING WELL

James 3:3-6

If we put bits into horses' mouths to make them obey us, we can guide their whole bodies as well. 4 And look at ships! They are so big that it takes strong winds to drive them, yet they are steered by a tiny rudder wherever the helmsman directs. 5 In the same way, the tongue is a small part of the body, yet it can boast of great achievements. A huge forest can be set on fire by a little flame. 6 The tongue is a fire, a world of evil. Placed among the parts of our bodies, the tongue contaminates the whole body and sets on fire the course of life, and is itself set on fire by hell.

There isn't much that I enjoy more in the outdoors than calling elk, deer and turkeys. Talking to animals and getting them in close. One time in the mountains of North Central Colorado I had a good bull elk coming my way when I tried to make one more call to "finish the deal". The sound that came out of the call was nothing like the one that was in my head and it ended the hunt short. Instead of speaking well, I used the call in a bad way.

How often we catch ourselves speaking badly of someone when we could have just as easily spoken positively or said nothing at all. We are given the ability to speak and the freedom to use this ability, yet we so often abuse it.

When we learn to hold our tongue or speak blessings we will find that we receive blessing as well.

Start practicing uplifting speech and verbal blessings... We will be amazed at how it will change our lives.

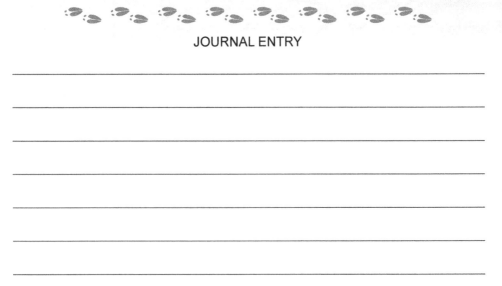

JOURNAL ENTRY

_____

_____

_____

_____

_____

_____

NOV 6

SWEET REST

Mark 6:31
"Then, because so many people were coming and going that they did not even have a chance to eat, he said to them, "Come with me by yourselves to a quiet place and get some rest."

For many people there is nothing better than a quick nap in the afternoon. Some like a 5 minute quick snooze while other people have to sleep for an hour to get rested. Most of my life neither kind of naps were possible. Except for when I have been sick I can count on both hands the times I've napped in the last 20 years. Until this year... I've finally learned the joy of napping and sweet rest.

God gives us rest if we seek Him out and find our rest in Him. He allows our spirit to find rest and comfort.

Tomorrow I will head out for a couple days of rest thanks to a few good friends. They saw the need and blessed me with the opportunity. I don't have to feel as though I'm missing out on anything... I can close my eyes and regain some strength.

The great hockey player of the 1900's, Gordie Howe, gave his all on the ice. He explains effort and restful reward like this... "You find that you have peace of mind and can enjoy yourself, get more sleep, and rest when you know that it was a one hundred percent effort that you gave—win or lose."

So it is with the life of a Christian. When we give our all for God, we know that we will be rewarded with the rest we deserve... But like salvation, we need to just accept that gift and allow rest to come over us.

All of us need a rest, there is no shame in it. Allow yourself the pleasure of a renewing of your body and mind. Work hard in what God has called you to, but then take the time to refresh so you can again move forward with strength.

Hebrews 4:11 Let us, therefore, make every effort to enter that rest, so that no one will perish by following their example of disobedience.

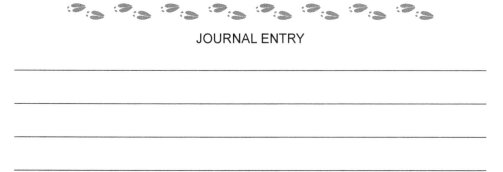

JOURNAL ENTRY

_____

_____

_____

_____

NOV 7

WEARY WITH SORROW? THERE'S HOPE!

Psalm 119:28
My soul is weary with sorrow; strengthen me according to your word.

"Weary with sorrow"... How often our souls feel this, how often we are at a point of being so emotionally weary that we just can't even get out of bed... It's at this time that we are most open to God changing us, for Him to fill us with what He wants in us.

William Faulkner once wrote, "Given the choice between the experience of pain and nothing, I would choose pain."

Why would we choose pain over nothing? God uses pain and sorrow in our lives to show us His greatness. When we are so low that we just don't see a way up out of the mud puddle of this life, we are suddenly open to what God has for us.

In Jeremiah 18:3-4, we see the potter (God) and the clay (us)

"Then I went down to the potter's house, and, behold, he made a vessel on the wheel. And the vessel that he made of clay was damaged in the hand of the potter: so he made it again another vessel, as seemed good to the potter to make it."

If we are the clay in God's hands, then we know that no matter how damaged or broken we become, God can make something beautiful and useful from our lives if we allow Him to do so.

By definition, clay is nothing more than any earth that forms a paste with water and hardens when heated or dried. If you are feeling low and filled with sorrow and pain... Look up, even if we see ourselves or our situation as hopeless and nothing more than earthly "mud". Allow the Potter to rework your life, to change your perspective.

Become a vessel for God.

JOURNAL ENTRY

NOV 8

NOTHING BUT THE BLOOD OF JESUS!

Hebrews 9:22
In fact, the law requires that nearly everything be cleansed with blood, and without the shedding of blood there is no forgiveness.

Blood is an amazing thing... In the physical and spiritual world both, the "lack" of blood means death. In the spiritual world the "loss" of blood means life.

I've written before that I love to blood trail animals. For a hunter, the bigger the trail, the more exciting the "track". Christ's blood is just the opposite... Only by the loss of His blood do we have hope for life, eternal life.

More than anything else in the body, blood is essential to life. It's what carries the fuel and oxygen to the billions of cells in our bodies. Blood supplies the brain and the heart with the necessary nourishment to function. It also carries waste materials to the digestive system, where they are then removed from the body. Without blood we couldn't keep warm or cool, fight infections, or get rid of our own waste products. Additionally, our very identity—our DNA—is located in our blood.

Blood is what gives life, period! Both physical and spiritual life is dependent on Blood.

"For the life of the flesh is in the blood" Leviticus 17:11

If you are counting on ANYTHING else to get you through life, both now and the afterlife, you are going to be shocked by what you find...

NOTHING but the blood of Jesus!

JOURNAL ENTRY

NOV 9

SUBMISSION TO THE DIVINE WILL

2 Peter 1:5-7
And beside this, giving all diligence, add to your faith virtue; and to virtue knowledge; And to knowledge temperance; and to temperance patience; and to patience godliness; And to godliness brotherly kindness; and to brotherly kindness charity.

These are all great attributes and right in the very middle is "Patience". This is one quality that can only be acquired by persistence and endurance. It is a drill that you have to do over and over and over again!

The original Webster's dictionary offers this definition of patience: "the suffering of afflictions, pain, toil, calamity, provocation or other evil, with a calm, unruffled temper; endurance without murmuring or fretfulness, from a kind of heroic pride, or from a Christian submission to the divine will."

Reading the definition two things really jumped out at me... first, "endurance without murmuring." I can get so frustrated sitting in a construction zone or waiting for my family to get ready to go somewhere... counting the wasted minutes when I could have been doing something else (maybe even something useful)! Yet, what an opportunity for me to use the delay to work on my patience! I need to stop murmuring.

The second thing that really hit me was, "a Christian submission to the divine will." WOW!!! I fail miserably at times with this. Read it again..."a Christian submission to the divine will." How many times are we placed in a difficult position, or forced to deal with an "impossible" situation or perhaps, an "impossible" person? These circumstances are always opportunities to grow in patience – or to learn to submit to God's providential will, and often, to minister in some special way.

Is your patience being tested today? Great! Remember, in 1 Cor. 13:4 Paul wrote that love is (first of all) patient. The Lord is training you toward godliness... and godliness is moving toward perfect love. With so much work to be done, He really wants to work patience into your character now. He wants to perfect your love, and with it to transform the world around you for His glory!

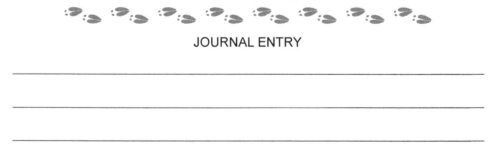

JOURNAL ENTRY

NOV 10

HOPE IN DISAPPOINTMENT

Romans 5:2-6

Through him we have also obtained access by faith into this grace in which we stand, and we rejoice in hope of the glory of God. More than that, we rejoice in our sufferings, knowing that suffering produces endurance, and endurance produces character, and character produces hope, and hope does not put us to shame, because God's love has been poured into our hearts through the Holy Spirit who has been given to us. For while we were still weak, at the right time Christ died for the ungodly.

Life is full of disappointments... Period!

Those verses and that statement say it all... We "rejoice in our suffering" and, "For while we were still weak, at the right time Christ died for the ungodly."

But how often do we rejoice in our suffering? I have to confess, I don't so it very often.

Sometimes disappointment can't be overcome, only endured. In moments like that it's important to remember that we have hope on our side. Hope in Christ's love, hope for better days to come, the hope to maybe even try again. So when the storms of life come your way don't let yourself be troubled, instead pick yourself up and remember with God there will always be hope.

There is hope in disappointment.

JOURNAL ENTRY

NOV 11

TIE IT ON YOUR HEART

Deuteronomy 11:18-19
Fix these words of mine in your hearts and minds; tie them as symbols on your hands and bind them on your foreheads. 19 Teach them to your children, talking about them when you sit at home and when you walk along the road, when you lie down and when you get up.

All of us that hunt have heard the stories of someone pulling their bow or rifle up into a tree stand and have the rope break or the knot come undone. I once watched my favorite rifle free fall 20' to the base of a large spruce tree. It is a sick feeling. I've got a friend that won't hunt one of my stands anymore because he saw his Mathews Bow clatter down the rungs of the tree stand.

Our hunting equipment is precious to many of us and we treat it like our babies at times. If only we were to treat our spiritual life with the same care and conviction all of the time. We passively live a "good life" and attend church on Sunday. We talk the talk on Sunday and maybe throughout the week... But do we walk the walk?

If we can just learn to cherish God's word like we do our "things" in this life. Verse 18 says to, "tie them as symbols on your hands and bind them on your foreheads". This is so we can never forget them or be without them.

Just as we are taught to do things as a child, we learn to do spiritual things by repetition and internalizing meanings... So it is with a close Christian walk. We need to continually surround ourselves with Godly people and Godly things.

Once when a skeptic expressed surprise to see him reading a Bible, Abraham Lincoln said, "Take all that you can of this book upon reason, and the balance on faith, and you will live and die a happier man."

Take all that is important and tie it on your heart.

JOURNAL ENTRY

___

___

___

___

___

NOV 12

ARE YOU LISTENING?

Deuteronomy 28:2
And all these blessings shall come upon you and overtake you if you heed the voice of the Lord your God.

Tonight I was sitting high on a ridge waiting for dark to pick up my brother coming off the mountain. Being without a radio to hear when he was down I was spending the time glassing some elk. When all of a sudden from the valley below, I hear a voice yell out "Hey Dean!" I jumped up and yelled back, "What?". No response. I whistled no response. So I drove the Ranger to the valley floor to find no one waiting. There was no one for 5 miles around.

I have no idea what I heard tonight on that quite mountain... It evidently wasn't human. Can God speak to us in an audible voice, He can do anything. I don't think that God called to me tonight, if He did, I'm not sure yet what He wanted.

But God does speak to us all the time. He speaks to us through His word, through other people that care enough about us to point out things in our lives, through His creation and many other ways.

Our job is to listen to His voice and respond.

In 1st Samuel chapter 3 we read of Samuel hearing God call to him... Samuel's response was what our response needs to be... Verse 10, Then Samuel said, "Speak, for your servant is listening."

Are we, "His servants" listening as Samuel did?

Everything that happens in our lives, great or small, is a parable in which God speaks to us and the true grasping of these messages is to honestly hear God.

Are you listening?

JOURNAL ENTRY

_____

_____

_____

_____

_____

NOV 13

ALL THINGS ARE POSSIBLE

Matthew 19:26
26 But Jesus looked at them and said, "With man this is impossible, but with God all things are possible."

How often we put God in a box. We struggle and fret and all too often fear... And deep down inside we know that God is bigger than anything we will face today, this week, this year or ever... He is all powerful and yet we forget.

What do you have to fear? Nothing. Whom do you have to fear? No one. Why? Because whoever has joined forces with God obtains great privileges: omnipotence without personal power, direct access to the King and life without death. All three gifts that can only be passed down from God to each of us.

A few days ago a friend sent me a devotional that had a quote at the bottom. I'm not sure who it came from but it was very powerful. "He is the God of boundless resources. The only limit is in us. Our asking, our thinking, our praying are too small; our expectations are too limited."

Jeremiah 32:27 Behold, I am the Lord, the God of all flesh: is there anything too hard for me?

It will always pay to remember, "With man this is impossible, but with God all things are possible."

JOURNAL ENTRY

NOV 14

THERE IS HOPE!

Romans 5:3-4
Not only that, but we rejoice in our sufferings, knowing that suffering produces endurance, 4 and endurance produces character, and character produces hope.

Long suffering is a fruit of The Spirit. But how long must we suffer, while we wait for things to turn our way?

There are many of God's people that suffered in the bible... Perhaps none more Job... He lost most everything. But how long did Job suffer?

We know that it was more than days. It had to be more than a month, it may have even been a year or more.

Whatever the length of time, Job certainly did suffer greatly. He lost 1000 oxen and donkeys, all 7000 of his sheep, his 3000 camels, most of his servants and probably worst of all, his 7 sons and 3 daughters. Finally, after all of this, Job was smitten from head to toe with painful boils which caused his skin to turn black and gave him a fever. Now that is real suffering.

So, if we're living in God's will, Satan will not like it... He will do whatever he can to stop us from having an impact for the Lord. If we are fighting against God then we bring some of the conflict and struggles on ourselves.

But, there is hope because in John 16:33 we have a promise

33 "These things I have spoken unto you, that in me ye might have peace. In the world ye shall have tribulation: but be of good cheer; I have overcome the world."

So how long must we put up with suffering? Until God has helped each one of us to overcome as well. So be of good cheer, Christ Jesus has gone before and has already overcome this world on our behalf.

Last, remember this, "suffering produces endurance, and endurance produces character, and character produces hope."

There is hope!

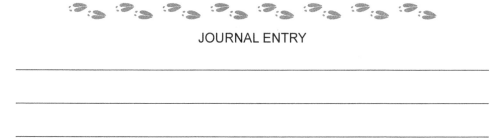

JOURNAL ENTRY

_____

_____

_____

NOV 15

CHASING AFTER THE WIND

James 4:1-3

What causes fights and quarrels among you? Don't they come from your desires that battle within you? 2 You desire but do not have, so you kill. You covet but you cannot get what you want, so you quarrel and fight. You do not have because you do not ask God. 3 When you ask, you do not receive, because you ask with wrong motives, that you may spend what you get on your pleasures.

Tonight at deer camp we were serenaded by a friend with his 12 string guitar. He played and sang amazingly. A couple of songs reminded me of the Rolling Stones song, "You can't always get what you want"... So I started writing about this thought. Before long I drifted to the old ballad, One Tin Soldier (The Legend of Billy Jack)... It was a late night.

Somehow through all the thoughts of how we long for things we want and what we will do to get it, I realized how much I will do for something I really want. I also came to realize that what I really want sometimes doesn't satisfy. What really satisfies is what God wants for me.

In Ecclesiastes 2:10-11 Solomon writes about his quest for satisfaction... Just to find emptiness.

10 "I denied myself nothing my eyes desired; I refused my heart no pleasure. My heart took delight in all my labor, and this was the reward for all my toil. 11 Yet when I surveyed all that my hands had done and what I had toiled to achieve, everything was meaningless, a chasing after the wind; nothing was gained under the sun."

We can search and search... We can kill for assumed treasure as the people did in the song "One Tin Soldier"... But in the end it is all meaningless if it isn't what God wants for us.

Later in Ecclesiastes 2, verses 24-26, Solomon finally explains what has meaning...

"A person can do nothing better than to eat and drink and find satisfaction in their own toil. This too, I see, is from the hand of God, 25 for without him, who can eat or find enjoyment? 26 To the person who pleases him, God gives wisdom, knowledge and happiness..."

True contentment comes from what we treasure, those things that God provides.

All else is "chasing after the wind."

JOURNAL ENTRY

NOV 16

BUILDING MEMORIES

Psalm 89:1
I will sing of the mercies of the Lord for ever: with my mouth will I make known thy faithfulness to all generations

I read this verse early this morning and it brought great memories of hymns that I remembered as a child. Recently I have come to a realization of how much was instilled in my mind as a child by what I was surrounded with.

I was blessed to be raised in a family where we heard strong Christian music played in the home and in the vehicles. Many of those same songs still resonate in my mind today.

Our world can so easily become filled by Ungodly "stuff" that overshadows the Godly influences that should be there. We don't realize that it is happening until it is almost too late at times. We accept things of this world too easily.

I've shared before about memories of coming into my mother's kitchen almost any day and hearing the songs from WRVM radio from Suring Wisconsin, or the preaching of J Vernon McGee. These things stuck with me and at times fill my mind with words and thoughts of praise.

What are we leaving as a legacy in the minds of our children and grandchildren? What music, TV and radio programs will influence their memories in the future?

Fill your life and that of your family with Godly things. Envelop yourself with a blanket woven by a love for Christ.

The memories will last for generations to come.

JOURNAL ENTRY

NOV 17

CALLED TO LOVE

Romans 12:20-21
Therefore if thine enemy hunger, feed him; if he thirst, give him drink: for in so doing thou shalt heap coals of fire on his head.

I can't say that I have many enemies in today's world. Trying to think of even one right now is tough. I watch the news and see the political battles going on and see battle lines being drawn. There are those here in our own country that would like to see their political enemies dead...

In the past year we have seen major attacks over what the Bible points out as sin. And if God said that it is sin... In my heart and mind it is sin! But does that mean that the sinner is my enemy?

A few years back the big craze was the bracelet with WWJD on it. So in our world today, WHAT WOULD JESUS DO?

Prostitutes, samaritans, tax collectors, gluttons, the diseased, mentally unstable, and all garden-variety sinners were at home with Jesus because of the Spirit of the Lord that was upon Him. In fact, the knock on Jesus was that His standards were very low when it came to His associations and locations of ministry. But HE didn't care what his critics said, HE was going to love those that the world today would call our enemy.

How about you? How about me? Does the world look at me and think "look at Dean, he has lowered his standards so far that he is caring for the sinners." I hope so.

We are all in the same boat... We are ALL sinners, it's just that some of us have accepted that God can forgive that sin. Romans 3:23 tells us that, "for all have sinned and fallen short of the glory of God."

But, the difference is that for those that know Christ... There is hope... Romans 5:8, "but God shows his love for us in that while we were still sinners, Christ died for us."

So; enemies, friends, sinners, saints, sick, healthy, black, white, Republican or Democrat... God calls us to love.

JOURNAL ENTRY

___

___

___

NOV 18

THE GREAT PHYSICIAN MAKES HOUSE CALLS...

Matthew 9:11-13

When the Pharisees saw this, they asked his disciples, "Why does your teacher eat with tax collectors and sinners? 12 On hearing this, Jesus said, "It is not the healthy who need a doctor, but the sick. 13 But go and learn what this means: 'I desire mercy, not sacrifice.' For I have not come to call the righteous, but sinners."

In Jesus' day, rabbis and other spiritual leaders were the highest members of Jewish society. Everyone looked up to the Pharisees. They were strict adherents to the Law and tradition, and they avoided those whom they deemed "sinners" because they had a "clean" image to maintain. Tax collectors, infamous for embezzlement and their cooperation with the hated Romans, definitely fell into the "sinner" category.

As Jesus' ministry grew, so did His popularity among the social outcasts of society. Now that Matthew was part of His "inner circle," Jesus naturally had more contact with the social outcasts in Matthew's circle. Spending time with the tax collectors and other sinners was part of Jesus' mission.

In Mark 2:17, Jesus declares, "I have not come to call the righteous, but sinners."

If Jesus was to reach the lost, He must have some contact with them. He went to where the need was because "it is not the healthy who need a doctor, but the sick."

So, in our lives it is very important to spend time with God's family members, remember, that if we aren't spending time with those that don't know HIM, we will never reach the lost.

Praise the Lord, the Great Physician makes house calls.

JOURNAL ENTRY

___

___

___

___

___

NOV 19

Psalm 139:13, 16
For You created my inmost being; You knit me together in my mother's womb... Your eyes saw my unformed body. All the days ordained for me were written in Your book before one of them came to be.

I've been with biologists when we've done postmortem examinations on dead female deer. I've seen unborn fetuses of deer, elk, buffalo and cows... You know what they look like? Little deer, elk buffalo and cows... They are the same animal. I'm sure you know that it is illegal to destroy an eagle's egg. Fines are as high as $5,000 and imprisonment up to 3 years. An eagle's egg is not an eagle, many may argue.

The law, written in 1940, makes it very clear that destroying an eagle egg is the same as killing a full grown eagle... Why? Because the life in that egg is, to all our country's people, the same as that of a mature eagle. Yet, somehow it is different when it is a human. HOW???

I could write all day on this and I realize that I might be "preaching to the choir" here. However, if this spurs one person to question one decision it is worth it. There is so much new evidence to prove now that the human embryo is living. It is a life, without a doubt. And we kill that life for the convenience of the mother. How?

God has so much to say on this subject;

Deuteronomy 27:25 Cursed is the man who accepts a bribe to kill an innocent person

Cursed! Dr's being paid for this murder, parents paying the father of the unborn baby to go "take care of the situation"... CURSED!

Deuteronomy 30:19 I have set before you life and death, blessings and curses. Now choose life, so that you and your children may live.

It's hard to argue with God's word. I'm afraid that God has blinded America and we need to change this quickly.

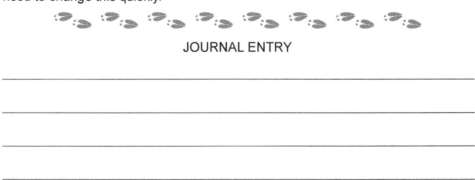

JOURNAL ENTRY

___

___

___

___

NOV 20

Romans 7:24-25
Wretched man that I am! Who will set me free from the body of this death? 25 Thanks be to God through Jesus Christ our Lord! So then, on the one hand I myself with my mind am serving the law of God, but on the other, with my flesh the law of sin.

How often when we struggle do we think, "I am so much worse than everyone else, why can't I overcome my sins?" There is never an excuse for sinning, ever, but EVERYONE goes through the same struggles. And there are times when the strongest stumble and fall.

Even the apostle Paul admits in Romans 7:15, "I do not understand what I do. For what I want to do I do not do, but what I hate I do."

But there is hope. 1 John 1:9 tells us, "If we confess our sins, He is faithful and just to forgive ours sins and cleanse us from all unrighteousness."

Charles Spurgeon once said, "There is no form of sinfulness to which you are addicted which Christ cannot remove."

King David is another prime example, a murderer, adulterer, liar etc... But in the end, he was a "man after God's own heart."

There is hope, don't give up or give in.

JOURNAL ENTRY

NOV 21

VOLUNTEER OR ONE THAT IS CALLED

Colossians 3:23-24
Whatever you do, work at it with all your heart, as working for the Lord, not for human masters, 24 since you know that you will receive an inheritance from the Lord as a reward. It is the Lord Christ you are serving.

We often hear of people who go sign up and volunteer for military service. Or we hear of local "heroes" that do volunteer work around our country. I am sure that most of those that serve are great people and do what they do without seeking glory in any way.

In God's family we also hear of volunteers that sign up to do a task or fill a position, these people are what we describe as "called" to His service... But are they volunteers?

Generally in a community a volunteer can come and go from a position as they find time to do their tasks. In God's work, if we are truly called we no longer have the ability to set our schedule for serving or quitting, we follow God's lead.

Yesterday I was told this very thing by a friend who serves for the "Gideon" organization. He told me, "we are not volunteers, we have been called into service by the Lord". I found this very interesting and accurate.

So the next time you feel called by the Lord to do something by serving, go into it as a soldier, called on to serve. As Christ came here to fulfill His calling by the Father so we ought to serve, not as a volunteer, but as one called into that service and being paid by the most holy God.

Heidi Baker, in her book "Learning to Love..." explains Jesus' calling and service and this gives us an example of how we are to serve.

"Jesus emptied Himself, He humbled Himself and He so yielded Himself to His Father's love that He had no ambition of His own. He was not looking to build an empire, He did not want praise or adulation or to impress people with who or how many followed Him. He stopped over and over again for just one person, for just one life."

That is not volunteering, that is being sent into service. Are you one of those called by the Lord or just a volunteer?

JOURNAL ENTRY

November

NOV 22

A HELPING HAND

1 John 3:17
If anyone has material possessions and sees a brother or sister in need but has no pity on them, how can the love of God be in that person?

We all have more "material possessions" than we need. We are blessed beyond most of the world. The poorest of Americans are rich by much of the world's standards. Yet we too often sit on our hands when it comes to serving the less fortunate.

What are you doing about helping others? How about that young man or the little girl that has grown up without a dad or a mom, can you sit with him or her once a week and teach them the Word of the Lord? What about the lady across the road that is too old to keep the outside or inside of her house in good condition, can you lend a hand – without expecting to be paid? As the Church we are called to love one another and one way that we do that is by helping others. When was the last time you put your love in action?

The words to a song by "Casting Crowns" tell a story of a girl in need of some care... She's right in front of our churches.

She is yearning
For shelter and affection
That she never found at home
She is searching
For a hero to ride in
To ride in and save the day
And in walks her prince charming
And he knows just what to say
Momentary lapse of reason
And she gives herself away

If judgment looms under every steeple
If lofty glances from lofty people
Can't see past her scarlet letter
And we never even met her"

It is great that we pray for people, we are called to do that, but we are also called to do more... Step up and step out to love those in need, and serve those around us.

Galatians 6:2 Bear one another's burdens, and so fulfill the law of Christ.

JOURNAL ENTRY

NOV 23

GOD IS GOOD

Psalm 34:8
Oh, taste and see that the Lord is good! Blessed is the man
who takes refuge in him!

If you're one of God's children, you will figure this out by the end of your life: God is good. There's no telling what He will take you through to bring you to that place. But eventually you will say, "The Lord is good!" Everything He allowed, everything He withheld, every difficult season, every stretching circumstance, God meant for your good.

Pastor James MacDonald wrote, "His disposition is kindness. His default action is for your benefit. You can know His goodness as certainly as you can taste and savor your favorite food."

Psalm 100:5 says, "For the Lord is good; his steadfast love endures forever, and his faithfulness to all generations."

Every generation learns the truth... God's goodness is something He wants us to experience. It comes to us as "steadfast love" and "faithfulness" and can be seen in everything He does.

Even God's timetable is good, but we may only see this after events have transpired. I've shared before how we can look back in our life and see a trail, how God has brought us from one point to the next and how we've grown through the journey.

So we need not question God's motives or His timing, both will ALWAYS be good.

Our prayer must be, "Father, I'm waiting for You because I've tasted and know You are good in what You do and in when You do it!"

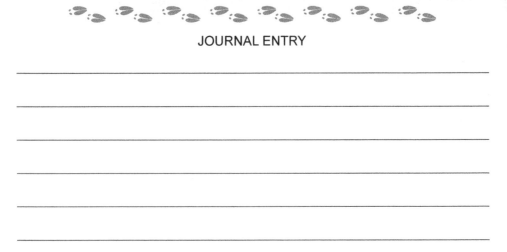

JOURNAL ENTRY

___

___

___

___

___

___

NOV 24

THE BLESSINGS OF SERVING

Philippians 2:5-7

"Have this mind among yourselves, which is yours in Christ Jesus, who, though he was in the form of God, did not count equality with God a thing to be grasped, but emptied himself, by taking the form of a servant, being born in the likeness of men."

It's been a long year of working on a house to sell. Each little job to make the house better turns into two more jobs... It feels as though it will never end. Yet with a couple days break, where am I? Helping friends with their projects, but what a blessing!

God calls us to serve. I have a skill or knowledge that someone else doesn't have, God put us together as a family for a reason.

Mark 10:45 tells us, "For even the Son of Man came not to be served but to serve, and to give his life as a ransom for many."

When Jesus speaks about serving, we should listen to Him. Here is the very God of the universe who came as a Man to serve. The word He uses for servant is the Greek word "diakoneō" which is where we get the name "deacon" and diakoneō means "to be a servant of, to serve, wait upon, or minister to." That is what every believer is called to do. Not to be a deacon but to be a servant of the members of Christ's Body, the church. He served to the uttermost, giving His very "life as a ransom for many."

How do we not serve others in simple ways, when Jesus did what He did for us? I've found that the serving others is a true blessing... We see these blessing in different ways, but they are always there. There is true reward for serving others.

If we look around and listen to the needs of others, we will see and hear of needs and opportunities to serve. There is little that is more gratifying than filling the needs of a friend.

Share the blessings.

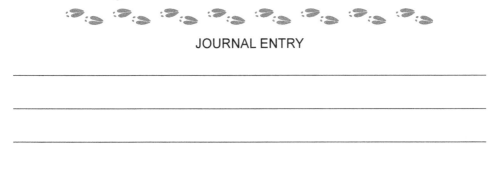

JOURNAL ENTRY

_____

_____

_____

_____

NOV 25

GIVE IT TO HIM!

Philippians 4:6-7 do not be anxious about anything, but in everything by prayer and supplication with thanksgiving let your requests be made known to God. And the peace of God, which surpasses all understanding, will guard your hearts and your minds in Christ Jesus.

It is easy to tell someone, "just don't worry about it"... But then a minute later we catch ourselves wondering how we will get through our own situation. Living the worry free life that God wants us to live can only be done one way. There is no secret formula, no special 10 step plan. It may not be easy, but it's simple... Give it to God... "In everything by prayer and supplication... with thanksgiving, let your requests be made known to God. And the peace of God, which surpasses all understanding, will guard your hearts and your minds in Christ Jesus."... Give it to God!

Most things that we worry about are things that we can't change anyhow... So why worry. In his gospel Luke tells us that worry won't add to our life. In Luke 12:25 he writes, "And which of you by being anxious can add a single hour to his span of life?" We can't add a minute let alone an hour. And actually medical science has proven worry can shorten your life.

A week ago I heard someone take credit for something that I had done. It hurt... badly. I worried about it for about 5 minutes; it was destroying my day... Then I thought, "I can't allow this to cause me a lost minute of time." I prayed continually to allow God to take that from me... Within minutes it was gone. No hard feelings, no worry.

Faith is the absence of worry and the confidence in He that has control... And it isn't us!

Mahatma Gandhi explained it well. "There is nothing that wastes the body like worry, and one who has any faith in God should be ashamed to worry about anything whatsoever."

God can, and will, take the worry and anxiety away, "through prayer and with thanksgiving"...

JOURNAL ENTRY

_____

_____

_____

NOV 26

Luke 12:15
"And he said to them, 'take care, and be on your guard against all covetousness, for one's life does not consist in the abundance of his possessions.'"

At midnight we started "Black Friday"... As the second hand on the clock hit twelve people all over America started trampling over each other to get sales... Just one second after a day where we were giving thanks for all that we already have... Kind of ironic, don't you think?

God is so good to us... Not many (if any) of us reading this devotional went to bed hungry last night. More likely we ended the day sick from all of the food we consumed throughout the day. Yet, we need more all the time. In The Apostle Paul's letter to the Philippians, he wrote in 4:11-13, "I am not saying this because I am in need, for I have learned to be content whatever the circumstances. 12 I know what it is to be in need, and I know what it is to have plenty. I have learned the secret of being content in any and every situation, whether well fed or hungry, whether living in plenty or in want. 13 I can do all this through him who gives me strength."

"The secret of being content." "Content" is defined as "satisfied with what one is or has." Contentment doesn't mean you are happy in the bad times. It means you are satisfied with life because you know that God has things in control.

How many of us have abundantly more than we need at times? We had some guests here with us this week... Not financially wealthy people. But they are blessed with a generous spirit and contentment... When they see a need they fill it. Wouldn't our world be an amazing place if we all lived like that?

Philippians 4:19 – "And my God will supply every need of yours according to his riches in glory in Christ Jesus."

JOURNAL ENTRY

___

___

___

___

___

NOV 27

PAY IT FORWARD

Philippians 2:3-4
Do nothing out of selfish ambition or vain conceit. Rather, in humility value others above yourselves, 4 not looking to your own interests but each of you to the interests of the others.

This week I've seen a commercial several times for a phone company that talks about celebrating "thanksgetting". I realize it is just a trick to get your attention (and it worked), but it worked in reverse on me. Thanksgiving should be a time to reflect on the blessings that we receive and be thankful for them.

If we think back in our lives, we (or at least I) can think of the blessing of so many that took the time to care for me and make a difference in my life... Linda, Mom, Dad, Grandma, Mr. Willis, Mr. Linn, Pastor King etc... These people have given of themselves spiritually and physically to make me what I am today.

At Thanksgiving do we remember to thank God for those who have blessed our lives? Do we put it into action I John 4: 11, "Beloved if God so loved us, we also ought to love one another?"

I challenge you today to first praise God for those that he has blessed you with in your life, those that have cared more for you than for their own needs at times. Secondly, pay that forward. Search out someone that is in need of a mentor, someone in need of you to come alongside to just love them and care for them.

Life is short you may change someone's life, like others changed yours... Pay it forward

JOURNAL ENTRY

NOV 28

CHEERFUL GIVING

Matthew 6:21
"Wherever your treasure is, there your heart and thoughts will also be."

It was Martin Luther who said, "there are three conversions necessary: the conversion of the heart, the conversion of the mind, and the conversion of the purse" (or wallet, as we would say today). But for many of us, the wallet is often the last thing to change.

If we believe that God really owns EVERYTHING, then we know that He really doesn't need the small amount that we can give... So why does He instruct us to give? What he needs is us, and the process of giving blesses us and changes us, as well as brings him glory.

In the Old Testament, Abraham was willing to give his only son (a son he thought he would never have) after God asked him to, and I believe that experience helped prepare him to be the man of faith that he was. God can do so much more through a wise, giving, mature person than a person who is overly concerned with possessions of this world. Our money and belongings can disappear or get destroyed at any time and if we place too much value on them, we will be devastated when they are gone. God wants our treasure and worth to be with those things that can never be destroyed or taken from us, namely himself and the people he has put in our lives.

So in the last week we've gotten through Thanksgiving, Black Friday, Cyber Monday and now Giving Tuesday... A day that gives us a chance to evaluate where and how our hearts match God's... Remember God doesn't need our money, He needs our hearts! Where is your heart today?

2 Corinthians 9:7 Each of you should give what you have decided in your heart to give, not reluctantly or under compulsion, for God loves a cheerful giver.

JOURNAL ENTRY

___
___
___
___
___
___

NOV 29

HEARING VOICES

1 Sam 15:22
"Does the Lord delight in burnt offerings ...as much as in obeying the voice of the Lord? To obey is better than sacrifice..."

How often we hear in our heart a prompting, "I should call him or her" and we think, "maybe tomorrow when I have time." How often we miss an opportunity to bless someone with something as simple as a quick phone call.

My wife is always telling me that I'm on my phone too much... She doesn't understand why when someone comes to mind I dial their number... Or send an email, text or just swing into their driveway. To me when I get that prompt, I know that it might be God wanting me to bless someone or I might meet a need in their life.

Our general problem is one of hearing God's "still small voice." What would the Spirit have us do next? This obedience comes through "promptings" to our hearts or minds, which are generally low-risk until we mature and listen more carefully. God tells us to call someone late at night; to give someone the money in our pocket; to offer to pray with someone about something very specific that we couldn't have known... He wants to know we are willing to listen.

Charles Stanley said, "Often times God wants us to sit before Him in quietness. He doesn't want us to do all the talking. As Is. 30:15 says "In quiet and confidence will be your strength."

John 10:27 My sheep hear My voice, and I know them, and they follow Me.

Listen to God's still small voice, you never know when you will be called on to make a difference in someone's life.

JOURNAL ENTRY

November

NOV 30

GOD'S ARMOR

Ephesians 6:12-13
For our struggle is not against flesh and blood, but against the rulers, against the authorities, against the powers of this dark world and against the spiritual forces of evil in the heavenly realms. 13 Therefore put on the full armor of God, so that when the day of evil comes, you may be able to stand your ground, and after you have done everything, to stand.

I'm not sure about everyone else but I struggle... I struggle to keep a good godly attitude at times, and I struggle with being beat down. But Paul wrote to put on God's full armor to defend against the struggles we face in life. Even when we face struggles with other individuals, it isn't a struggle against that person but with satanic attacks. Attacks meant to bring us down, to diminish our usefulness to God, to diminish our testimony to others.

In the bible we've learned that man's armor is of no use in God's fights; Saul's armor did not fit David, Goliath's armor was useless against David's stone. And a stray arrow found a crack in Ahab's armor, killing the wicked king. "So much for the value of armor!"

So don't fight these fights as if we were fighting a person... Trust God's armor to protect us and to advance forward in battle. Prepare for battle by utilizing the pieces of armor that God provides to us.

Ephesians 6:14-18 14 Stand firm then, with the belt of truth buckled around your waist, with the breastplate of righteousness in place, 15 and with your feet fitted with the readiness that comes from the gospel of peace. 16 In addition to all this, take up the shield of faith, with which you can extinguish all the flaming arrows of the evil one. 17 Take the helmet of salvation and the sword of the Spirit, which is the word of God. 18 And pray in the Spirit on all occasions with all kinds of prayers and requests. With this in mind, be alert and always keep on praying for all the Lord's people.

And remember, "our struggle is not against flesh and blood, but against the rulers, against the authorities, against the powers of this dark world and against the spiritual forces of evil in the heavenly realms."

JOURNAL ENTRY

DECEMBER

Philippians 4:19

And my God will meet all your needs according to his glorious riches in Christ Jesus

Trophies of Grace

DEC 1

STRADDLING THE FENCE

Romans 1:16
For I am not ashamed of the gospel of Christ: for it is the power of God unto salvation to everyone that believeth; to the Jew first, and also to the Greek.

Yesterday Linda and I were riding in the car and on the radio we heard that someone was "straddling the fence" on an issue. Linda said, "That sounds painful." I chuckled and agreed... I've accidentally straddled wooden fences, barbed wire fences and even one electric fence... They were all painful.

I'm getting too old to straddle fences, both literally and figuratively. We have to come to a point in our lives where we take a stand and live through it. If you are a Christian you have to eventually say, "I'm not ashamed of the gospel of Christ" and stick to it. If you don't you are wasting the greatest gift that God can give, the Gift of His one and only Son (John 3:16)

There is an Aaron Tippin song named YOU"VE GOT TO FOLLOW SOMETHING. If we read into this song as the "family" being the Family of God, it speaks right to our need to stand up for what Christ has done for us.

You've got to stand for something or you'll fall for anything
You've got to be your own man not a puppet on a string
Never compromise what's right and uphold your family name
You've got to stand for something or you'll fall for anything

We are coming into a time where we will be called out to stand for something... Where will you stand?

Matthew 5:10 Blessed are those who are persecuted for righteousness' sake, for theirs is the kingdom of heaven.

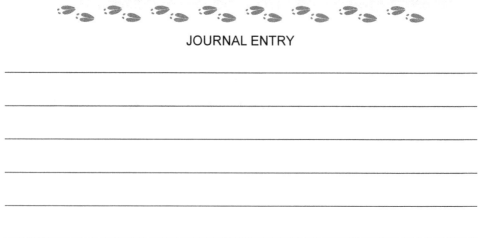

JOURNAL ENTRY

December

DEC 2

STILL ON THE THRONE

1 Chronicles 29:11
Yours, O Lord, is the greatness and the power and the glory and the victory and the majesty, for all that is in the heavens and in the earth is yours. Yours is the kingdom, O Lord, and you are exalted as head above all.

In the last week we've seen some drastic changes in our country. Our Supreme Court said same sex marriage is acceptable, we've made treaties with our enemies and more...

All this makes it easy to get drawn in & side-tracked by everything going on right now. So, it's time for a reality check; GOD is still on the throne & still in control!!

With all the religious views, tolerances, & expanded beliefs in everything from spiritualism, to witchcraft, to the 'New Age' stuff, Christians out there need to be reminded that prayer is our most powerful tool and we need to be praying for the lost. GOD uses us to reach others, and our lives & attitudes should be an example to those who both know Christ & to those who do not know Him.

We need to be careful of our own 'tolerance levels' and remember that we're merely tools & vessels in the hand of an all powerful GOD who will soon open the heavens & put this sinful world under His feet.

Come quickly Lord Jesus...

JOURNAL ENTRY

_____

_____

_____

_____

_____

_____

_____

DEC 3

HIS DESIRES, BECOME OUR DESIRES

Psalm 37:4-7(a)
Delight yourself in the Lord, and he will give you the desires of your heart. 5 Commit your way to the Lord; trust in him, and he will act. 6 He will bring forth your righteousness as the light, and your justice as the noonday.
7 Be still before the Lord and wait patiently for him...

Will God really give us the desires of our heart? Will He answer our "wish list?" Yes and maybe.

In the last couple of months two friends of mine lost their jobs. The first one prayed with his wife on a Monday night for God to direct him on whether or not he should purchase the company he was working for. Very early on Tuesday morning he got a call telling him to shut the doors, the company was closed and because of a legal issue, the company couldn't be sold. The second friend, just yesterday, was praying for God to clearly show him what God wanted him to be doing. Half way through the day he was let go from his long-term job. Before he got home, he was hired at a new job. How can you argue with those answers?

Neither of these friends "desired" to lose their jobs. But, like verse 5 says, they; committed their ways to the Lord; trusted in him, and God acted. They know that God has it under control and that He has a plan that is greater than our plan.

My friends, if you are truly delighting in Him, trusting in Him, committing your ways to Him, and waiting on Him, yes, He will give you the desires of your heart. Scripture tells us He will, but God's timing may not be your timing. We must wait patiently on the Lord and understand that the scripture does not say "He will give you what your heart desires" but rather it states "He will give you the desires of your heart." Note the difference, the scripture promises us that the Lord will *give us the desires* of our heart. He gives us the desire! He has a desire for our hearts and lives and when we delight in Him, He implants *His* desire into our hearts; He *gives us the desire* of our heart. His desire literally becomes our desire, as it is God almighty that instills in us His desire for our lives. He places His desire in our hearts! We delight ourselves in the Lord and *He gives us the desires* of our heart.

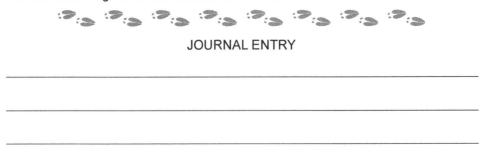

JOURNAL ENTRY

December

DEC 4

Matthew 5:9
Blessed are the peacemakers: for they shall be called the children of God.
The headline read, "KABUL, Afghanistan Five American troops with a special operations unit were killed by a U.S. airstrike called in to help them after they were ambushed by the Taliban in southern Afghanistan, in one of the deadliest friendly fire incidents in nearly 14 years of war."

Friendly fire has taken more people out of action in the Christian church than we care to admit. The Bible tells us that the peacemakers are blessed... But too often we fake peace instead of making peace. And by faking peace, many will be hurt and their service to God diminishes greatly.

In Romans 12:18 the Bible tells us, "If it be possible, as much as lieth in you, live peaceably with all men."

We are to be peacemakers... But we've become a Christian family of "peacefakers" to try to avoid conflict or hurting anyone's feelings.

Avoiding conflict isn't peacemaking. Avoiding conflict means running away from the mess while peacemaking means running into the middle of it. Peacemaking means addressing those issues that caused conflict in the first place. Peacemaking can never be separated from doing justice. They go hand in hand. Peacemaking means having to stir the waters on the way to peace. Peacemaking means speaking the truth in love, but speaking the truth nonetheless. The only way we can truly be peacemakers is if we first have peace with God. One must understand that we cannot have the peace *of* God until we first have peace *with* God. The only way sinful man can have peace with God is to surrender their lives to the Lord Jesus Christ. The Holy Spirit will then have the liberty to equip us to be God's peacemakers!

If you truly love those around you, you won't fake peace, you will meet conflict head-on. Become a peacemaker... You will be blessed because of it.

JOURNAL ENTRY

DEC 5

GOD'S TROPHY

Jude 1:24-25
Now to Him who is able to protect you from stumbling and to make you stand in the presence of His glory, blameless and with great joy, 25 to the only God our Savior, through Jesus Christ our Lord, be glory, majesty, power, and authority before all time, now, and forever. Amen.

As a kid we all love to put a trophy on the shelf of our bedroom or the family room of the house. It shows some sort of significant accomplishment in life. Then as hunters and fisherman we grow to hang mounts and photographs on the wall. These are not only accomplishments but memories of time spent in the field and with friends and family. Memories that will always a bring smile when we see that trophy.

Did you ever think that we are a trophy of God, or more accurately, a trophy of God's grace? Think about what God's grace is towards us. The most common definition of grace is, "God's unmerited favor." That is a great definition, but let's go a little further.

God's grace is to offer each and every one of us the gift of eternal life. He loved us enough to send His only Son, leaving heaven, to come to earth and die on our behalf. He did all this while not a single one of us deserved in any way at all. It was done totally independent of our own merit.

If you've accepted God's beautiful gift of grace think of your picture on God's wall. When He looks at it, He smiles knowing that you are His. If you haven't yet taken hold of that gift of a loving Father, do it now. Repent of your sins and put your faith in the Lord Jesus Christ. He died on the cross 2,000 years ago so you could be a recipient of God's grace. Receive the gift of Salvation and forever be a Trophy of God's Grace.

JOURNAL ENTRY

DEC 6

Romans 12:2
And be not conformed to this world: but be transformed by the renewing of Your mind, that you may prove what is good, and acceptable, and perfect, will of God.

Joyce Meyer once said, "I've discovered that when we take time to renew our minds with God's Word, we learn how to think like God thinks, say what God says, and act like He wants us to act."

As believers, we ought to be different from the world. Our goal should be to be more conformed into the image of Christ so that we can better display the nature of Jesus: forgiving, loving, and helping others... How can we do that? By walking by faith in the blood of Jesus and renewing our mind in God's Word. With our faith ever-anchored in the cross of Jesus Christ, we cultivate a relationship with Him is by spending time in His Word, spending time with Him in prayer and surrounding ourselves with His people.

When we have renewed our mind, as the verses direct us to do, we will be transformed from this world and we will have a much more powerful impact for God. A godly lifestyle will attract some people to you, and it will drive others away. But sometimes the same people who resist the gospel will seek out a Christian for help when life gets difficult.

We have some awesome responsibilities; first to God, second to those around us that are watching us and also to our own heart.

So don't conform... "But be transformed, by a renewing of your mind" and be ready and willing to do the will of God.

JOURNAL ENTRY

_____

_____

_____

_____

_____

_____

DEC 7

SUPER POWERS

Ephesians 3:20-21

Now unto him that is able to do exceeding abundantly above all that we ask or think, according to the power that works in us, 21 Unto him be glory in the church by Christ Jesus throughout all ages, world without end. Amen.

Yesterday I took Micah, my grandson, on the road with me for some meetings. While driving he asked, "Grandpa, if you could have one super power what would it be?" Hmm, I really didn't know for sure.

This morning while reading Ephesians 3 I realized that we already have super powers! However, we probably rarely ever take advantage of that power.

The twentieth verse of this chapter states that God is able to do "Exceeding abundantly above all that we ask or think, according to the power that works in us,"... Wow! More than we ask or think? And the power is already working in us? Yet how often do we call on Him? Always understand it's faith in the cross of Christ that allows the Holy Spirit latitude to move and operate in the heart and life of the believer! We sit on our hands and feel like we can't request of God those things that are good in life. I'm not talking about personal selfish things... But the really "good" things; peace, love, ability to serve, health, provision, etc...

Lailah Gifty Akita asks an interesting question in her writings... "What do you have that the Lord didn't provide? What do you need that the Lord can't provide?"

Our living God can provide all truly good things, we just need to request of Him. Don't be afraid to ask... Then if your heart is right, expect to receive.

JOURNAL ENTRY

_____

_____

_____

_____

_____

_____

_____

DEC 8

FOR THOU ART WITH ME

Psalms 18:30
As for God, his way is perfect: The Lord's word is flawless;
he shields all who take refuge in him.

In the midst of David being pursued by Saul David knew that God was protecting him.

We quite often feel as though our whole world is caving in around us, friends have turned on us, and no matter what we try fails. But we need to know that if we praise God in the hard times as well as the good times, He is faithful to protect and provide.

The most memorized chapter in the Bible is psalms 23... It's all about God's provision and protection... Read it here with the mindset of God pulling us close as His child.

1. The Lord is my shepherd; I shall not want.
2. He maketh me to lie down in green pastures: he leadeth me beside the still waters.
3. He restoreth my soul: he leadeth me in the paths of righteousness for his name's sake.
4. Yea, though I walk through the valley of the shadow of death, I will fear no evil: for thou art with me; thy rod and thy staff they comfort me.
5. Thou preparest a table before me in the presence of mine enemies: thou anointest my head with oil; my cup runneth over.
6. Surely goodness and mercy shall follow me all the days of my life: and I will dwell in the house of the Lord forever.

We have to realize that our safety does not come from the distance we keep from danger; it comes from how close we stay to God. Allow Him to be your shield.

JOURNAL ENTRY

DEC 9

YESTERDAY'S A CLOSING DOOR

Psalm 103:12
as far as the east is from the west, so far has He removed our transgressions from us.

Over the years of guiding I've had many people come through with many different attitudes. I've had hunters with the attitude that says, "By being in camp I'm already successful" and they have a wonderful time no matter what. I've also had hunters that came in defeated before arriving at camp. They decided they couldn't climb the mountain before they tried. They knew they would miss if they got a shot and they did just that.

Unfortunately, we see the same thing every day in our lives as well. There are Christians that act defeated and they never grow because of it. They carry their past around like a mule that has more than he can carry.

Psalm 103:12 makes it clear that our past defeats have been removed from us. How far? As far as the east is from the west, that means infinitely.

Danny Gokey sings a song named, "Tell Your Heart to Beat Again". Part of the chorus tells to say goodbye to our last and move on.

"Yesterday's a closing door
You don't live there anymore
Say goodbye to where you've been
And tell your heart to beat again"

Today's a new day... Let your past go, God already has.

JOURNAL ENTRY

DEC 10

DON'T BE AFRAID

Isaiah 41:10
Don't be afraid, for I am with you. Don't be discouraged, for I am your God.
I will strengthen you and help you. I will hold you up with my victorious right hand.

It's not always easy for me to trust God and follow him. There are tough patches of life that drain me and test my faith. "God, you've told me to leave my job and follow you, but where will the money come from? How will I pay my rent?" It's hard to trust Him. Or, "God, you've given me this ministry, but nothing seems to be sinking in. I can't make everyone happy." It's hard to trust Him. It's easier to worry and become discouraged.

God says, "I am with you." He is with me. No matter what I go through, he is by my side. No matter if I can't pay my mortgage, He is with me. No matter if the world seems to be against me, He is with me. I don't need to fear. No matter if I hear more criticism than encouragement about my leadership, I don't need to be discouraged. He is my God—He is in control of it all. All I need to do is have faith and trust His promises.

You know what the best part is? I don't have to do it alone. He gives me the strength I need when I don't feel I can take another step. He helps me in those times when I want to give up. He holds me up to see the fruits of my ministry and find victory in doing His service. I can trust Him.

Are you struggling with trusting God? Does the future seem hazy and impossible? Do you doubt your impact on people's lives? Don't be afraid. Don't be discouraged—nothing is impossible with God. He will help you through your times of doubt. Run to Him. He provided a way thru the death, burial and resurrection His son Christ Jesus. The atoning work on the cross 2,000 years ago is what allows us to "come boldly unto the throne of grace, that we may obtain mercy, and find grace to help in the time of need." Jesus promises us "He who comes unto me, I will in no wise cast out." Run to Jesus and He will give you all the strength and help that you need to accomplish His purposes for your life.

JOURNAL ENTRY

_____

_____

_____

_____

DEC 11

STAND STRONG... TOGETHER

Ephesians 4:16
from whom the whole body, joined and held together by every joint with which it is equipped, when each part is working properly, makes the body grow so that it builds itself up in love.

What's the largest living organism on Earth? No, it's not a blue whale. It's a tree, a Quaking Aspen. That's right, a single Quaking Aspen in Utah covers 106 acres of land and is estimated to weigh more than 6,000 metric tons. By some estimations the Aspen grove known as Pando, Latin for "I spread," could be shoots from a spreading root system that is as much as several thousand years old.

What makes this aspen grove survive for this long? It's the fact that each tree has a common root that supports all the other trees around it. They are connected and hold up one other. That is the way that God created His family to function, as a working team with a common root source. If we can allow God to weave our lives together, around Him, we can withstand the worst possible storms.

Chris Bradford said, "Only by binding together as a single force will we remain strong and unconquerable."

1 Corinthians 1:10 encourages us in this way. 10 "I appeal to you, brothers, by the name of our Lord Jesus Christ, that all of you agree, and that there be no divisions among you, but that you be united in the same mind and the same judgment."

Stand strong, together.

JOURNAL ENTRY

_____

_____

_____

_____

_____

_____

_____

DEC 12

YOUR MOUNTAIN TOP

Mark 9:2-3
Six days later, Jesus took with Him Peter and James and John, and brought them up on a high mountain by themselves. And He was transfigured before them; 3 and His garments became radiant and exceedingly white, as no launderer on earth can whiten them.

I love the mountains. Spending time looking out over God's amazing creation is a great way to lift my spirit. I cannot sit up high on the mountain without feeling the presence of my Savior. And going there with another person or small group raises conversations that we normally couldn't or wouldn't have.

God graciously gives us these experiences so we are able to navigate the many valleys in our lives, not so we can stay on the mountain. So, I cherish these mountain top experiences, and draw from them in the valleys.

Maybe you can't get to the mountains. But we all need somewhere to have these experiences in life. Places where it is just you and God, or a place to build a relationship stronger between you and others that are working together toward a common goal.

God has given us all a "mountain" where we can meet Him face to face. This place is there to rebuild our heart and soul by allowing God to reach out and touch us.

Go to the mountains if you can, or just go to God and ask Him where your mountain top is. He will meet you there.

JOURNAL ENTRY

DEC 13

THE LOST HAS BEEN FOUND

Luke 15:31-32

31 "'My son,' the father said, 'you are always with me, and everything I have is yours. 32 But we had to celebrate and be glad, because this brother of yours was dead and is alive again; he was lost and is found.'"

The parable of the Prodigal Son is a story about God's redemptive grace and mercy. It is a story of His unconditional love and forgiveness. The story starts earlier in Luke 15 with the younger brother taking his inheritance and running off.

The younger brother had taken the money and run off, spending his wealth on "wild living" (v 13) and "prostitutes" (v 30). These are some of the worst things imaginable in the Christian church of today... Yet, the father welcomed him home and threw a huge celebration.

It doesn't matter how far we've roamed away from God, He is always waiting with open arms. He's waiting with unconditional love for us to return to Him.

So no matter what you've done or how far you've gone, even if you've squandered what God has given you... Turn around and run to Him.

We have an amazing, loving God that just wants us home with Him. Today if you are struggling, turn around and run home to him

JOURNAL ENTRY

December

DEC 14

KEEP CLIMBING

Philippians 3:13-14

Brethren, I do not regard myself as having laid hold of it yet; but one thing I do: forgetting what lies behind and reaching forward to what lies ahead, 14 I press on toward the goal for the prize of the upward call of God in Christ Jesus.

It's hard to forget what's behind... The hurt, the memories (good and bad), etc... But Paul told the people of Philippi to do just that.

If you've ever climbed a mountain you know what false summits are. You think that you are nearing the top and you find that you aren't quite there. But you keep looking ahead plotting forward toward the goal of the top. You don't look back down behind you... You keep looking ahead...

A true close relationship with Christ is the goal, the pinnacle, the summit... We strive to reach that place, not looking back but looking ahead at the goal.

Dag Hammarskjold wrote, "Never measure the height of a mountain until you have reached the top. Then you will see how low it was."

Don't worry about what you've left behind, look to what is ahead and when you've reached the goal, you will be blessed by the Lord. It isn't an easy trip but when you've reached it, you can look back down at all the obstacles, the rocks, the rushing streams you had to get past in life, and say, "it was worth the climb."

Keep climbing

JOURNAL ENTRY

_____

_____

_____

_____

_____

_____

_____

DEC 15

LOVING WORDS

Proverbs 15:1-4
A gentle answer turns away wrath, but a harsh word stirs up anger.
2 The tongue of the wise adorns knowledge, but the mouth of the fool gushes folly.
3 The eyes of the Lord are everywhere, keeping watch on the wicked and the good.
4 The soothing tongue is a tree of life, but a perverse tongue crushes the spirit.

I love calling to animals when hunting or just while in the woods walking. I've been so blessed to be able to travel across the country to call turkeys, elk, deer and one almost fatal calling of a Kodiak brown bear. But I also love talking to owls, cardinals, chickadees, bobwhite quail, etc.

Learning to "say" the right thing at the right time when calling animals will make us a more successful hunter/caller. The same is true in dealing with our speaking with people. Talking to them in a soft loving fashion will get far more accomplished than raising our voice in anger. People will gravitate to someone with loving talk and a caring personality.

Read these verses and then reread them, "bind them on your heart" as the scripture says. They will change your life and will definitely change the lives of others around you. We need to pray that God would help us to "bridle" not only our tongues, but also the attitude by which words are said. As I've been told and tell others, "It's not so much what you say, but how you say it". Let's make sure that tongues give a SOFT ANSWER.

JOURNAL ENTRY

DEC 16

TRUSTING GOD'S GRACE

Jonah 4:9,
But God said to Jonah, "Is it right for you to be angry about the plant?"
"It is," he said. "And I'm so angry I wish I were dead."

That's pretty angry. I'm not sure I have ever been so angry that I wished I were dead. Jonah was. But, why?

Jonah had just seen 120,000+ people turn to God (just what God had sent him to do...) He was mad about that so he went out and sat to watch and see what God would do. It was terribly hot and God made a plant grow overnight for Jonah's comfort, then God took it away. And Jonah was again mad.

We so often say we trust God to take care of us and He does... Then we hit a little bump in the road and we become angry that we are not getting our way. We need to start trusting that our all-powerful, loving God, the one that saved Jonah from the ocean's fury, the one that saved 120,000+ Ninevites from death, the one who made a tree grow over Jonah's head for his comfort, will provide for all of our needs according to His riches in Christ Jesus. We need to trust Him in all the big and little things in life.

Verses 10 & 11 go on to put Jonah in his place...

10 But the Lord said, "You have been concerned about this plant, though you did not tend it or make it grow. It sprang up overnight and died overnight. 11 And should I not have concern for the great city of Nineveh, in which there are more than a hundred and twenty thousand people who cannot tell their right hand from their left.

JOURNAL ENTRY

Trophies of Grace

DEC 17

INHERITANCE

Psalm 37:27-29
Turn from evil and do good; then you will dwell in the land forever.
28 For the Lord loves the just and will not forsake his faithful ones.
Wrongdoers will be completely destroyed; the offspring of the wicked will perish.
29 The righteous will inherit the land and dwell in it forever.

There are promises through the bible about the inheritance of the righteous. What is this inheritance? Our eternal inheritance is a life with God in a place beyond compare. This is enough, but as younger people look at it and think of a long life ahead of them, what is the "here and now" benefit?

There are promises of peace and joy for those who love the Lord. In Galatians 5 Paul talks about the fruit of the spirit which include, love, joy, peace, forbearance, kindness, goodness, faithfulness, gentleness and self control... These are all benefits (inheritance) of a Godly life.

As we get older these promises from Galatians are worth more and more to us. We can't buy these things; we can only receive them freely as reward for a righteous life.

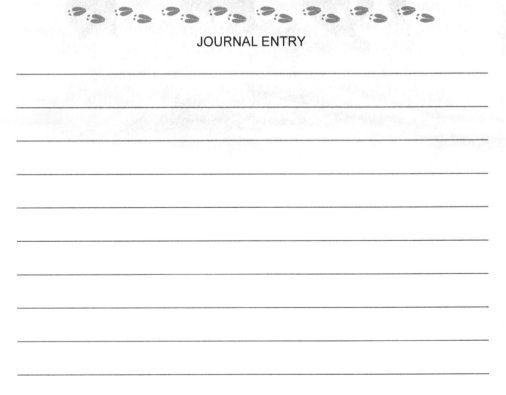

JOURNAL ENTRY

DEC 18

CREATE IN ME A CLEAN HEART

Psalm 51:1-12

Have mercy on me, O God, according to your unfailing love; according to your great compassion blot out my transgressions. 2 Wash away all my iniquity and cleanse me from my sin. 3 For I know my transgressions, and my sin is always before me. 4 Against you, you only, have I sinned and done what is evil in your sight; so you are right in your verdict and justified when you judge. 5 Surely I was sinful at birth, sinful from the time my mother conceived me.
6 Yet you desired faithfulness even in the womb; you taught me wisdom in that secret place. 7 Cleanse me with hyssop, and I will be clean; wash me, and I will be whiter than snow. 8 Let me hear joy and gladness; let the bones you have crushed rejoice. 9 Hide your face from my sins and blot out all my iniquity. 10 Create in me a pure heart, O God, and renew a steadfast spirit within me. 11 Do not cast me from your presence or take your Holy Spirit from me. 12 Restore to me the joy of your salvation and grant me a willing spirit, to sustain me.

As a hunter, I put every effort to recover an animal that I (or a hunting partner) shoots at. I've spent days tracking, searching, walking and sometimes praying to try to find a wounded, or shot at, animal. And at times it has brought tears.

Considering that effort and emotion, how do I react when I've sinned? When I've drifted away from God's perfect plan for me? Do I lament over my actions like I do a misplaced or all together missed shot?

The scripture above was written by David when Nathan came to confront him about his sin of adultery. David was heartbroken over what he had done and he laid it all out before God.

We should consider David's response the next time we become aware of our sinful actions and lay ourselves right out and open before the Lord... Not just saying, "God I sinned, forgive me." But allow your sin (and more importantly God's forgiveness) to change you.

10 Create in me a pure heart, O God, and renew a steadfast spirit within me.

JOURNAL ENTRY

_____

_____

_____

_____

DEC 19

ASSOCIATION WITH CHRIST

Acts 5:41
The apostles left the Sanhedrin, rejoicing because
they had been counted worthy of suffering disgrace for the Name.

'Tis the season... Signs reading, "Keep Christ in Christmas" and "Christ has been stolen from Christmas" are popping up for the month of December. And the war over whether to say, Happy Holidays or Merry Christmas is raging everywhere.

As we approach Christmas I fully expect that many of those that stand up for the worship of Christ will run into people that want to put us down for our belief. That is fantastic! As hard as it is sometimes to be put down, especially by a friend, it should be exciting to know that people see Christ in us. As we go through this the season that generally brings us closer to God, remember that if we are persecuted for Christ we are blessed.

1 Peter 4:16 tells us that if we are associated with Christ we should not be ashamed, but should praise Him for it. "However, if you suffer as a Christian, do not be ashamed, but praise God that you bear that name."

Enjoy the season and take pride in your association with Christ.

JOURNAL ENTRY

DEC 20

A PLACE FOR HIM?

John 1:11-12
"He came unto his own, and his own received him not. But as many as received him, to them gave the power to become the sons of God, even to them that believe on his name."

They didn't receive Him and we didn't receive Him.

Luke 2:6-7 tells us that "While they were there, the time came for the baby to be born, and she gave birth to her firstborn, a son. She wrapped him in cloths and placed him in a manger, because there was no guest room available for them."

Not much has changed since then. Check out verse 7. There was no room for Jesus. Even today people don't want to make room for King Jesus. It's no different during Christmas time. People reject the one true God that created them and wants to have a relationship with them. They otherwise seek comfort in the very things of the world that distract them from the true meaning of Christmas."

Have you made room for Jesus? Does your heart have room? Do the distractions of this world take you away from making a place for Christ? If you have made room for Him already, are you living as if He has filled that place in your life? Or are you living like those that don't know Him? Are you like the innkeepers with no room for Christ or have you made a place for Him?

Remember, Jesus is the reason for the Season! Give Him a place in your life today.

JOURNAL ENTRY

DEC 21

"CHRISTMAS...PERHAPS...MEANS A LITTLE BIT MORE!"

Luke 2:6-7
While they were there, the time came for the baby to be born, 7 and she gave birth to her firstborn, a son. She wrapped him in cloths and placed him in a manger, because there was no guest room available for them.

This morning I was thinking back on Christmas gifts of the past... Childhood gifts and those more recent... Simple things my kids have given me or my grandkids made, things that took personal effort, those where the gifts that stuck with me, the little things. Some of the most memorable items were a walnut bowl my dad turned on the lathe himself and signed and dated the back, just a couple years before he passed away.... My first bible when I was around 12... A framed deer license that was my dad's first when he was 12.

Last night we watched a movie where someone was trying to make a big deal out of the decorations and all his family wanted was to celebrate as a family. Little things were important.

Frank McKibben made a profound statement of what Christmas is and isn't... "This is Christmas; not the tinsel, not the giving and receiving, not even the carols, but the humble heart that receives anew the wondrous gift, the Christ."

Christ didn't come with a loud flashy entrance and Christmas doesn't have to be that way either. I challenge you to take the time to quietly enjoy the small things this Christmas... Enjoy the time with your family (our second greatest gift from God)... Share with the little ones around you God's greatest gift, His Son.

It might seem strange to quote "The Grinch" In a devotional... But... "Then the Grinch thought of something he hadn't before! What if Christmas, he thought, doesn't come from a store? What if Christmas...perhaps...means a little bit more?" It does mean more. Celebrate the quiet arrival of Christ to earth, the small gift that brought hope to a world headed for death. Thank you Jesus!

JOURNAL ENTRY

DEC 22

Matthew 20:28
28 even as the Son of Man was born not to be served but to serve, and to give his life as a ransom for many."

As we approach another Christmas morning we anxiously await the celebration of the Christ's birth. While this is a beautiful story of Christ coming to earth, it isn't a story of all happiness and joy. First consider the hardship that Christ was born into. He was laid in a manger (a feed trough), maybe in a stable or a cave, Herod wanted Him dead as soon as he learned of Him.

But most exciting and sad is that the little baby born to Mary that day came here to die for our sins. We celebrate His birth, but if we only celebrate His birth and that is as far as we go, we lose the real meaning of His coming. If Christ came to earth, lived a full life and died of natural causes, if He was not nailed to cross died and rose again, we would have no hope.

So this week, celebrate His birth. Through all of the parties, shopping, preparation, hustle and bustle, celebrate His birth. But at the same time thank Him for what He did on that terrible cross 33 years later that was the other half of truly the "greatest gift of all".

For unless we believe that Christ came down from heaven as a baby and was born to a virgin and the later was crucified to take all the punishment for all of my sins and yours and then was laid in a tomb, but rose again three days later... Unless we not only celebrate his birthday this week, but also the rest, we lose the entire meaning of Christmas.

The gift isn't completed at Christmas. Without His death and resurrection, it would be "an incomplete gift."

JOURNAL ENTRY

DEC 23

OVERCOMING CHRISTMAS

Luke 19:9-10

⁹And Jesus said to him, "Today salvation has come to this house, because he, too, is a son of Abraham. ¹⁰For the Son of Man has come to seek and to save that which was lost."

Christmas is a time of celebration, of love and sharing. A celebration of the gift that is the greatest gift ever given that brought salvation to a dying world. A love that is beyond human comprehension to those that are undeserving. Sharing of love from one to another here on earth, that is reflective of the love that God showed each of us.

The stress of Christmas at times overwhelms the passion and love. There are people that worry for months leading up to Christmas. The fear of the lack of money to buy gifts is a depressing feeling that can destroy that which is Christmas. There are those that can't be with family to celebrate the season. Loneliness is painful and can paralyze some.

The celebration of love and sharing can overcome the worry, fear and loneliness that we deal with each year. There is so much more to Christmas that isn't dependant on these things. Allow the love of Christ to take over the worry, fear and pain and when you decide this, you will completely focus on the greatest gift of all you will have the best Christmas of your life.

JOURNAL ENTRY

_____

_____

_____

_____

_____

_____

_____

_____

December

DEC 24

Luke 2:4-7

4 So Joseph also went up from the town of Nazareth in Galilee to Judea, to Bethlehem the town of David, because he belonged to the house and line of David. 5 He went there to register with Mary, who was pledged to be married to him and was expecting a child. 6 While they were there, the time came for the baby to be born, 7 and she gave birth to her firstborn, a son. She wrapped him in cloths and placed him in a manger, because there was no guest room available for them.

I have been in situations where I was traveling in areas unfamiliar to me and felt totally lost. Last year it happened to me on the way to some friends lodge. I was late and I got to the point where I just wanted to turn around and go home. When I get myself in those situations, I feel so totally alone and desperate.

Can you imagine the feeling of Mary and Joseph on that original Christmas Eve? Knowing your baby is coming soon and having no place to stay and no one to help take care of you. It must have been very lonely and probably very scary for a teenage girl.

Today, because of Christ's birth and then His death and resurrection, we are never alone... Not only do we have access to God 24/7... But if we have that special relationship with Christ we are part of a much greater family. We are always close to others in our immediate family.

Because Mary was obedient to her calling, and Christ gave us the ultimate gift, we are never alone

Please remember today that through all of the busyness, all of the family stress, all of the loneliness for many... We are never alone... Even one of the names for Christ, Immanuel, means, "God with us."

JOURNAL ENTRY

_____

_____

_____

_____

_____

Trophies of Grace

DEC 25

UNTO US A CHILD IS BORN

Luke 2:1-20

2 In those days Caesar Augustus issued a decree that a census should be taken of the entire Roman world. ² (This was the first census that took place while Quirinius was governor of Syria.) ³ And everyone went to their own town to register.

⁴ So Joseph also went up from the town of Nazareth in Galilee to Judea, to Bethlehem the town of David, because he belonged to the house and line of David. ⁵ He went there to register with Mary, who was pledged to be married to him and was expecting a child. ⁶ While they were there, the time came for the baby to be born, ⁷ and she gave birth to her firstborn, a son. She wrapped him in cloths and placed him in a manger, because there was no guest room available for them.

⁸ And there were shepherds living out in the fields nearby, keeping watch over their flocks at night. ⁹ An angel of the Lord appeared to them, and the glory of the Lord shone around them, and they were terrified. ¹⁰ But the angel said to them, "Do not be afraid. I bring you good news that will cause great joy for all the people. ¹¹ Today in the town of David a Savior has been born to you; he is the Messiah, the Lord. ¹² This will be a sign to you: You will find a baby wrapped in cloths and lying in a manger."

¹³ Suddenly a great company of the heavenly host appeared with the angel, praising God and saying,

¹⁴ "Glory to God in the highest heaven, and on earth peace to those on whom his favor rests."

¹⁵ When the angels had left them and gone into heaven, the shepherds said to one another, "Let's go to Bethlehem and see this thing that has happened, which the Lord has told us about."

¹⁶ So they hurried off and found Mary and Joseph, and the baby, who was lying in the manger. ¹⁷ When they had seen him, they spread the word concerning what had been told them about this child, ¹⁸ and all who heard it were amazed at what the shepherds said to them. ¹⁹ But Mary treasured up all these things and pondered them in her heart. ²⁰ The shepherds returned, glorifying and praising God for all the things they had heard and seen, which were just as they had been told.

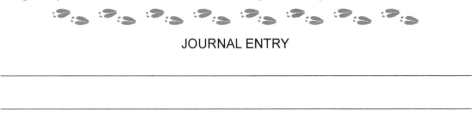

JOURNAL ENTRY

_____

_____

_____

December

DEC 26

THE FARM TREE

Philippians 2:3-4
Do nothing out of selfish ambition or vain conceit. Rather, in humility value others above yourselves, ⁴ not looking to your own interests but each of you to the interests of the others.

When my brothers, sister and I were young we would always get a real Christmas tree from the tree lot in town. It was a family tradition to decorate the tree. Other traditions were things like hand pulling taffy, making cookies and Christmas Eve at Grandma's house. Dad would talk about the Christmas tree that they would have on the farm when he was a kid. The tree's limbs had to be a large distance apart in order for the candles not to light the other limbs on fire. Grandma and Grandpa's farm didn't have electricity at that point and candles had to be used for lighting.

Dad talked about the "farm trees" for many years but we laughed and said that it wasn't what the rest of us wanted. Then one year we gave in and allowed dad to have his way. He was so happy to have a tree that reminded him of his childhood. Why did we wait so long to let him have that memory?

The Apostle Paul wrote that we should "do nothing out of selfish ambition"… Why is that so hard? Dad was so proud of his farm tree, if we had known we would have given in sooner and everyone would have been happier.

Acts 20:35 tells us the blessing. " In everything I did, I showed you that by this kind of hard work we must help the weak, remembering the words the Lord Jesus himself said: 'It is more blessed to give than to receive.' "

JOURNAL ENTRY

_____

_____

_____

_____

_____

_____

DEC 27

Romans 8:1-2
Therefore, there is now no condemnation for those who are in Christ Jesus, 2 because through Christ Jesus the law of the Spirit who gives life has set you free from the law of sin and death.

TGIF... Thank God I'm Free... Free "from the law of sin and death." Once I've accepted the gift of life and freedom from Christ, I no longer live as someone that is chained to a life of this sinful world. This doesn't give me a license to sin, but assures me that when I do sin, I'm forgiven.

Yet, we are still here in this sinful world. The good news is that we are in this world but we don't have to be part of it. We will suffer with it but Romans 8:18 says, "I consider that our present sufferings are not worth comparing with the glory that will be revealed in us."

So start today living as a person free from this sinful world, a person with a promise of coming glory.

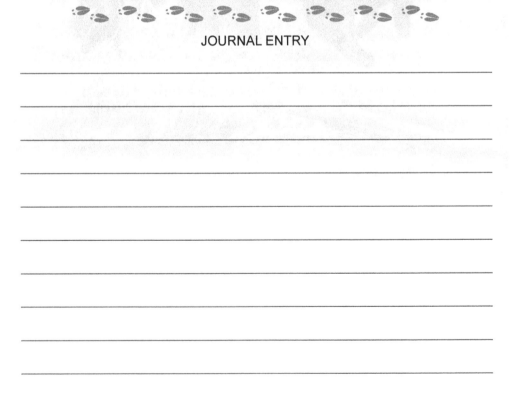

JOURNAL ENTRY

December

DEC 28

Hebrews 12:2
"Let us run with endurance the race that is set before us . . ."

Hunting elk can be a terribly strenuous sport. Depending on the type of country you hunt in, it can actually be a dangerous endeavor. As I've guided in the Colorado mountains, I've had to continually tell myself or my hunter, "just a little further" or let's just "keep going" for bit more. Sometimes in my head I just hear, "keep going, keep going, keep going..." Without that continual prodding there would be little chance for success.

Many people have no idea how critical those two words are to success in life and in the Christian life. The biblical word is endurance or perseverance, the ability to keep on doing the things you have committed yourself to doing when you feel like it and when you don't feel like it. Nothing is more essential to success in the Christian life than perseverance. Faith gets you started; perseverance keeps you going.

Here's the question. What do you do when the pressure is on? It's easy to start the climb. All kinds of people come to the mountain, get up in the morning and put their hunting boots and start the climb. But when the miles click past and the muscles start to fatigue and life isn't easy anymore, what do they do? What do you do?

In James 1:2-3, James tells us that we can look at the challenge of "keeping going" with joy... "My brothers, consider it pure joy when you fall into various trials knowing that the trying of your faith produces perseverance."

Staying power! Did you know that if God could get that one thing into your life, He could give you everything else? James 1 goes on to say in verse 4, "But let perseverance have its perfect work that you may be perfect and complete, lacking nothing," Perseverance, Finishing strong. Keep going.

This week we stand on the ridge line between two years. How will these two years mark your life? Look back on this year for a moment. If your year was like mine, you can see some pretty significant peaks and valleys. Praise God for them. Praise God that at this year's end, you can stand before Him in faith and humility and say, "No matter what is behind me, I finish this year strong in Christ." Like Paul in Philippians 3:13—4 "but one thing I do: forgetting what lies behind and reaching forward to what lies ahead, I press on toward the goal for the prize of the upward call of God in Christ Jesus." I press on (I keep going) that's perseverance. Now look ahead to next year. You don't know what the year will bring, but you can be sure of this, God is faithful. His mercies will be new every morning of every day of 2016. Start each day with faith in God and a commitment to perseverance. There is power in it!

Keep going... Keep going...

DEC 29

HIS RESOLUTION FOR OUR NEW YEAR

Philippians 3:13-14
One thing I do: Forgetting what is behind and straining toward what is ahead,
I press on toward the goal to win the prize for which God has called me
heavenward in Christ Jesus.

Today I spent some time with friends looking over some of my leased lands making plans for next year. How will we hunt them next year? How can we get better at how we hunt? In order to get better at anything in our lives we have to remember what the past was to make a plan for what the future should be. Yet we can't completely forget about the past or we would never grow.

So, in this Scripture, Paul cannot be telling us to forget the past by wiping our brain clean of its memories. But he is telling us not to dwell on the events of the past, but to live in the present (while remembering the past) so we don't miss God's best for our future.

Many people begin the New Year by making New Year Resolutions. They think of things they would like to change, such as their weight or things they would like to do in the New Year. But most of our resolutions are forgotten within a few days of having made them. Quick enthusiasm for something new will never stand the test of time.

But what would happen if all believers approached the New Year with a different question and asked God what were His plans for them? And then we spent some time with God waiting on Him so that we could listen to His voice? We would then have better vision for the year ahead, and if it is vision from Him then we wouldn't run out of quick emotional energy in no time at all, but we would discover His sustaining power, helping us to press on toward the goal He has put before us.

So the challenge is then to go to God, ask Him to direct what He wants for your future. Allow Him to show you the lessons from yesterday and the promise of tomorrow.

JOURNAL ENTRY

DEC 30

Isaiah 43:18-19
"Forget the former things; do not dwell on the past. See, I am doing a new thing! Now it springs up; do you not perceive it? I am making a way in the wilderness and streams in the wasteland."

As we pass the threshold of a new year we look ahead, not knowing what we are looking at just yet. Each day will be an exciting adventure of trusting God has control, as long as I allow Him to take it.

There are many "sayings" related to bringing in a new year... A couple of my favorites are from Brad Paisley and Lucy Maude Montgomery...

Brad wrote... "Tomorrow is the first blank page of a 365 paged book, write a good one.

And In Anne of Green Gables, Lucy wrote, "Isn't it nice to think that tomorrow is a new day with no mistakes in it yet?"

What kind of book will you write in the new year? A Godly book wIth reliance on Him?

Life is so short, we don't know if we have any years past 2016 or if we do, how many we have left. We only know that we have one "page" at a time to write. Tomorrow will be that first "page" of the year. I challenge you to start 2016 out strong with God leading and directing... Then write each page like it might be your last. Fill the page with love, joy and a hunger to grow closer to your Lord...

He desires to grow closer to you!

JOURNAL ENTRY

_____

_____

_____

_____

_____

_____

_____

DEC 31

BE THE BLESSING

Genesis 22:14
Abraham called the name of that place The LORD Will Provide, as it is said to this day, "In the mount of the LORD it will be provided."

Oh, New Year's, a new beginning, a time to look forward with hope and a time to look back with thanks. There are many traditions that come with The New Year, singing Auld Lang Syne, The Ball Drop and New Year's resolutions to name a few. One very interesting tradition is a southern thing. eating black eyed peas on New Year's day. The reason for this tradition is for the hope of good luck and a prosperous new year.

History tells us that as General Sherman marched across the south his soldiers destroyed pretty much everything in their path. They ate or stole most all of the food. At one point the southern people were finally able to come out of hiding, many of them facing starvation. The Union army had taken everything that they thought had value... Including all the food they could carry. The one thing that was left behind was the silos filled with black eyed peas. The Union army thought that the beans were used as cattle feed and seeing they has taken or killed all the cattle the beans had no value.

Southerners awoke to face a new year in this devastation and were facing massive starvation if not for the blessing of having the black eyed peas to eat. From New Years Day 1866 forward, the tradition grew to eat black eyed peas on New Year's Day for good luck.

I consider it God's blessing and provision as opposed to good luck... But nonetheless it shows that in the midst of devastation, God still provides for our needs. For the Israelites it was manna and quail for a time. For the southerners it was black eyed peas.

Matthew 6:26 tells us that we have great value to God and He will provide for our needs:

"Look at the birds of the air, that they do not sow, nor reap nor gather into barns, and yet your heavenly Father feeds them. Are you not worth much more than they?"

Maybe you are the blessing that your neighbor needs. Maybe you and I can make the difference in the lives of someone that needs that hope this new year.

Matthew 10:8 tells us to pass the blessings on that we have gotten. "Heal the sick, raise the dead, cleanse those who have leprosy, drive out demons. Freely you have received; freely give."

Be the Blessing

December

JOURNAL ENTRY

About the Author
Dean Hulce

There is no place like a campfire to tell hunting stories and Dean excels at storytelling. His experiences while hunting, fishing and guiding all across North America have given him an endless supply of material for his writing and speaking engagements. From the Mountain tops of Alaska to the Rio Grande River Valley of Texas, the successes, the failures and near death experiences have added to the depth of his relationship with God.

Dean has written for several National magazines such as; Buckmasters, Rack, Safari, Safari Times, Whitetails, Christian Bowhunters of America and more. In addition, he has been writing a daily devotional for several years, many of them based on his hunting and outdoor experiences.

Along with his family, Dean has been fortunate to hunt many states and Canadian provinces for deer, bear, turkeys, bison, alligators and many others species.

Dean speaks on a regular basis at many outdoor events each year. He continues to write devotionals and is also producing Christian hunting videos. Living the Dream!

Allow Dean to take you on these adventures while learning what God wants us to learn from His Word.

Printed in the USA
CPSIA information can be obtained
at www.ICGtesting.com
LVHW041551081023
760506LV00035B/406